VΣ

# Hi-Fives

PETER LANG
New York • Washington, D.C./Baltimore • Boston
Bern • Frankfurt am Main • Berlin • Vienna • Paris

# Hi-Fives

## A Trip to Semiotics

Edited by
### Roberta Kevelson

PETER LANG
New York • Washington, D.C./Baltimore • Boston
Bern • Frankfurt am Main • Berlin • Vienna • Paris

**Library of Congress Cataloging-in-Publication Data**

Hi-fives: a trip to semiotics / edited by Robert Kevelson.
p.  cm.
Includes bibliographical references and index.
1. Semiotics. 2. Semantics (Philosophy). I. Kevelson, Roberta.
B840.H5   302.2—dc21   98-25588
ISBN 0-8204-3842-1


**Die Deutsche Bibliothek-CIP-Einheitsaufnahme**

Kevelson, Roberta:
Hi-fives: a trip to semiotics / ed. by Robert Kevelson.
–New York; Washington, D.C./Baltimore; Boston; Bern;
Frankfurt am Main; Berlin; Vienna; Paris: Lang.
ISBN 0-8204-3842-1

Cover design by James F. Brisson.

The paper in this book meets the guidelines for permanence and durability
of the Committee on Production Guidelines for Book Longevity
of the Council of Library Resources.

© 1998 Peter Lang Publishing, Inc., New York

Printed in the United States of America.

# Contents

## Part Three
### *The Visible Sign*

## Part Four
### *The Spirit of Semiotics*

# Acknowledgements

This book is a tribute to the power of thought on a two-way street: one lane for the countless travellers, named here and not named, whose work has gone before us; the other for those who, in passing through, carry the significance of semiotics forward.

Special thanks to Cindy Palecek for preparing the contributed manuscripts into this one-of-a-kind semiotics "reader".

*Introduction*

# Chapter 1

# Introduction:
# When Old is New Again

Roberta Kevelson*

## I

This book is a reply to questions heard: What is Semiotics? Explorers of ideas of any age see that Semiotics cuts across the boundaries of cultures, of disciplines, of languages.

Semiotics is a maker of relationships. By way of answer to questions raised about semiotics, by students in classrooms as well as students of lifetime learning, we have brought together between these covers a group of world class scholars, each a specialist in a major "subject".

Semiotics is not about any particular subject, as subjects are called in the academic world. Semiotics is about a *way of exploring* any subject-idea whatsoever. Semiotics is a way of seeing, of asking questions that open yet unexamined aspects of the world of concern to us as being human beings.

Semiotics does not set out to challenge traditional study of subjects taught in college classrooms around the world. But semiotics brings another dimension of *asking about* all of the above, and all those not yet identified. The semiotics process of looking at and looking into creates new meaning. The more one investigates the more the object of investigation grows, and so grows the investigator. Semiotics begins with the idea — a brainchild of one of its chief founders, Charles Sanders Peirce — that knowledge is an infinite resource if and only if people continue to want to know. This infinite resource feeds on curiosity and is nourished by exchanges of whatever matters, between people.

It sounds simple. It's not. It's as hard to do semiotics as it is to do anything of importance that sustains and enriches the human experience, like love and friendship and experimentation and creating. Just as you cannot exhaust the significance of any person or activity or that part of the natural world that you love, but rather that loving is an ever-renewing activity, so is semiotic investigation ever-flowing. It takes the known and the familiar, and by a shift of perspective, or the disclosure of another dimension of seeing something as if for the first time, the old becomes new again. Grasping this core aspect about semiotics is the really tough part. The chapters of this book, each a focus on a special facet of semiotics, will give the newcomer something to hold onto: a hand down a strange path.

While there are several differences between coexisting semiotic theories which are represented in this collection, the authors share in common the assumptions that 1) semiotics presents an alternative to academic subjects in little boxes; 2) the process of semiotics is based on dialogic exchange of ideas between equals, and not on authoritative instruction; 3) whatever we may claim to know is by means of representation or signs, and not directly by intuitions, or by introspection.

But this may say not quite enough about semiotics. What is usually wanted is a *definition*. When one asks, What is Semiotics?, the usual expectation is a definition: Semiotics is... But the best definitions, according to Peirce and others, don't tell you *what* something is: they say what it *does* and *how it does it*.

The traditional type of definition, the *Semiotics Is* kind of definition, is what we may call artificial; since it is essential to analysis, it keeps definite ideas in definite, closed places, and it maintains a kind of stable order.

But the other kind of definition which Peirce calls the "real" definition, is like the natural world itself: it is vague, ever-changing, and even *intentionally ambiguous* (Peirce CP 5.393,491).

We begin with a verbal or artificial definition here. The real, vague, "natural" definition will follow, less explicitly in the examples offered in the various papers presented.

A good verbal definition I offer paraphrases from Peirce's writings: Semiotics is a theory of signs. It is a theory which is produced by a particular method of exploring signs. A sign is a thought. Signs interpret other signs. Each stage of sign-interpretation increases the meaning of the thought. Signs connect thoughts, and connect thinkers with thinkers *and* thoughts. Signs mediate, or act as connectors in making relationships between signs, between people, between whole worlds of discourse. The main business of a sign is to represent meaning. The very process of exchanging meaning-representations *increases* that meaning. An exchange of meaning is always in the same code, just as a commercial transaction in any country is always in the currency of that country. It is possible, and very desirable, to translate from one code to others, just as one exchanges one kind of currency for another when travelling. This kind of code-translation also takes place when one switches from one subcode to another, as from slang to formal speech: from standard speech to talk that's "all in the family." This whole process of exchanging and making new thought — *new value* — is what Peirce calls Pragmatism. This Pragmatism, *as method*, is a go-between, or mediator that brings about meaning-relations. Pragmatism is a kind of matchmaker.

Every language is a code. A language may be verbal, as in the natural languages of English, German, or Swahili. Or a language may be formal, as in symbolic logic, the mathematics, or any notational system which is not directly verbal, e.g., dance, music, cultural gestures, shrugs, grunts, shrieks, and raising one's eyebrows. Each of these codes or subcodes are sign-systems. Each system of signs is a complex of sign-relations. Sign-relations may begin with the instincts, but as we use them with intentional purpose they are conventions, or symbols of habits of thought and use between persons, like "high-fiving". Many semiotic investigators study semiotic processes of biological type forms at micro- and non-human levels. But Peirceans, by and large, are primarily concerned with the evolutionary conceptual signs, i.e. thoughts.

A sign, as representation, stands for something which it is not, to someone or to some other sign. All signs function in three main ways: 1) as Icon; 2) as Index; 3) as Symbol.

An Icon is a spatial, visualizable relation that *may* look like the object it represents but *need not resemble* it, just as a map does not look like the portion of the earth it represents, nor does a mathematical equation look like the two "things" in balance.

An Index represents the experiential aspect of the sign; it is, in this way, representing the structure of opposition, of struggle, of the *actual world*.

A Symbol represents that character of the sign relation which has come to be conventionalized, like a social custom or a personal habit or a name or a part of a language code such as its grammatical order or the letters of an alphabet.

Depending on what the purpose is at any given use of the sign, one or another or a third of these sign-functions may be predomanant; the others are also present, but not predominant.

Signs are not of things, as Peirce sees it. They represent stages in the semiotic process of the evolution of an idea or thought. Peirce has compared the whole process of thinking to a motion picture process I think that if he lived in our age he would have also understood the growing of thoughts as a *cyberreality*. Peirce *suggests* that we think in holograms.

We move on here, to talk just a bit about that other kind of definition: the "real". This definition is not fixed by custom or habit, but is more flexible, improvisational. There is always a sense of free play in this "real" definition. It is not governed by rules; it seems to break rules by hitting against a rule in the background as a reference. It is not governed by authority, but by *ad hoc* law-like authorization. There is always room in this kind of definition for something not given, but is invented, or happening by chance. Thus a genuine novelty may enter into the world and become a part of the world, influencing — possibly influencing — every other part of every other process.   Sometimes this chance happening is detectable only by its consequences, by a "trace".   Whatever has meaning is consequential, says Peirce; significance makes a difference or is *non-sense*!

Every growing idea in this unfinished universe, this evolving universe, is a live idea, says Peirce.   And like life itself, any complete definition can never be accurate, i.e. "true", but may be used *as if* it were true, as a representation or sign of what is "truly true" or "really real".

Semiotics is about the exchange of meaningful representations or signs which result in the increase or surplus of meaning in the worlds of sign-users. Meaning grows in the direction of the future, asymmetrically.   "Time" is *not* reversible!

## II

Semiotics is ancient, traceable to the Stoics and working "underground" in the development of western civilizations.   It emerges in various transitional periods, such as the birth of universities and fusions of law and logic; in the overlapping of alchemy and a "scientific" chemistry a few centuries later; and most importantly in the work of John Locke.   Locke is the platform upon which 19th and 20th century semioticians stand, i.e., more semioticians of the Peircean cast.

At the least, Locke is Peirce's intellectual support for his own emerging theory of signs.   But the idea of a semiotics was not unique to Peirce's thought only.   We find strong schools of semiotics in the years prior to World War I in Russia's Universities of Tartu and Moscow, moving to Prague (for political reasons) in the 1920's.   We find substrata for semiotics among linguists of the 19th and 20th century elsewhere in western Europe, drawing largely upon the work of de Saussure and developing to a semiology or structuralist approach to sign-theory shortly after World War II.   The ability of scholars to move more freely since the middle of the 20th century has resulted in the shaping of a global framework for modern, present-day semiotics.

Through the teaching and intellectual influence of actual people, great scholars such as Roman Jakobson, Juri Lotman, I.A. Richards, Colin Cherry, Charles Morris, Umberto Eco, Roland Barthes, Thomas Sebeok — and many others — Semiotics took root everywhere and burgeoned.

The fact that Semiotics and Structuralism seemed to share on the surface many concepts led to a fusing of these quite dissimilar ways of making meaning more meaningful.   Structuralism, which clearly died back in the early 1980's produced a brief flowering of "poststructuralism" and "postmodernism", but these movements appear to have had their season while Semiotics continues.   Semiotics is a continuum idea which seems to evade classification, primarily because the kind of definition which best suits it is not merely verbal, analytical definition, but one which represents the dynamical pattern of life as it lives.

Semiotics is not something to catch and cage. It is that quintessential idea which comes out of the authors and their work represented here, out of relationships which, invisibly, bind them into a community.

But if newcomers to Semiotics want a bit more tangible notion of what it is that Semiotics does, we can say that it is the dynamical response to something surprising that is noticed in the world; this surprise sets off a response to examine the "surprising fact", and thereby change one's mind.

One does this by taking a relationship apart: ' e.g., by taking the redness out of its customary strawberry ground. In actuality this is not imaginable for people: one cannot "see" red unless one sees it *on something*, as part *of something*. But semiotically it is possible to lift this Quality of redness out of its habitual place, and see what happens, with respect to a perceived qualitative change in redness, to the very idea!

This investigation of the *Quality* of *something* — both of which are phenomenal, that is, are entities of the world — prepares for a closer semiotic examination. A quality, which corresponds to the elemental adjective in natural language grammar in some languages, is like a "primitive" of thought and perception. Therefore, when one is surprised to perceive some change in this presumed primitive idea it is important to investigate it. By separating this Quality under review from its usual, habitual associations — like red to strawberry — we deform what we thought we knew. We make it seem strange. We shake up the bag of knowledge that we thought was in good order. What we formerly took for granted will then appear unfamiliar, not known. This shake-up is an irrepressible energizing force. It is the *poetic force* (Kevelson 1998).

One of the great mathematicians of the late 19th and early 20th centuries, Bertrand Russell, notes that by the middle of the 19th century "People have discovered how to make reasoning symbolic," (Russell, in Newman, 1956, Vol. 3, at 1577). This ability, on the one hand, contributes to understanding how to "make our ideas clear" (as Peirce wrote), and to reduce vagueness and ambiguity. But this tendency to habits of thought also tends to devitalize and make meaning mechanical. Therefore what was needed was a counteraction, a way of admitting spontaneity to thought. That meant *reaffirming the vague and the living*. The problem is, in part, that if ideas are continuous, and continuity is a special kind of order, then this order is reducible to quantification. But there are great losses when methods of quantification are applied to all creative activity. Peirce relates the quantifiable with the nonquantifiable by introducing the idea of play — of interludes of Musement: — an order of a different nature, and with play the notion of the infinite; the "enumerable infinite".

Peirce's logic of relatives, Russell tells us, reinterprets the symbolic and offsets its tendency to be fixed and definitive (Russell, above at pp 1577-1578). Peirce invents a new symbolism, Russell says. Without going into details here, it is enough to note that what Peirce accomplished was a means of making the easy and automatically habitual *new and difficult*. By providing a means of reintroducing the "difficult" Peirce provides a way to make the old new again.

Semiotic inquiry, based on logics of relatives, of possibility, of paradox, provides a mode of operation which takes the presumably known and makes it less familiar, i.e., makes it difficult. It is for this that Russell especially praises Peirce.

What this does is to reinvest a "mainstream" of knowing about anything whatsoever with analogous counter-entropic force: with new energy, with fresh perception, with vitality.

The contributors to this book are introduced in the following, each with a special perspective on making the old new again.

## III

There is no hierarchy among the variety of disciplines which are here represented by a wide range of semiotic investigators. This is not to say there is no order in semiotic transactions of ideas. Rather, the order which characterizes idea or sign-exchange is between persons as sign-systems in themselves, or between systems of signs representing discourses. In these respects order is not a linear top-down, nor a linear bottom-up, i.e., is neither from authority nor from the basic "simple" or nonreducible "element". Order in semiotics is nonlinear, presuming crossing and recrossing in self-referential and self-representable manner.

Yet Peirce does also present hierarchical orders, namely between most to least abstract of the sciences, from the most abstract mathematical sciences to the least abstract practical sciences such as law, economics and politics which come close to the actual level of human affairs as lived. Jakobson also speaks of a hierarchy which distinguishes the several linguistic levels, the highest of which is at the level of poetics and poetic creativity in discourse, and the lowest which is at the level of nearly automatic, nonintentional level of the phonetic. These levels are not fixed, neither in Peirce's schema nor in Jakobson's, but rather the very boundaries which are implied are not fixed, but are permeable, so that there is crossing and recrossing in and over these unfixed and vague boundaries.

Some of the authors here discuss this notion of several co-existing orders in semiotic systems. In fact, most semioticians are people of more than usual curiosity, openness to ideas, and considerable comfort level in two or more academic "fields". This is certainly true of all contributors to this volume. Yet each is a specialist in that particular topic in the semiotics gamut which s/he has chosen to talk about.

The outstanding scholars who come together in this book do so because they share a commitment to this idea of Semiotics. They have each taken on semiotics as a life's work. Most of the people here not only have worked as a community of inquirers over the several decades of the history of modern semiotics, but share as well a deep wish to take others, students of all ages, into this great adventure of an idea. Individually they are inspiring. As a group they represent the best of what a faculty of teachers can be: *people to learn with*.

It is the "role of the reader" as Umberto Eco tells us (1979) to contribute to the meaning of the text. Here is a feast of appetizers for follow-up semiotic study, from Architecture to Zen (among other "wizardry"). The topics focused on are Folklore, Psychoanalysis, Law, Graphics, Poetics/Literature, History, Architecture, Linguistics, Language/Culture, Music, Drama, Religion, Media and Semiotics-as-Such. This book could be called essays on and about a semiotics of culture. Semiotic studies of physical sciences as well, of biology, mineralogy, neurology, and, in fact, semiotic approaches to whatever traditional departmental study one might find in modern universities, are available and possible as material for a sequel to this *Hi-Fives*.

As long as we use the media of the written languages we have to respect what they are and what they are not. For one, media do not permit us to break with a dominantly lineal order; and we must, at least on the surface level, write one word after another, and have one chapter follow another. What may happen between the lines is another and nonlinear story.

The order of presentation I have chosen is arbitrary. It tells a tale not unlike the way a cartoon strip tells a story in one serial order; but if we shuffle the frames around we have a somewhat different story. The story I tell is intentionally familiar: it starts with the images of things and moves inward, to the emotions for which images have to be invented, *as signs*, to share in the external social worlds.

I don't give the reader a list of test-yourself questions. Instead I leave three suggestions on which to focus:

- 1) unifying themes
- 2) overlapping theory and theoretical references

- 3) contrasts and comparisons between the manner in which a *traditional* "subject" might be presented and the way that subject is represented through a *semiotics lens*.

Any number of projects — of cooperative or individual nature — will come to mind through the reading of this book: some may be verbal while others may take shape through the construction of models, making of films, experiments with different materials and thus the production of all kinds of hybrids. Such projects will want an accompanying explanation, so that the experimenters will not be tempted to credit inspiration only with the project, but to explain the hows and the whys.

## IV

Part One is called *Of Street Signs and Pop Culture*. In this section Arthur Asa Berger's paper on the advertising media takes us to ground level, through the "looking glass" of window displays. This paper is followed by Myrdene Anderson's walking us through enchanting paths of folklore and folklife. Anderson interweaves among folkloric icons a wealth of sources for follow-up research. The third paper in this opening triad is Paul Bouissac's, on the semiotics of popular performance. Bouissac's now classic work on the semiotics of the circus is implicit in this chapter which connects the entertainment of "everyperson" with the theory of signs.

Part Two is titled *Mapping Semiotic Plots*. Here the reader is introduced to Peirce by Roberta Kevelson and to some of the key ideas of this Pioneer of Semiotics as he knew himself to be. Robert Hatten's chapter examines how semiotics from various theoretical frames of reference has brought about a creative interaction, a creative evolution in our understanding of emergent music theory. Hatten especially uses linguistics as a model to frame his work in the nonverbal medium of music. The semiotics of linguistics is Linda Waugh's chapter. She leads the reader through the incomparable greatness of Roman Jakobson's thought spanning almost three-quarters of a century. Waugh points out that the term, semiotics, actually occurs rarely in Jakobson's writings. Yet it was he who "discovered" Peirce's importance for a semiotics of language, and it was he who brought, in his person and through his work, all the coexisting theories of semiotics which had not previously been related. The bibliography of Jakobson's publications is invaluable, and presented here as a study tool in itself.

Indeed, all the contributors to this volume have appended to their papers bibliography that may serve as a resource to be used over and over, in the discovery of this semiotics world. Included in this section is William Pencak's paper which discusses, from the perspective of history, the way semiotic investigators may reinterpret the past. Pencak provides theoretical signposts to show how scholars now and again, shape and reshape the malleable matter of human history.

Part Three is *The Visible Sign*. Included in this section are two papers: one by Steve Skaggs on graphic design. The other is by Shelagh Lindsey whose paper on the semiotics of architecture has brought together, in direct consultation, the most important spokespersons who still continue to work together on this aspect of semiotics. Skaggs' paper, "Making Marks" is in the verbal form of a dialogue between a Dr. Pearce (no relation, I think to the infamous Charles S., except, I suspect, as a same-sound take-off) and a Kathy Bishop who plays the part of student. Skaggs' paper includes original graphics, graphs and other nonverbal highlights and illustrations. He shows how one mode of expression, of making marks, may interpret another.

Lindseys' paper, as noted above, is the tracing of a continuum idea by the very semioticians she cites. Here, too, the visuals become "marks of a mark".

The last part of this book, *The Spirit of Semiotics*, brings together several important viewpoints on the concept of relationships. According to premises held by semiotic theorists of all stripes, the minimal unit of significance is not a *one*, but is at least a pair, i.e., *a relationship*.

Three of the papers in this section are directly concerned with psychology of significant relations. The penultimate paper examines the relational aspects of the law from a semiotic point of view, when law, among the practical sciences, draws directly from life as actually lived in the sphere of human interactions. Vivian Curran's paper takes law as pivotal between actual society and abstract values.

The last paper which brings our venture into semiotics home again takes us to the persistent relation between the games of "wizardry" and real encounters; this paper by Terry Prewitt discusses a variety of religious structures which are markedly significant. In relation to ordinary life, these relations between "sacred and profane" are implicitly foreshadowed in the three earlier papers of this last section; those of Bruce Arrigo, Laurence Rickels and Thomas Beebee.

Beebee's paper is concerned with the development of the tragic, from ancient to modern times. The tragic, as a semiotic phenomenon, permits us to understand the psychological action of the tragic upon theater audiences. Beebee argues that the tragic sign is not intuited nor innate but is learned: a complex, symbolic theatrical strategy.

Laurence Rickels uses literature as genre of a psychoanalytic kind: — a "cryptology" — to explore the process of understanding "dead," "ruin," "unmade". Literature is the sign-vehicle through which Rickels guides us: it is an awe-filled passage.

In the third paper of this section, and the final paper of this introduction, Bruce Arrigo takes us back to the surface level of the criminal justice system, from the "psychoanalytic underground." Lacan's semiotic psychoanalytic theory is the primary frame for Arrigo's paper. He invites us to consider, via semiotic pathways, new, nontraditional ways of talking about, hence of understanding, "socio-legal truths."

As mentioned at the outset of this introduction, ordering is provisional, has little or nothing to do with protocol, and everything to do with present purpose: A trip through blinking orange lights and other signs.

*\*Roberta Kevelson is Distinguished Professor of Philosophy Emeritus and Director of the Center for Semiotic Research, Penn State.*

## REFERENCES (Selected)

Barthes, Roland, 1977, *Elements of Semiology*, trans. A. Lavers and C. Smith. New York: Hill and Wang.

Eco, Umberto, 1976/1979, *A Theory of Semiotics*. Bloomington: Indiana University Press.

Kevelson, Roberta, 1987, *Charles S. Peirce's Method of Methods*. Amsterdam: John Benjamins.

-------, 1990, *Peirce, Paradox, Praxis*. Amsterdam: Mouton.

-------, 1993, *Peirce's Esthetics of Freedom*. New York and Bern: Peter Lang.

-------, 1996, *Peirce, Science, Signs*. New York and Bern: Peter Lang.

-------, 1997, *Peirce's Pragmatism*. New York and Bern: Peter Lang.

-------, 1998, *Peirce and the Mark of the Gryphon*. New York: St. Martin's Press (forthcoming).

Peirce, Charles S., 1931-35, 1958, *Collected Papers*, eds. Ch. Hartshorne, P. Weiss, A. Burke. Cambridge: Harvard University Press.

-------, Microfilm edition of Peirce's unpublished manuscripts, 33 reels, Harvard University.

Russell, Bertrand, 1956, "Mathematics and the Metaphysicians" in J. Newman, ed., *The World of Mathematics*, 3, 1576-1592.

Sebeok, Thomas A., 1976, *Contributions to the Theory of Signs*. Bloomington: RCLS with the Peter de Ridder Press.

# Part One

## *Of Street Signs and Pop Culture*

# Chapter 2

# The Sign in the Window:
# A Semiotic Analysis of Advertising

Arthur Asa Berger*

HAMLET      Do you see yonder cloud that's almost in shape of a camel?

POLONIUS    By th' mass, and 'tis like a camel indeed.

HAMLET      Methinks it is like a weasel.

POLONIUS    It is backed like a weasel.

HAMLET      Or like a whale.

POLONIUS    Very like a whale.

The signs I'll be discussing have two different meanings. Literally speaking signs are print advertisements and television commercials. (The convention, incidentally, is to use the term advertisement for the print media and the term commercial for electronic media.) The window, for my purposes, is the television screen or pages in magazines or other kinds of publications with advertisements on them. But semiotically speaking, they refer to Saussure's and Peirce's analyses of signs and the science of semiotics.

## Two Perspectives on Signs

Saussure split signs into signifiers (sounds and images) and signifieds (concepts) and argued that the relationship that existed between signifiers and signifieds was arbitrary — that is, based on convention. As he wrote in his *Course in General Linguistics (1966: 67):*

I propose to retain the word sign [signe] to designate the whole and to replace concepts and sound-image respectively by *signified* [signifié] and *signifier* [signifiant]; the last two terms have the advantage of indicating the opposition that separates them from each other and from the whole of which they are parts.

Peirce had a different theory of signs and elaborated a trichotomy in which he suggests there are three categories of signs: *icons* (which signify by resemblance), *indexes* (which signify by cause and effect) and *symbols* (whose meanings are conventional which means they have to be learned.).

Peirce stressed the importance of having some signs interpret signs and wrote that a sign "is something which stands to somebody for something in some respect or capacity." (1977:27) He believed that signs pervade the universe. As he explained:

> It seems a strange thing, when one comes to ponder over it, that a sign should leave its interpreter to supply part of its meaning; but the explanation of the phenomenon lies in the fact that the entire universe...is perfused with signs, if it is not composed exclusively of signs, (Peirce; epigraph in Sebeok, 1977: vi).

If everything in the universe is a sign then semiotics becomes the master discipline for interpreting and analyzing everything. I will not pursue the implications of this "imperialistic" notion. For our purposes it is useful to think of everything in a print advertisement or television commercial as a sign and therefore meaningful. The implication of Peirce's statement is that everyone is a practicing semiotician, with varying degrees of expertise, even though most people have not heard the term and are not familiar with the theories of Saussure or Peirce. That is because we all find meaning in signs — not just in words but in all parts of signs, as I will explain shortly.

Traditionally, Saussure's theory is known as semiology and Peirce's as semiotics; I will use the term semiotics, which is the term conventionally used nowadays, to cover both approaches.

There are certain problems we should be aware of when using semiotics. There is the matter of "aberrant decoding," the fact that people who see a commercial or glance at an advertisement may not have the same background as the people who made the commercial or advertisement and thus may interpret it differently from the way its creators thought it would be interpreted.

But even if there are some aberrations in the decoding, that does not mean the decoders (the readers and interpreters of commercials and advertisements) completely misinterpret things or misinterpret everything. We're all different. We have different backgrounds, levels of education, interests, incomes, occupations and so on — but we probably understand most of the messages that are found in commercials and advertisements. Or, at least, enough of us do to make it worth while advertising products and services.

There is also the matter of lying with signs. As Umberto Eco points out, if you can tell the truth with signs, you can also lie with them. So we have to be careful when we analyze signs and distinguish between people who are using signs to tell the truth and people who are using signs to lie to us. For example, many blondes we see are really brunettes who have "dyed by their own hands" or someone else's.

## Signs in Signs: a Primer on Applied Semiotics

I'd like to offer a metaphor that might be useful here. Think of yourself as a "practicing semiotician" as being analogous to Sherlock Holmes or some other detective investigating a crime. He's looking for clues and everything is potentially significant. The difference between detectives and readers of crime novels is that the detectives don't miss important signs that readers gloss over. Often these important signs are buried in descriptions, to which readers pay little attention.

So, let me ask — what might be important in an advertisement or commercial? (In scholarly discourse, works of art are generally called "texts" and I will use that term at times. This enables us to avoid having to write the word commercial or advertisement or whatever, over and over again.) What is important in a text? The answer is — everything! It is possible to make a distinction between the sign/advertisement and the signs/semiotically speaking in the advertisement. To make it easier to discuss advertisements from a semiotic perspective, let me suggest that we think of each sign within an advertisement as an elemental sign or *signeme* — a fundamental sign that cannot be broken down any further. The following chart lists a number of important non-verbal signemes but it does not cover all possible signemes in a print advertisement or commercial. The list can easily be expanded upon; but it does offer an idea of the most commonly found signemes that, depending upon the particular advertisement or commercial, can have varying degrees of importance.

(This list is as follows - *ed. note*)

| | |
|---|---|
| Hair Color | Clothes |
| Hair Style | Body Language |
| Eye color | Setting |
| Eyeglasses (styles) | Relationships implied |
| Earring/other body adornments | Occupations |
| Facial structure | Age |
| Makeup | Gender |
| Figure (women) | Race |
| Body type (men) | Actions going on |
| Facial expressions | Sound effects, Music |
| Spatiality | Design |
| Type faces in text | Color |
| Lighting | |

*Fig. 1: Non-Verbal Signemes in Print Advertisements*

When we come to verbal matters, we might consider the following matters, listed in the chart below.

| | |
|---|---|
| Words used | Arguments & Appeals used |
| Metaphors & Similes | Slogans |
| Associations (Metonymies) | Headlines |
| Negations made | Paradoxes generated |
| Affirmations offered | Questions asked |
| Tone | Style |

*Fig. 2: Verbal Signemes in Advertisements*

We must remember that a word is a kind of sign and the definition of a word is based on convention and must be learned. That explains, in part, why dictionaries are always being revised.

### The Maiden in Paradise: A Case Study
Let's take a very interesting print advertisement as a case study in applied semiotic analysis. The advertisement is for Fidji perfume and appeared a number of years ago in many fashion magazines. We see a photograph with part of the face of a Polynesian woman (from just below her nose) who is holding a bottle of Fidji perfume in curiously intertwined fingers. Her fingernails are red. She has long dark hair, full red lips (slightly parted), and has a yellow orchid tucked into her hair on the right hand side of her face. Around her neck we see a snake, part of whose body forms something that looks like an infinity symbol, whose head faces down, slightly covering the

top of the Fidji bottle. The lighting is rather dramatic, using chiaroscuro (which means, in essence, both clear and dark). Parts of the photograph are light but other parts, particularly the upper right of the photograph, is quite dark.

Let me list some of the things a semiotician would think about in interpreting this advertisement.

1. *The formal design of the ad.* In our minds formal design (approximating axial balance), simplicity and spaciousness (a great deal of white or "empty" space) is associated with class, wealth and sophistication. Advertisements for expensive and "classy" objects often are full of white space and, relatively speaking, empty.

2. *The warm colors.* The maiden's yellow orchid and full red lips and finger nails. Red is commonly used to suggest passion.

3. *The partial showing of the woman's face.* Because we only see the bottom part of her face, it is possible for women to "identify" with her more easily than if we saw her complete face. Her lips are partly open and the lighting emphasizes her long and slender neck. The open lips may suggest current (or future) sexual passion or something of that nature.

4. *The woman is a Polynesian.* In the popular imagination we connect Polynesia with fantasies of natural love and sexuality. Gaughin abandoned France for Polynesia and this story, of his "escape" to paradise is known to many people.

5. *The woman has dark hair.* Dark hair, in American culture, is often associated with warmth, heat, and sexual passion. Women with blonde hair, on the other hand, are often thought of as Nordic and as cold, icy, innocent and sexually unresponsive. Her hair is long, also — which, let me suggest, is connected in the popular mind with youth and sexual "abandon." That explains all those commercials with young women, their long hair flying in the breeze, racing through meadows toward — presumably — their lovers. It is quite common for women to cut their hair short, so they don't have to bother with it as much, when they get older.

6. *The name of the perfume.* The name, "Fidji," makes the connection between this perfume and Polynesia (and all that goes with it) explicit. The copy in this advertisement reinforces this notion.

7. *The yellow orchid.* Flowers are the sexual apparatus of a plant...so there is a hint of sexuality in the use of this orchid, which due to the lighting, is prominently displayed. We often talk about women "flowering" which means becoming physically developed and with that, sexually receptive.

8. *The snake.* Snakes, Freud explained, are phallic symbols by virtue of their shape — an example of iconic semiotic and psychoanalytic interpretation. (It should be pointed out that in some countries that advertisement was run without the snake.) This image, a woman with a snake

around her neck (it looks like a corn snake) is also found in Piero Di Cosimo's "Simonetta Vespucci" and other paintings and works of art as well — an example of intertextuality (one work that either consciously or unconsciously borrows from another work.)

The relationship between women and snakes goes back a long way, to The Garden of Eden, and the outcome of that relationship, Adam's temptation, has been of considerable importance in Western history. One might argue that the snake, in the story of the Garden of Eden, is the prototypical advertising executive. Let me quote from Genesis here. "Now the serpent was more subtil than any beast in the field which the Lord God had made" and he convinced Eve that if she ate from the tree of knowledge of good and evil she wouldn't die but her eyes would be opened. After she ate from the tree and convinced Adam to do the same, they were both thrown out of the Garden of Eden.

Eve's excuse was "The serpent beguiled me, and I did eat." Advertising executives have been beguiling the progeny of Adam and Eve since then — though they have not been required to slide on their bellies and eat dust.

There is also, in Greek mythology, Medusa — the goddess whose hair was made of snakes. They turned any man who looked upon her into stone. Hair, this myth suggests, has power.

9. *The intertwined fingers.* The fingers are curiously intertwined...with one finger shown between two other fingers — approximating, vaguely, a penis coming between two legs. We find intertwined fingers in some works of art, such as Sandro Botticelli's "Primavera" so there is another intertextual relationship in this work that might be considered.

10. *The bottle.* The bottle has a large stopper and highlights that run across it. It has a perpendicular black line in the middle of the bottle and a horizontal black ribbon between the stopper and the bottle.

11. *The woman is naked.* The woman is not wearing any clothes, which reinforces its paradisical image. Before Adam and Eve ate from the tree of knowledge, they were naked and nakedness is associated in Western consciousness with innocence (and in the case of nudists, for example, with a desire to regain the innocence of paradise). Curiously enough we do not see any indication of her breasts. They seem to have been airbrushed out. Showing breasts might suggest maternity and related matters which would not be conducive to fantasies of primitive sex with a natural (read uninhibited) woman. Showing breasts is much different, I should point out, from showing cleavage and indicating breasts — which is a sexual turn on.

12. *The use of the French language.* The ad only has French in it and French here is used because of its metonymic qualities — because we associate the French (whether this association is correct or not is beside the point) with style and sophistication and with sexiness. The French language

also acts as a means of separating those with "class" and who know French (or, at least can understand the French used — which is not very difficult) with the "masses."

13. *The headline used.* In the upper right hand corner of the advertisement, in relatively small type, we see the following words:

*Fidji: le parfum des paradis retrouvés*

I would translate this as "Fidji: the perfume of paradise regained (or rediscovered)". You don't have to know French to understand most of the headline. And the phrase "paradise regained" is one that people with any degree of education are familiar with. So even if they don't know what "retrouves" means, they can most likely figure it out. So you don't really have to know French or be "sophisticated" to be able to understand the headline.

On the bottle we read "Parfum Guy Laroche Paris" and see the logo for Fidji on the right hand side of the bottle as we look at it in the ad (it is actually on the left hand side of the bottle). The only other verbiage we find is at the bottom of the ad on a light band below the image of the woman and the snake, which reads in a roman face:

## *Fidji* de Guy Laroche

and then in small italic:

*De la Haute Couture à la Haute Parfumerie.*

This translates, roughly, as "from high fashion to high perfume." There is, then, rather little in the way of copy. The image is used to sell Fidji, not any arguments made by the copy in the advertisement. But that is rather common in perfume ads because what they are selling, one way or another, is fantasies of sexual abandon, paradisical sex and similar notions.

14. *The "hidden word" in the advertisement.* If you look at the way the snake's body folds back from its head, without stretching things too much you can make out an "S." Then if you look at the highlights on the top of the bottle's stopper, on the top of the bottle and on the bottom of the bottle, you can see an "E." And if you look at the woman's fingers crossing one another, you can make out an "X." Thus the word "SEX" is hidden away or embedded in the image and, so some theoreticians argue, even though people who look at the advertisement may not consciously see the "sex" hidden in the image, unconsciously they pick it up and are affected by it.

15. *The crucifix.* If you look at the vertical black line and the horizontal ribbon on the bottle, you find a highly stylized crucifix form, another bit of symbology that possibly links the passion of Christ with sexual passion in ordinary people. The way the "F" in Fidji is designed also vaguely suggests a crucifix.

16. *The infinity sign formed by the body of the snake.* Part of the way the snake loops around on the woman's shoulder forms an infinity sign — perhaps an indication of the infinite nature of the passion that will be generated by wearing Fidji?

17. *The painted fingernails.* There is something incongruous, one might think, about having a "natural" woman, in Polynesia, wearing painted red fingernails. Maybe the subtext of this advertisement is that you can have the best of both worlds — modernity, sophistication (the perfume is French and therefore, in the popular mind, sophisticated) and elegance *and* the kind of innocence and passion we associate with the innocent and natural woman.

This duality is, in fact, at the core of the advertisement: a natural woman holding a bottle of French perfume. The bottle mediates between the primitive woman "in women" and their socialized, enculturated, everyday lives.

## A Paradigmatic Analysis of the Fidji Advertisement

One of the most famous statements Saussure ever made explained how people find meaning in their experiences. As he explained, "Concepts are purely differential and defined not by their positive content but negatively buy their relations with other terms of the system." (Saussure, 1966:117) "The most precise characteristic" of these concepts, he added, "is being what the others are not." (Saussure, 1966:117) In essence, it is the way language works, by forcing us to see differences, that explains how we make sense of things. Meaning is relational, not based on some kind of essence in things.

The French anthropologist Claude Lévi-Strauss developed a method of analyzing myths that involves finding oppositions in them. I will adapt his method of analysis, paradigmatic analysis, and apply it to the Fidji advertisement. What I will do is look at the oppositions generated by the Fidji ad — suggesting what it is not. My thesis is that when people look at the ad, they go through the same process — if they are to find meaning in it.

| Woman of Color (Polynesian) | White Woman |
|---|---|
| Nature | Urban Society |
| Escape | Imprisonment |
| Paradise | Hell |
| Dark Hair | Light Hair |
| Free Sexuality | Sexually Inhibited |
| Magic | Rationality |
| Fidji perfume | Other perfumes |

*Figure 3: Polar Oppositions in Fidji Advertisement*

I'm not suggesting that people consciously make this paradigmatic analysis when they see the Fidji advertisement, but if Saussure is correct and concepts have meaning differentially, they must do something like this, unconsciously, if the advertisement is to make sense to them. These oppositions are, then, implicit in the advertisement.

There is a good deal of redundancy in the Fidji advertisement to help get the message across. We see the word "Fidji" three times — in the caption, on the bottle, and in the textual matter in the upper right hand part of the ad. And the image of the woman with a flower in her hair (like the women in Gaughin's paintings) and the snake reinforce the Fidji-paradise theme. The perfume promises magic — to transport women back to earlier times, before life was so complex, and their lives were so full of everyday bothers...back to when sexuality was natural and uninhibited. The irony, that this primitive maiden is holding a bottle of very expensive French perfume, is, no doubt, lost on most of those to whom the advertisement is directed.

Let us make a quick trip, now, from paradise to hell — and consider the famous Macintosh "1984" commercial that was broadcast in the 1984 Olympics. It is often found in lists of "top ten commercials" and is, I would suggest, a brilliant piece of work. I have a Quick-Time video of this commercial on my computer, thanks to "The 1997 Apple MacAdvocate CD-ROM" which works on both Macintosh and IBM PC type computers.

## On the Semiotic Analysis of Television Commercials

Television commercials are infinitely more complicated texts for semioticians to deal with than magazine advertisements. It is possible to think of a television commercial as being composed of a huge number of "shots," each of which is equivalent to a magazine or print advertisement in terms of the signemes found in it. To this we must add matters such as dialogue, music, narrative structure, sound effects, editorial manipulation, and the power of the human voice.

If a commercial is made on film, which runs at 24 frames a second, a fifteen second television commercial would contain approximately 360 frames. A thirty second commercial would contain 720 frames. We do not have the same discrete unit — the film frame — in commercials that are done on video, but we can substitute — without doing too much violence to the truth — the shot as our minimal unit. Of course many of the frames or shots in any given commercial would be similar in nature, but some commercials have numerous quick cuts in them so it is conceivable we could end up with a thirty second television commercial that has thirty or forty (or even more) shots, in the form of quick cuts, in it.

It is impractical to make the same kind of detailed semiotic analysis of every signeme in a television commercial that I made in the Fidji advertisement. But we must deal with important signemes and tie these to the narrative structure of the commercial. And we must also consider Saussure's suggestion that the mind finds meaning differentially — which means we must also look for the patterns of opposition in narrative texts, except that in commercials the polar oppositions are generally shown, not merely implied.

## The 1984 Macintosh Commercial

This commercial was made by the distinguished British director Ridley Scott for around $600,000. (That figure was quoted to me by someone from the agency that hired Scott to make the commercial.) Let me offer a brief synopsis of this text:

> It starts out with an extreme long shot of a group of men marching in a huge and strange building. We see they have shaved heads (it was made using skinheads) and are wearing coarse uniforms. They are being led to a vast auditorium for a brainwashing session. In one of the shots we see their heavy boots marching in unison. We have a sense that they are prisoners in some kind of prison or total institution. Then there is a cut of a beautiful blonde woman who is shown running ahead of a group of troopers, with plastic head protections, who are chasing her. The skinheads file into a huge auditorium where they watch a man's face on a gigantic television screen, indoctrinating them. His talk is ideological gobbledygook. The woman races into the auditorium, spins and throws a small sledgehammer at the screen. There is an explosion as the sledgehammer hits the screen. The inmates stare, open mouthed, at what they have seen. Then we read that 1984 won't be like 1984 (the Orwell dystopian novel) and that a new kind of computer, the MacIntosh, is to be introduced.

Let me list a few of the important signemes in this text.

1. *The building*. It is a very strange building, with corridors that vaguely remind one of veins and arteries in the human body.

2. *The skinheads*. The men are all shown marching, like forced laborers, toward some destination. Their faces are sullen, their clothes ill fitting and drab, their boots heavy and ugly. We have a sense that we are in a concentration camp, a prison, or some kind of total institution.

3. *The boots*. The shot of the boots may possibly have reference to Eisenstein's film *Potemkin*, which has a famous shot of the boots of the Tsar's soldiers as they massacre people.

4. *The blonde woman*. The existence of this woman shows that there is resistance in this institution. Her blonde hair and vitality contrast with the sullen, zombie-like prisoners. Wearing a white jersey and red shorts, she races ahead of the police. In this text, Apple is represented by an attractive blonde woman and IBM by a "faceless" bureaucrat. The woman liberates the prisoners but they have been so brainwashed that they cannot do anything at the moment of their liberation.

5. *The police*. The blonde woman is chased by a band of burly men, wearing uniforms and plastic head protectors. We have a sense, from the way the police are shown — and the condition of the inmates — that the police are powerful and brutal.

6. *The indoctrinator or brainwasher*. A bald man, perhaps in his fifties, with eyeglasses, presumably from the bureaucracy that runs the prison, is shown on a television set, brainwashing the prisoners. We only see his face. His words don't really make sense. He talks about "the first glorious anniversary of the information purification repentance" and gardens of "pure ideology" and suggests that "our enemies shall talk themselves to death...."

7. *The sledgehammer*. The blonde woman spins and hurls the sledgehammer, with a mighty effort, toward the gigantic television screen in the front of the auditorium. When the sledgehammer finally hits the television screen, it explodes and the imagine of the man disappears. The brainwashed inmates can only stare, open mouthed, at what has happened.

There is an element of intertextuality at work here. One thinks of the Bible and the story of David slaying the giant Goliath with a slingshot. The blonde woman can be thought of as a David figure, representing Apple computers, and the huge bureaucratic face as a Goliath figure, standing for International Business Machines. The sledgehammer is the Macintosh computer, which will — due to its superior technology — defeat Apple's much larger and more power rival, IBM/Goliath.

One might also think of Eve who rescued Adam from his ignorance, but convincing him to eat from the tree of the knowledge of good and evil. The blonde woman is attempting to rescue the skinhead prisoners from their condition of indoctrination and is bringing not knowledge of good and evil but the possibility of knowledge of reality to the inmates.

8. *The Announcement*. After the image of the brainwasher has been shattered, we see the following announcement:

> On January 24th, Apple Computers will introduce Macintosh and you will see why 1984 won't be like "1984."

Here the intertextual relationship between the commercial and George Orwell's novel is made most explicit.

**Paradigmatic Analysis of the 1984 Commercial**
What are the primary oppositions in this text? Let me suggest the following ones.

| BIG BROTHER | THE INMATES |
|---|---|
| commands | obeys |
| hair | hairless |
| regular clothes | ill fitting uniforms |
| speaks | listen |
| brainwasher | brainwashed |
| is looked at | look at |
| calculating | mindless |
| dehumanizing | dehumanized |
| heartless | emotionless |

This Brainwasher/Inmates polarity is "resolved" by the blonde woman, who destroys the image of the brainwasher Big Brother figure and in doing so, it is suggested, destroys the power he has over the inmates. This set of bipolar oppositions is contained in the text and even though viewers might not be conscious of it or articulate it, they must approximate it if they are to make sense of what is going on. The blonde mediates between the inmates and the Big Brother figure.

There is one other important bipolar opposition I would like to discuss here, and that is between the blonde woman and the inmates.

| BLONDE | INMATES |
|---|---|
| Female | Male |
| Active | Passive |
| Bright Clothes | Ill fitting uniforms |
| Liberates | Liberated |
| Freedom | Imprisonment |

There is a question about who the inmates represent. One interpretation suggests that they are IBM employees, who in 1984 supposedly were very regimented and controlled by the IBM corporation. The other interpretation suggests that the inmates represent the American public, who will — with the release of the Macintosh — have the power to escape from their imprisonment (or ignorance) at the hands of governmental bureaucrats and other who control the communication process. Some conspiracy theorists might see the IBM corporation and the American government as being tied to one another, so the blonde is liberating both those who work for IBM and the American public at the same time.

This brief semiotic analysis of the 1984 Macintosh commercial cannot do justice to this micro-drama, to its texture, to the startling nature of the imagery, to its narrative excitement. But it suggests, at least, some of the things to consider when doing a semiotic analysis of a television commercial: analyze the most important signemes (nuclear signs, monosigns, whatever you will), look for examples of intertextuality, and consider the bipolar oppositions that give the text its meaning.

The advertising industry is so all-pervasive and generates so many interesting print advertisements and commercials that there's no lack of work for those interested in using semiotics to interpret advertising and, indirectly of course, American culture and society. For advertising grows out of American culture and society. Which leads to an interesting question: if advertising is the symptom, what is the disease?

## On the Matter of Authorial Intent

One question that arises involves to what degree the people involved in making the Fidji advertisement and Ridley Scott and the others involved in the creation of the 1984 Macintosh commercial were aware of all the things I've found in these two texts. Am I "reading in" material that isn't there, or am I "discovering" material in the text but not generally noticed by ordinary readers or placed in the texts intentionally by the creative individuals involved in making these two works. (This is sometimes known as the "hocus-pocus" versus "God's truth" debate about signs and meanings in texts. The "hocus-pocus" theorists would say that semioticians and other textual critics "read in" all kinds of things that aren't there; the "God's truth" theorists argue that they are merely writing about material contained in the texts being studied but not always recognizable.)

I would argue that creators of texts have a certain sense of what they are doing but that they are not conscious of all the signs, signemes, symbols, and so on found in their creations. That is, writers and artists in all media create works, tapping upon unconscious sources, using conscious intentions, being influenced by other artists and other matters (sexual, political, etc.) and they have certain things that they try to realize — but they do not recognize what they are doing, to a large extent. That is why semioticians and other kinds of scholars are needed to investigate and explain texts, for they are very complex works and, as the analyses of the Fidji advertisement and 1984 commercial suggests, often have an enormous amount of material in them.

As Yuri Lotman, the distinguished semiotician argued in *The Structure of the Artistic Text* (1977:23)

> Art is the most economical, compact method for storing and transmitting information. But art has other properties wholly worthy of the attention of cyberneticians and perhaps, in time, of design engineers.

> Since it can concentrate a tremendous amount of information into the "area" of a very small text (cf. the length of a short story by Chekhov or a psychology textbook), an artistic text manifests yet another feature: it transmits different information to different readers in proportion to each one's comprehension: it provides the reader with a language in which each successive portion of information may be assimilated with repeated readings.

What semiotics does is teach us how to be good (by which I mean "deep" or "perpicuous") readers, how to discover the ways artistic texts — whether they be paintings, novels, or print advertisements and commercials — generate meaning and affect our consciousness and, in many cases — especially the case of advertisements and commercials — our behavior.

And as the *Sign Wars* (to quote the title of a recent book on advertising) heat up, and advertisers work more and more frenetically to capture our attention, it is imperative that we learn how these messages attempt to manipulate us and gain, from our knowledge, to whatever degree we can, a means of insulation from their effects.

*Arthur Asa Berger, Broadcast & Electronic Communication Arts Department, San Francisco State University.* Copyright © *1997.*

## REFERENCES

Barthes, Roland, 1972, *Mythologies,* A. Lavers, trans., New York: Hill & Wang.

Baudrillard, Jean, 1996, *The System of Objects,* J. Benedict, trans., London: Verso.

Berger, Arthur Asa, ed., *Semiotics of Advertisements,* Aachen, Germany: Edition Herodot.

Berger, Arthur Asa, 1989, *Signs in Contemporary Culture: An Introduction to Semiotics.* Salem, Wisconsin: Sheffield Publishing Company.

-----, 1996, *Manufacturing Desire: Media, Popular Culture and Everyday Life.* New Brunswick, New Jersey: Transaction Publishers.

-----, 1997, *Seeing is Believing: An Introduction to Visual Communication.* Second Edition. Mountain View, California: Mayfield Publishing Company.

Goldman, Robert and Stephen Papson, 1996, *Sign Wars: The Cluttered Landscape of Advertising.* New York: Guilford Press.

Lotman, Y., 1977, *The Structure of the Artistic Text.* Ann Arbor: Michigan Slavic Contributions.

Vetergaard, Torben and Kim Schroder, 1985, *The Language of Advertising.* Oxford, England: Basic Blackwell Ltd.

# Chapter 3

# Folklore, Folklife, and other Bootstrapping Traditions

Myrdene Anderson*

Culture is elusive. It passes secretly, often silently, telepathically, between a parent and a child who does not even realize she has been looking on or listening until years later, when she somehow discovers what she has learned and can now do herself; it ripens, untended ... Cantwell 1993: 80.

## I
## Signs and/in/as Life

Each person's life is preceded by one sign of firstness, of potentiality — singled out from a whole cascade of signs in ontogeny (development) and phylogeny (evolution) — the gleam in his or her parent's eyes. This "gleam" initiates a fresh web of stories *about*, *to*, and *by* the individual, the former sources of stories not even ceasing with death of the person, who will live on in narrative and even be addressed silently and out loud.

Meanwhile during a lifetime, the individual is at the nexus of a timeline running from past to future, intersected by the immediacy of here and now. Human experience precipitates from this stream of signs constituting biology, culture, and language, sandwiched Janus-fashion between the fact and fiction of the past and the prescriptions and anticipations of the future. Most especially this experience is mediated by language, that system of signs unique to *Homo sapiens*.

Humans, along with other creatures, negotiate the kinky path from past to future, mostly with conspecifics, in a restricted but never closed community sharing an array of customary habits we can call "culture". This behavior is carried out in a culturally constructed environment "natural" to the group, relying on many sign systems from the senses (such as pheremonal via smell, and haptic via touch) and from habits couched in memory, whether from shallow-time, linear, ontogenetic *development* or deep-time, nonlinear and indeterminate, phylogenetic *evolution*. Superposed on and sometimes subsuming these zoosemiotic systems, humans enjoy language. Human language is fundamentally a symbolic (arbitrary, opaque) systems of signs, buttressed with indexical (pointing) and iconic (representative) elements. Folklore, largely linguistic, is organized into forms which are symbolic at still higher levels, which parallel in some instances the semiotic systems in dreams.

According to Bascom (1968:497), the term "folklore" entered English in 1846 through William John Toms' interests in British traditional culture, probably inspired by the German studies by the Grimm brothers and others. Folklore, the folk- learning inclusive of folktales, legend, and myth, are explicitly linguistically encoded and primarily oral. Even folklife customs, learned through imitation — such as dance, musical arts, ethnomedicine, and handicrafts — are accompanied by beliefs and instructions in language. To further fuzz this juncture between languaging and other cultural behavior, oral folklore forms are themselves supported by extralinguistic constraints and behavioral practices, from prescriptive settings to gestural accompaniment. For instance, folktales, unlike legends or myths, are usually recounted after dark (Bascom 1965/1984:9).

## II
## Language and/in/as Narrative

Language *permits* humans to "decline" their actual and imaginary worlds in an *infinite* number of scenarios, and to "conjugate" these worlds in trajectories of *infinite* dynamicity. Permits? Well, it would be more accurate to say that language and culture make these processes virtually obligatory. Infinite? Well, near-infinite and decidedly indeterminate, while constrained by habit, culture, and language itself — would be a more careful assertion. The constraints both *limit* and *enable* the worlds we inhabit, and that inhabit us. The constraints provide us with conventional rationales and goals, couched in our language and culture, yet give us plenty of slack, like rope, from which to construct a *developmental* noose, an *evolutionary* macrame, or a limp line between here and there, now and then — or an invitation to be overlooked or ignored. See below for the semiotic dynamics referred to as relatively closed, linear, developmental and very open, indeterminate, evolutionary processes.

Other creatures may have interior "discourse" and past-recall and future-anticipation even more richly embellished than we can document for them, but we can be quite certain that these other creatures do *not* have "not", *nor* can they lie! Their communication systems permit no negation, no constructive fantasy, no manipulations of other times and places, and no sustained prevarication. Other animals cannot "re-call" a pheromone indicating "fear" and replace it with another saying "not-fear" or "hungry" — nor can we, in the medium of smell. The odor, the touch, the sigh, the taste, the raised eyebrow, cannot say, "this pertains to the day-before-yesterday". In fact, most such signs leak out without being presented with deliberation; they are less symbolic than indexical or iconic.

Humans, thanks to language, find it easy to lie and deny, to transport both sender and receiver to other actual and imagined situations, and to construct elaborate shared narratives, and simultaneously to modify and contradict these stories. Indeed, human life itself suspends from these webs of possibility, probability, and actuality, impossibility, improbability, and counter-factuality. This is tantamount to saying that human experience is organized by, through, and into stories. Even science, oral or written, relies on the discursive habits of its practitioners.

## III
## Developmental and Evolutionary Narratives

In everyday speech we impute digital factuality and couterfactuality, or analogue gradations and provisionalities pertaining to facts and fictions, about the relative "reality" feature in stories. We don't need a metalanguage to deal with fact and fiction in everyday life. Socially situated, fact and fiction (and faction) slip into and out of each other. Children believe the fable, *not* believe *in* the fable. And adults "lie with statistics", or so the folk saying has it.

But both fact and fiction can be rendered in either straightforward, linear, developmental fashion, or in nonlinear, perhaps spiral or metaphoric, evolutionary fashion.

In western cultures and languages, the common form of any story often has a beginning, a middle, and an end. The explicit plot-driven form typifies the semiotic process of *development*, while stories riddled with nonlinearities and streams of consciousness typify the semiotic process of *evolution*. (See Salthe 1991; Salthe and Anderson 1989). Developmental genres, such as tragedy (and proverb and fable), lend themselves to ends with explicit didactic messages, while evolutionary genres, such as comedy (and riddle and often myth), invite the recovery of possibly implicit messages or just the acceptance of the narrative as a means to no obvious extrinsic ends whatever. Development, exemplified by tragedy, engenders suspense; evolution, such as comedy leads to surprise.

The consumer of narrative has as much a role in shaping these two vectors of sense-making as does the teller. Much has to do with the habits conjoining speaker and hearer, and the intentions and context as well. Both developmental and evolutionary discourse can entrance and addict both speaker and hearer, the more so perhaps when not subjected to close, critical analysis. The participatory response to developmental narratives is — "and then?, and then?, oh!", because these stories have a temporally linear, syntagmatic construction. The participatory response to evolutionary narratives is more like — "I continue to listen, I'm enjoying it, don't stop!", as the convoluted, open-ended but holistic, paradigmatic construction acts as a sink for impressions, not an invitation for closure.

Both developmental and evolutionary narratives support repeated renderings. Like muscle, and culture itself, they become stronger through use rather than wearing out. While evolutionary narratives by definition may be unique and intransigent to comparison, except analysis between versions in space or time, developmental narratives have a common linear structure with built-in stages. Of course, an evolutionary narrative in the telling has a beginning, middle, and end, but these ensue from its enactment in real time. For example, "trickster" tales can be very convoluted, while the figure wobbles between wisdom and folly (Anderson 1998, Spinks 1991). On the other hand, the beginning, middle(s), and end of a developmental narrative pertain to the form, which invites comparison across quite distinct stories. As discussed below, diverse versions of the Hero myth recounts a quest with an explicit end (Campbell 1968, Segal 1978/1984).

# IV
## Genres of Folklore and Folklife

Human language as interior experience, as somatic aural-oral speech, and for some languages as extrasomatic inscribed signs such as writing, dominates the pragmatics of cultural behavior. People talk, tell, gab, and mumble to themselves, sometimes thinking that it's all invented for the occasion. We scarcely notice when these narratives derive from the deep historical or prehistorical (before written records) past, or how they project into the proximate and distant future, through their repetitions and translations into other actions. This is the realm of folklore and folklife. "[W]e imitate, impersonate, incorporate, and figure forth our culture..." (Cantwell 1993:82).

Folklore and folklife articulate, obviously, at the informal, naturalistic level of "folk". They need never be written, described, analyzed, compared, questioned; they are learned without being taught. Folklore comes from the past through linguistic forms, always nuanced by changing circumstances, and, like a virus, finds carriers into future generations of the tradition. Folklife is typically propelled by material as well as mental and linguistic practices; in other words, folklife may be more shaped by feedback based on perceived functionality, while folklore persists independent of logical or analytic justification. Folklore and folklife refresh themselves through repetition and through outright new invention, as in contemporary urban tales, which may also be variations on older, established themes. In fact, all things considered, folkloric versions can persist with remarkable stability (Dundes 1962/1984:274), especially when constrained by a developmental narrative form (analagous to the ontogeny from birth to death shaping secular lives and practices), or when referenced to a universal psyche (Kluckhohn 1959:268).

Without a doubt, folklore and folklife joined language and culture to define our species. Mysteries as well as wisdom are carried by folklore, in dense capsules such as folktales, legends, and myths (Bascom 1965/1984:8-9). Folklore tends to be in shorter, well-shaped, translucent, developmental prose forms, while poetry, as found in epics, can carry longer, sometimes inscrutable, rhythmic, opaque, evolutionary forms. Poetry may be as motivated by its form as its content, so that its learning may require explicit teaching, while the prose stories may permit of some ad-lib renditions. Folklore seeps from generation to generation. Children may be exposed to fables, riddles, aphorisms, folktales, legends, and myths, and even become adept at reciting them, before any levels of meaning are evident. Indeed, once internalized like this, there may be little call for dispassionate analysis. The lore satisfies both carrier and audience "as is". In fact, even children may resent variations on the familiar form, and demand "authenticity", (for a select bibliography of folklore sources, see Anderson and Kirby 1997; and for a comprehensive introduction to folklore and folklife, consult Georges and Jones 1995).

Folklife is even more social than folklore, if that is possible. The practices constituting folklife range from the manifestly pragmatic to the murky habits that may or may not obscure some latent functions. Both folklore and folklife are performed, and re-performed without much reflection, with or without deliberate or incidental deviation, indefinitely. They can also be re-performed self-consciously, as in folk music recitals, historical event re-enactments, cultural revivals, and museum exhibits (Cantwell 1993). Folklife forms have also been compared across time and space with rich results; Alan Lomax's ethnology (1968) of folksong styles is among the most impressive.

# V
# Sacred and Secular Lore as
# Received Fact (Myth and Legend)

Following Bascom (1965/1984; Sebeok 1958), sacred lore, such as *myth*, is believed, as fact and truth, on faith. It is believed by both narrator and audience. Such sacred stories are set in the deep historical or even prehistorical past, when perhaps different forces and extra-human personages regulated the cosmos, or were regulated by it.

Myths can be dogmatic, even didactic, or they may simply relate the givens of the cosmos and human existence within it. Proscriptions, as taboos, outnumber prescriptions, perhaps because humans learn best from negative examples to be avoide — the positive ones being either vague, general, or unattainable. A tally of the Ten Commandments is instructive in this regard.

Often, cosmology is human ontogeny writ large, as the body grounds the metaphor motivating developmental stories. Myth deals with human birth and death, and with the creation and dissolution of the world as well. When/how/why did time begin, when/how/why will it end? Where/what/why is space/place besides the familiar here and there?

Creation myths relate how the culture, and the cosmos, took shape. Sometimes embedded in the creation story is a formula for the end of the world, or in other cases separate myths of dissolution may exist. In western culture, we have at least three contemporary instantiations of the dissolution of the world, two by fire (AIDS through sex, and global warming), one by ice (nuclear winter) (Anderson 1989).

In myth, the gods carry on their human-mimicking families and foibles, and through myth, the landscape becomes animated as well. Myths classify and name, often justifying the social reality.

This is not to say that myths are just-so stories. They deal with big questions having slightly smaller answers — contradiction can not be dismissed. Contradiction, ambiguity, paradox — between real and ideal, between good and bad, between the past and present, between the superior and the inferior — are sometimes domesticated through transformations (Eliade 1962). The chief could be reborn as a fly; and the virtuous weak do enter the Kingdom of Heaven, leaving powerful sinners relegated to hell.

Hence, the reconciliation of contradiction in myth often aligns it with religious functions. In any event, myths are mulitfunctional, and can be read, understood, and analyzed on different levels and from different perspectives.

The main distinction between myth and *legend* is that the latter is not necessarily sacred, but may be secular, and set in a more recent historical past. Both narrator and audience believe the legend, as they do the myth, but adults realize that they have been party to the promulgation and also initiation of legends — family stories about an ancestor, tall tales from traditional lore and from the internet (Dundes and Pagter 1996), renditions from "real life" that take on a life of their own.

Legends are situated in a familiar world, inhabited by humans. The relations of concern may be culturo-historically grand (developmental rises and falls of dynasties) or focused on individuals. Individuals may be named, with or without their identy being confirmed in the historical record (Buffalo Bill, versus Paul Bunyan). Or extraordinary and non-human creatures may be the players; the ghosts and fairies of legend are believed, if not believable by wider audiences, which takes these legends to be folktales instead.

Somewhere on the less remote side of myth and legend, history takes over. But this is hardly a progression. History generates myth and legend, and conversely, scholars mine myth and legend for insights on history and society. The important distinction is that folklore forms are more social, more somatic, more visceral, more imperative, more compelling, more inscrutable, than history (Barthes 1972:124-131). This is to say that, compared with a developmental history, the folklore forms are holistic and evolutionary. Yet, a history of the unique would be evolutionary, and certain folklore forms with formulae, as the Hero sequence, are quintessentially developmental.

A suitable example here would be the two "theories" of history: the hero (or villain) makes (evolutionary) history, versus the view that (developmental) history makes the hero (or villain). Taking Hitler and the holocaust, the evolutionary story would present Hitler as the author of the holocaust, something that would never have happened in the absence of that unique actor. The developmental story would present the socioeconomic conditions of the times, positing that something drastic would have happened at this conjunction even without a Hitler. Of course, the evidence points to both strains of sense-making having merit, and that will always be the case. No analytical categories are intended to reduce analysis to classification, nor should they, however persuasive a fit, foreclose open-ended investigations.

As mentioned, the Hero of myth and legend, is often marked by or before birth. He, or she, due to powerful circumstances embarks on a journey, or is thrust on its path. The Hero does not, of his or her own volition, merely travel about, in an evolutionary fashion. No, the Hero is a dependent variable in a developmental script that integrates larger forces. Between embarking on the journey (separation, like a birth) and the return (with a prize, the grail, the gold at the end of the rainbow — consequently less like death than eternal life), the Hero undergoes trials and tribulations, and follows cues and clues. The Hero faces challenge and earns insight, and may even fail at the task posed. Failure and death would make the story truly tragic, but even when successful, the Hero story is tragic in a semiotic sense, in that it provokes suspense in carrying out a linear, developmental formula.

# VI

## Secular Lore as Constructed Fiction
## (Folktale — and Science)

While legend may be either sacred or secular, *folktales* are recognizably fiction. Folktales may be situated in any place, at any time, familiar or unfamiliar; they may also be timeless and placeless. And they may be told anytime, anywhere, as well, but especially after dark (Bascom 1965/1984:11). However, folktales often feature a formulaic beginning and closure, such as "Once upon a time" and "They lived happily ever after". Perhaps because of this, a person could easier presume to author a folktale than either a legend or myth.

Folktales come in several genres, including fables (moral tales), animal talks, trickster tales, and human talks. Fairy tales don't qualify as folktales, however, as their protagonists are usually believed in, and consequently fairy tales are apt to be legends.

Various other verbal art forms fall under or near the rubric of folktales: riddles, tongue-twisters, proverbs, and other aphorisms. Folktales in general appeal to young children as well as adults.

In *science*, and social science and humanities, scholars construct still other narratives. Science is, after all, making sense, making stories. Some of scientific narratives derive from the semiotic study of folklore and folklife themselves. The pioneers in this venture include Vico (1725/1984), a prescient Italian philosopher seeking universal laws of society, and, much later, Van Gennep (1909/1960) who posed that rites of passage, often aligning with myth, generate for the participant a transformation through first separation from a past state, then transition into a liminal borderline state, and finally integration with a new emergent state. Victor Turner (1969) among others elaborates on this system in the analysis of performance. Stith Thompson (1946) and Vladimir Propp (1968) concentrate on the comparative elements in the folktale. Perhaps the most recognized analysts of myth are Claude Levi-Strauss (1966), who takes a structural semiotic approach generating numerous contrasting features, Mircea Eliade (1975) who is also interested in symbolism, and Joseph Campbell (1968) who seeks universal patterns and processes.

# VII
## Bootstrapping, Defying, and Jump-starting Culture

The "functions" of folklore and folklife include education and instruction in practical and ethical culture, social control through explicit didactic messages, sociopsychological release through the fantastic and through violations of norms (trickster tales, dirty jokes ) (Bascom 1968), and validation of social disjuncture in liminal states accompanying ritual performances of myth in particular (Turner 1969).

As we explore still other "functions", no one can justify the reduction of any subject matter to function or even to functions. Folklore and folklife also resist because they exist; people enjoy these fundamental elements of culture, and through this dissipative aspect alone, folklore and folklife would thrive so long as they were not terminally "dysfunctional".

While folklore and folklife practices constitute the generative habits of nonliterate societies, they are obviously crucial to literate societies as well, whether formalized or not. Interestingly, political functions cannot be underestimated in today's world.

Different sectors of society imprint on distinct folklore and folklife practices, which practices — whether secret or specially coded or not — can also be used to excluded outsiders. These phenomena are most evident among the youth and within closed congregations, including religious ones.

Whole nation states have reinvented and deployed folklore and folklife in a mission to foreground their unique histories and claims to territory, language, and culture (Herzfeld 1982, 1997). Hence, semioticiams (especially linguists, folklorists, anthropologists, and archaeologists) may be conscripted to serve these larger political agendas.

Without political agendas, people commonly use folklore for social solidarity. This becomes particularly evident when the solidarity is not only positive, but negative, against others. An excellent example of this occurred in Nazi-occupied Norway during the Second World War, when folklore and humor in the Norwegian language could ridicule and undermine the occupying Germans, without them necessarily noticing (Stokker 1997).

Folklore and folklife ground folk culture, and folk culture itself is the generator of any other configurations of culture, however "high" or "formal" or "text-based". Folklore and folklife habits shape, limit, and enable the practices beyond the everyday. New nation-states feed on their pasts to project their images into the future, just as old neighborhoods gather for new year's fireworks, just as family gatherings are incomplete without the recitation of stories.

The folklore and folklife we experience constitute the node between past and future, even as they inevitably tinker with the representation of the past and have no confident prediction or control over the future. Our heritage in this regard is generous, maleable, enduring — and forgiving.

*\*Myrdene Anderson is Professor of Anthropology at Purdue University.*

## REFERENCES

Anderson, Myrdene, 1991, "Cosmological Semiotics: Rhymes and Reasons in the Cosmos." *Das Ganze und seine Teile — The Whole and Its Parts,*

Walter A. Koch, ed., 21-30, Bochum Publications in Evolutionary Cultural Semiotics, 19. Bochum, Germany: Brockmeyer.

Anderson, Myrdene, 1998, "Pricking Trickster," *The American Journal of Semiotics*, 13.3 (Fall 1996, forthcoming 1998).

Anderson, Myrdene, and John T. Kirby, 1997, "Folklore," Chapter 9. *The Comparative Reader: A Handlist of Basic Reading in Comparative Literature,* John T. Kirby, ed. New Haven, Connecticut: Chancery Press.

Barthes, Roland, 1972, *Mythologies,* translated from the French (1957) by Annette Lavers. New York: Hill and Wang.

Bascom, William, 1984, "The Forms of Folklore:  Prose Narratives," *Sacred Narrative:  Readings in the Theory of Myth,* Alan Dundes, ed., 5-29. Berkeley:  University of California Press.  Reprinted from *Journal of American Folklore* 78: 3-20 (1965).

-----, 1968, "Folklore", *The International Encyclopedia of the Social Sciences* 5: 496-500, David L. Sills, ed. New York:  The Macmillan Company and The Free Press.

Campbell, Joseph, 1968, *The Hero with a Thousand Faces.*  Princeton, New Jersey:  Princeton University Press.

Cantwell, Robert, 1993, *Ethnomimesis:  Folklife and the Representation of Culture.*  Chapel Hill:  University of North Carolina Press.

Dundes, Alan, 1984, "Earth-Diver:  Creation of the Mythopoeic Male," *Sacred Narrative:  Readings in the Theory of Myth,* Alan Dundes, ed., pp. 270-294.  Berkeley:  University of California Press.  Reprinted from *American Anthropologist* 64:  1032-1050  (1962).

Dundes, Alan, and Carl R. Pagter, 1996, *Sometimes the Dragon Wins:  Yet More Urban Folklore from the Paperwork Jungle.*  Syracuse, New York: Syracuse University Press.

Eliade, Mircea, 1962, *The Two and the One,* translated from the French by J.M. Cohen.  Chicago:  University of Chicago Press.

-----, 1975, *Myths, Rites, Symbols:  A Mircea Eliade Reader.*  New York: Harper and Row.

Gennep, Arnold Van, 1960, *The Rites of Passage,* translated from the French (1909).  London:  Routlege.

Georges, Robert A., and Michael Owen Jones, 1965, *Folkloristics:  An Introduction.*  Bloomington:  Indiana University Press.

Herzfeld, Michael, 1997, *Ours Once More:  Folklore, Ideology, and the Making of Modern Greece.*  Austin:  University of Texas Press, 1982.

-----, *Cultural Intimacy:  Social Poetics in the Nation-State.*  New York: Routlege.

Kluckhohn, Clyde, 1959, "Recurrent Themes in Myths and Mythmaking," *Proceedings of the American Academy of Arts and Sciences* 88: 268-279.

Levi-Strauss, Claude, 1966, *The Savage Mind,* translated from the French. Chicago: University of Chicago Press.

Lomax, Alan, 1968, *Folk Song Style and Culture.* Washington, D.C.: American Association for the Advancement of Science, 88.

Nuckolls, Charles W., 1996, *The Cultural Dialectics of Knowledge and Desire.* Madison: University of Wisconsin Press.

Propp, Vladimir, 1958/1968, *Morphology of the Folktale.* 2nd edition. Austin: University of Texas Press.

Radin, Paul, 1955/1956, *The Trickster: A Study in American Indian Mythology.* New York: Philosophical Library.

Salthe, Stanley N., 1991, *Development and Evolution: Complexity and Change in Biology.* Cambridge: MIT Press.

Salthe, Stanley N., and Myrdene Anderson, 1989, "Modeling Self-organization," *Semiotics 1988,* Terry J. Prewitt, John Deely, and Karen Haworth, eds., pp 14-23. Lanham: University Press of America.

Sebeok, Thomas A., 1958, ed., *Myth: A Symposium.* Bloomington: Indiana University Press.

Segal, Robert A., 1978, "Joseph Campbell's Theory of Myth," *Sacred Narrative: Reading in the Theory of Myth,* Alan Dundes, ed., pp. 256-269. Reprinted from *Journal of American Academy of Religion* 44.1: 97-114.

Spinks, C.W., 1991, *Semiosis, Marginal Signs and Trickster: A Dagger of the Mind.* London: MacMillan.

Stokker, Kathleen, 1997, *Folklore Fights the Nazis: Humor in Occupied Norway, 1940-1945.* Madison: University of Wisconsin Press.

Thompson, Stith, 1946, *The Folktale.* New York: Dryden Publishers.

Turner, Victor, 1969, *The Ritual Process Structure and Anti-Structure.* The Lewis Henry Morgan Lectures, 1966. Chicago: Aldine Publishing Company.

Vico, Giambattista, 1984, *The New Science.* 1st edition 1725. Translation from the Italian of the 3rd edition of 1744, by T.G. Bergin and M.H. Fish. Ithaca, New York: Cornell University Press.

# Chapter 4

# The Semiotic Approach to Performing Arts: Theory and Method

Paul Bouissac*

## I

In modern societies, the performing arts form a distinct category of public entertainment by opposition to the mass distribution through the media of expertly staged performances which have been recorded and edited. By contrast, theater, ballet, circus, concert, rodeo, puppetry, storytelling, etc., unfold their signs in real space and time, and engage spectators who respond cognitively and emotionally on the spot. Performers and spectators are involved in reciprocal gratification, or sometimes frustration, which occurs within the boundaries of a ritualized event. In industrialized and computerized cultures, the performing arts become economically fragile because the institutions which sustain them increasingly depend on public and corporate funding. However, they retain their fascination for large, if not massive audiences, which prize the experiential, risk-loaded and one-timeness quality they afford. In traditional and local cultures, performances still strive and provide their spectators with cognitive and emotional fulfillment in smaller scale, economically sustainable institutional settings. All performing arts can be considered as two-way communicative processes involving crafted signs in ideally noise-free channels. They embody the values of the societies in which they are perpetuated, and often reflect cultural changes and social tensions while trying to symbolically negotiate and overcome such disturbances. For all these reasons, the performing arts, both in traditional and modern settings, are of prime interest to semioticians who can observe, in quasi experimental conditions, the crafting, combining and trading of signs in well defined contexts. But conducting a semiotic inquiry in any of the performing arts is a daunting task because the observer is necessarily at the same time a spectator. It ensues that the difficulties in establishing some measure of post-positivistic objectivity are compounded. Can a semiotic analysis of a performance be anything more than a mere hermeneutic account of its reading from the spectator/observer point of view? Or is it possible to construct a consensual theory of the performing arts and elaborate a reliable method which would allow the observer to distance himself/herself from this engrossing experience and reach a semiotic understanding encompassing both the pleasure of the spectacle and its cultural production? There are, expectedly, some differences depending whether the observer operates within his/her own culture, and whether the performance considered belongs to "high" (formal, elitist, textualized, mainstream) culture or to "low" (popular, oral, traditional, marginal) culture.

## II
## The Implicated Observer

The study of traditional performances, in particular, poses a host of challenges to the researchers. A clear assessment of these problems in the cases in which they are most obvious can help develop a more acute sensitivity to a general condition which may easily be glossed over when one deals with performances in one's own culture. The first difficulty comes from the fact that all observation perturbs to various degrees the event that is observed. There is the risk, for instance, that the observed performance has been somewhat tailored by the performers in view of what they assume to be the investigators' specific goals and interests. Traditional performing groups are increasingly coming into contact with people external to their social environment through global tourism and cultural exchanges. Consequently, a set of marketing constraints such as the location and duration of the performances, or the contents of dialogues and gestures of performers may be modified in order to meet the real or supposed expectations of spectators whose standards of acceptable behavior may be markedly different from those prevailing in the culture in which the traditional performances originated. If some traditionally accepted elements are considered too crude or offensive, or politically incorrect, they can be changed through a process of self-censorship to suit the taste of the outsiders who may be in search of exotic experiences as long as these experiences remain within the limits of their sense of decency. Furthermore, when traditional performances are closely linked to religious or ritualistic values, as it is often the case, their secularization implies a transformation into spectacles governed by the laws of entertainment. Their purely aesthetic reception and the feedback this sort of reception generates, such as clapping of the hands or *ad libitum* photographing, adulterate the experience of the performers themselves and has a definite impact on the performance.

With respect to the understanding of traditional performances in their original context, there is always a danger that the "scientific" observers be considered by the performers as just another kind of outsiders toward whom the same rules of behavior apply as toward the tourists and cultural events' audience in general. Performers have learned how to negotiate such situations in which they are confronted to audiences which do not share their cultural background and values. Economic necessities do not leave much choice to the traditional performers besides complying with customers' expectations, mainly at a time when urbanization and industrialization transform their own society into a population of tourists whose taste and attention have been molded by the constraints of city life and the narrative patterns of popular film industry. In some circumstances, the researchers may be perceived by the performers as a particularly desirable kind of outsiders who have often precious connections with official agencies and whose expectations should be satisfied because of their potential support in facilitating access to the market structures of tourism and the politic arcane of cultural exchanges.

For example, in research on the circus, some anthropologists who have conducted interviews with the performers in order to gather information about circus performances have discovered that, whatever their efforts to establish their status as academic researchers, they have been lumped with journalists and used as a public relation commodity. In a highly competitive social and economic context such as the circus, "being written about" may confer both symbolic and material advantages. Moreover, a researcher's interaction with individual performers has always a political dimension with respect to the group's power structure. At the beginning of her anthropological career, Mary Douglas experienced this pitfall of fieldwork precisely in the circus. Her point of entry in this social microcosm — that is, who has given her access to the performers — determined all further modalities of her interfacing with them, including the kind of information she could gather. (Douglas 1991:201-204).

Whatever a performance researcher may fancy about his/her "scientific neutrality" with respect to an "object" of study, his/her very presence and the circumstances of the initial contact distort the production and subsequent perception of the performance and its ensuing documentation. Even when researchers chose to conduct their observation as mere member of an audience, their presence is immediately noticed. Performers are indeed extremely sensitive to the composition of their audience. Any unusual person or behavior is instantly scrutinized and must be ascribed to a category of spectators. Although it is true that the presence of investigators in the audience does not always alter in major ways the usual proceedings of the performance, the impact of outsiders must be taken into account. Even in the best cases of participant observation the mere visible presence of some recording device often changes the nature of the event by bringing a measure of enhanced self-awareness in the performers as well as in the audience.

Conversely, an observer can become so involved in the event that the entrancing experience itself overpowers all her or his efforts to stick to a pre-established analytical program. Although it might appear that such an experience from inside, so to speak, provides a privileged insight into the nature of the performance, it also opens the way to erogenic interpretations, that is, interpretations conditioned by another cultural context than the one in which the observed traditional performance originated and now functions, principally if there is a great cultural distance between the participant-observer and the regular audience.  Cultural perceptions and values may drastically transform such an experience and make it incommensurable to the form and meaning of the traditional event, let it be story telling, dance, drama or music, whose relevance to the culture goes well beyond the immediate context to involve broad societal factors and the whole spectrum of other cultural artifacts.

In brief, any student of performance must keep in mind that, even within his or her own culture, the gaze of the observer has always an impact on the performance that is observed.  This general phenomenon does not necessarily invalidate a systematic observation but indicates that one should always attempt to evaluate the perturbing factor of the outsider's gaze, mainly, but not only, if recording equipment is present.  A pragmatic solution to this general problem is to ensure that more than one performance of the same item is observed.  With time it can be expected that the degree of perturbation declines and even totally disappears.  Moreover, if the observer succeeds in establishing his or her status as friend of the performers and connoisseur of their art, and can also become sensitive to the perturbations caused by other outsiders, it can be confidently assumed that the study and analysis of the performance which are achieved in such conditions have some validity. However, the potential for the manipulation of the researchers by the performers which such relations of intimacy imply should never be underestimated.

## III
## The Predicaments of Description

The second challenge confronting the student of performance comes from the temporal mode of traditional cultural events, their usually multilineal unfolding, which requires a great deal of methodological ingenuity of the part of the observer if most of it is not to be lost through selective, untrained attention.  Even if the first sort of challenge which has been discussed above, has been successfully met, or at least taken into consideration and assessed, the second one remains intact.  An apparently easy solution such as sound or video recording is in fact loaded with methodological fallacies.  First, because the film of the event does not solve the problem of how to analyze the event. Not only it merely postpones the challenge (the film or video remains to be analyzed), but also it makes the challenge more formidable because the recording freezes the performance as a single instance from a single visual point of view, which is further transmogrified by the framing, distance, focusing and rhythm of the cameraman. The resulting footage can be at most an accessory element for the final analysis. In fact, it could be claimed that only a performance which has been thoroughly analyzed can be usefully filmed and preserved. Moreover, with the exception of "happenings", performances are repeatable events, which can be observed again and again, and it seems impossible to built a reliable model of such performances unless they are closely observed several times through their variations across different contexts. It is indeed important to understand what can vary in a traditional performance, and how much the variable elements can vary, without jeopardizing the performance's integrity; what is context-sensitive and what is not so; at which nodes can improvisation take over, and within which limits; how much it can be condensed or expanded depending on what circumstances: and so on.

But the greatest challenge, which is the subject of this essay, is the transformation of the performance experience into a single code: its textualization. Even if iconographic elements are introduced in the researcher's descriptive output, such diagrams and drawings are useful only in as much as they are framed by a text which gives them meaning by specifying their representative status. For instance, a waving line whose direction is marked by an arrow is meaningless by itself unless it is specified that it represents the trajectory of a dancer, or of a group of dancers, or the motion of a dancer's hand. It could also be a decorative motive, or even a melodic line. Only a verbal message is able to disambiguate such a graphic representation. Because a performance is by definition a temporal object which unfolds more or less rapidly, sometimes with a succession of various speeds, it challenges the attention and memory capacities of the investigators. Because it is characterized by a flow of events whose various streams blend with each other in time at various rates, it cannot be functionally sliced into still frames except for the identification of particular components such as costumes, make-up, or postures of a certain duration. But once again, the latter need to be integrated into an explanatory text. Therefore the main problem is to devise a method of textualization of the performance.

There are several reasons why "description" is not a sufficient concept for determining and guiding such a process of textualization, that is, the transformation of a multilineal and multisensorial temporal experience into an unilinear verbal object: the text upon which further analysis of the performance will be conducted, and the form in which it will be preserved. If we want that this new object encodes all the information relevant to the performance so as to be able to serve as a self-sufficient score for recreating the performance, we must develop a demanding method which cannot be characterized as a mere description, unless we redefine the word description for our purpose. This is why it may be useful to use a different expression such as "verbal copy" to designate the methodical transformation on the performance into a new object which will encapsulate all the relevant information pertaining to the performance which is to be studied and preserved. The notion of verbal copy of an object or situation has been thoroughly discussed in logical semiotic terms by Maria Nowakowska (1979) who provides the following definition: "A verbal copy is a description of the situation, in the form of a conjunction of sentences of the form '*x* is such and such'. [...] [T]he successive bits of information contained in sentences '*x* is such and such' cannot be completely arbitrary; they must concern the attributes specified in the system, which, of course, is a natural requirement. There is, however, another requirement, namely that the successive bits of information must be expressed in an 'admissible' way, that is, by using only those expressions that are allowed" (Nowakowska 1979:142). The question which can be asked then is: under which conditions are exact verbal copies possible at all? The answer is that it depends on the richness of attributes and labels which have been elaborated concerning any possible objects. In Nowakowska's words: "[E]xact verbal copies exist if every element in each of the sets of descriptors is expressible as an intersection of some sets in class L i" (143). (L i is the class of all those sets of descriptors on i-th attributes, which have their own name). The abstract definition given by Nowakowska in logical terms will be made more user friendly in the last section of this article, when it is applied to actual instances of performance. But for the time being, it is important to understand the advantage of adopting a well-defined logical model, rather than the ill-defined, fuzzy notion of "description" in the recording and study of performance.

"Description" is indeed a dangerous word because it conveys a false sense of objectivity and because it is associated with literary gestures and social practices which include their own implicit norms. It is neutral only in appearance. Students are instructed how to make "good" descriptions when they learn how to write creatively with respect to some particular literary models. Original metaphors are thus encouraged in some pedagogical contexts. On the other hand, "scientific" description promotes the use of quantitative data and particular rhetorical devices such as distanciation of the describing subject from the described object, and elimination of all emotional components. Therefore there is a risk that the researchers who undertake the daunting task of "describing" actual performances fall upon one or the other kind of descriptions mentioned above and use as guidelines a set of implicit norms which were devised for completely different purposes. Literary descriptions must be vivid and entertaining, and often play a distinct function in narratives and poetry. The scientific description must be quantitative and dispassionate, and meet some well defined pragmatic requirements. A "verbal copy" must be far more inclusive and must obey a different set of selective constraints. Unless we want to investigate exclusively the naïve reception of a performance by asking spectators to provide spontaneous descriptions of what they have seen and experienced, such texts are not valid objects for a study of the complex socio-cultural events formed by traditional performances. Further more, their high degree of selectivity and their usual reliance on descriptive stereotypes could not serve for the effective recreation of these complex objects.

In order to produce an effective verbal copy it is first necessary to construct an exhaustive model of performance, and to derive from it a set of classes and their corresponding labels. Only then can we devise methodical strategies of textual representation and verbal encoding. Naturally the goal is not to create the equivalent of a performance with words. This can be achieved with greater or lesser success by literary descriptions which may indeed convey similar values and emotions for a sensitive reader. The goal is rather to encode and order all the information which is sufficient for a reconstruction of the performance (its objects, situations and transformations). The verbal copy is an artifact elaborated through implementing a series of tasks which are determined by an abstract model of performance, and which consists of laying out on a two-dimensional space a three-dimensional event. All the constants and variables of the model must be determined in the verbal copy of the particular performance which is the object of the research. The first step is therefore to elaborate a model which is sufficiently general but whose parameters are at the same time very finely determined. It must be like a net cast upon the performance, which actually captures all the essentials. (For tentative attempts to achieve such a goal, see Bouissac 1990, 1991). In order to build such a model we must specify the general pragmatic conditions which define a performance, as well as the rules of implementation of the performance itself.

## IV
## The Rules of Performance

The term "rules" should not be taken here in a strict normative sense but refers to a set of general pragmatic conditions which seems to account for the difference which we experience between a successful performance and a failure. This sort of difference is not a matter of all or nothing but rather a question of degrees. One or several of these "rules" can be more or less respected by the performers whose level of professionalism can vary. They are similar to the "felicity" conditions, which Paul Grice (1975) called "maxims", of linguistic communication, in particular conversation. In fact these "rules" are relatively easy to uncover by simply reflecting upon failed performances, an experience which is actually more common than unqualified successes. It is through trying to locate the source of the failure — that is what Erving Goffman (1974) called a "negative experience" — that we can pin-point violations in the implementation of the performance, and become aware of the extent to which success depends on the respect of these "maxims".

The first maxim could be informally expressed as "meet the audience expectations". This is the principle of accountability. All performers are in a contractual relation to his/her audience. Any advance announcement of a scheduled performance constitutes the terms of a proposed contract bearing upon the kind of skill of the performers, the genre of work they will performed, the place, time and duration of the event. Usually an audience is requested to pay an admission fee before the performance, but even when the attendance is free, as it is often the case in traditional performances, the members of the audience are providing their own time during which they abstain from any productive activities. Sometimes the performance is commissioned by a donor for religious, corporate or political reasons. Whatever the form and modality through which a performance is produced, there is always a give and take structure which binds the performer to live up to the terms of a contract. This general condition may remain implicit and be regulated by oral tradition, or it may be explicitly stated, sometimes in great details and in legal jargon as it is the rule in modern societies in which performance has been industrialized, and involves considerable financial risks.

The second maxim deals with the act of communication which a performance fundamentally is. It could be stated as: "communicate effectively". Any member of the audience must be able to clearly see, and/or hear the performer(s) as the performance is implemented, and this unfolding must be clearly articulated in all the media it involves. This is the rhetorical rule. It demands that the desired effects of the performance upon the audience be taken into consideration by the performers as they produce it. This rule has also important consequences for the organization of the semantic contents of the performance.

The third maxim concerns the semantic contents of the performance. It can be expressed by the injunction: "Be relevant". There always is a certain semantic gap between the way in which a performer understands an artistic or ritualistic tradition and the reception of the corresponding performance by an audience. Even within a particular culture the semantic mapping of experience is not perfectly homogenous, much more so naturally across cultures. A century or so of anthropological effort to comparatively map the semantic universes of a large sample of world cultures has revealed marked discrepancies in the ways natural objects and social behaviors are classified and lumped together in constructive cognitive categories. Given the fact that traditional performances make sense in the most absolute manner within the cultural areas in which they originated and continue to strive, culture-specific semantic categories and their mutual relations form necessarily the core of these performers. Performers cannot engage an audience whose system of cognitive relevance does not overlap, at least to some extent, with the system upon which the meaning of their performance rests.

The fourth maxim is: "Be proper", that is "behave properly toward the audience according to the social conventions of the culture". A performer acts indeed on two registers at the same time, or at least successively, since there is a logic of actions which belongs to the message intrinsic to the performance, and in addition there is a form of social behaviors toward the audience, a sort of performers' etiquette correlative to the conventional behavior of the audience which is expected to show various degrees of appreciation. Admiring whistling in North America is not congruent with the European code according to which aggressive whistling in the context of performance is a strong mark of disapproval. These social behaviors, or their absence, are an important part of performance because they frame the whole experience in a way which has an impact on the deep meaning of the performance. Are the performing identities spirits who possess the performers for the time of the performance, or are the performers skilled artists who manufacture the illusions of the personae they represent and gleefully take credit for their performing success?

The fifth maxim concerns time. It actually involves so many aspects that it is difficult to express it with a single injunction. It comprises "Be in time", "Be timely", "Keep time in mind", "Keep the tempo". It has to do with time structure and duration, tempo and rhythm, speed and intervals. It could be called the rule of "timeness" to include all the above aspects which must be taken into consideration when a performance is analyzed.

The above considerations bearing upon the pragmatic conditions of performances provide a tentative framework which should help a researcher to conceptualize performance in a more comprehensive manner than a naïve approach could afford. By "naïve approach" I mean the frame of mind of an observer who studies the performance by focusing on what is happening in the performing area without questioning the assumptions which make this experience possible. Any performance presupposes an institution produced by, and embedded within, a culture, and a set of implicit rules whose observation ensures the felicitous implementation of the patterned event. It is only once a particular performance has been assessed with respect to these pragmatic conditions that a verbal copy can be productively undertaken.

# V
# How to Make a Verbal Copy

It is not possible to start making a verbal copy of a performance until a cognitive matrix has been developed. A cognitive matrix is a structure or a conceptual graph which determines which kind of information is relevant to the performance and should be entered as a part of the copy. It lists the choices which can be made by the performers in the implementation of the performance. For instance, and performer must make a first contact with the audience for the performance to start. The contact can be sudden or progressive. It can involve the *dramatis persona* right at the onset of the performance, or it can first introduce the civil identity of the performer who, after having been acknowledged as the real substrate of the character will then endow her/his performing identity and will initiate the performance. It is obvious that further choices are involved in each one of these modes of starting points. Is a social contact established with the audience, or only with the other performers, or even with some deity as it is the case in many Hindu performances through the burning of incense or the reciting of a mantra? It may be that, in some cases, the three types of contacts will be present in a particular order. A performer may represent the transition from civil to performing identity, or adopt the epiphany mode of appearance, hence possibly never relinquishing the performance identity to the extent that the audience cannot relate the *dramatis persona* to any known real person, as it has been often the case with circus clowns for the general audience of their performances. Many traditional performers use masks or make-up which so transform their face that the two identities can not be intuitively related.

In view of the above, a descriptive proposition such as: "at the beginning, performer *x* enters the stage and walks toward its center" cannot be considered a verbal copy because it leaves out a large number of relevant information. There are many ways of walking, some indicating that the performer walks as an ordinary person who goes and takes the place he/she is supposed to occupy at the beginning of the performance, some other signifying that it is the *dramatis persona* who walks for some performance related purpose to this particular spot of the stage area. Therefore the gait is one of the relevant parts of the cognitive matrix which must be specified in the verbal copy. Other such parts are the visual and auditory attributes of the performing identity. These attributes belong to identifiable categories either as categories which are functional in the contextual culture and may denote social class, age, mood, etc., or as categories pertaining to the code specific to a particular genre of performance such as a princess, a warrior, a monster, a clown, etc. What is said, and how it is said, the music being performed if any, the reaction of other characters, whose attributes have also been specified, are equally relevant parts of the cognitive matrix.  Such a matrix can be conceived as a fairly wide-mesh net whose purpose is to catch selectively the information which could be used later for reconstructuring the performance rather than duplicating it with a perfect match including elements which are not perceived by the audience and therefore are not relevant to the performance such as the real age of the performers, their blood pressure, the color of their undergarments, and the like.   The descriptive matrix is exclusively sensitive to the cognitive categories through which the meaning of the performance is produced for its audience.  For instance some colors may or may not be relevant as an attribute of a performer's clothing. Similarly some qualities or modifications of the voice, some accompanying tunes, etc.

It should be obvious at this point that a verbal copy is a methodical enterprise which requires first the careful elaboration of an appropriate cognitive matrix.  This elaboration can be achieved only through multiple reflexive experiences of the kind of performances one wants to study.  The all-purpose matrix which as been sketched above cannot be directly applied to any type of performance.  It must first be fine tuned.  There is in this process a certain circularity, but it is a constructive circularity since the researcher is lead to start with tentative verbal copies which can be compared to further experiences of the same performance.  At first the researchers must train their observation skill with the general matrix in mind, then a tentative copy is made through taking notes and using short term memory.  Then it must be formatted, so to speak, that is, the propositions must be standardized and made readable by a larger community of researchers.  This first stage will reveal many gaps in the information collected.  Only further experiences of the same performance, or the complementary memory of the other research team members, will make it possible to saturate the matrix.  Naturally, drawings, diagrams and sketches can be inserted in the verbal text to economically specify some stable or dynamic patterns.

The final verbal copy will be the result of a consensus.  It will take the form of a lengthy text in which natural syntax will indicate clearly what is perceived simultaneously and what is perceived successively.   Which attributes are permanent for the duration of the performance, which ones are changing at which points of the performance.  The fine tuning of the copy is facilitated by the numerous analyses of human communicative behavior which have been produced over the last fifty years, both in the auditory and visual channels.   The works of human ethologists such as Irenaus Eibl-Eibesfelt (1989) or psychologists such as Paul Ekman (1982) have provided a standardized terminology which can be very effectively used and several researchers have produced ways of noting in great details gestures, postures and choreographic movements (e.g. Rudolph Laban 1974).   On the other hand, the semiotic attention given to the function of structured space in determining meaningful positions, movements, social categories, etc., (for instance Edward Hall 1969), represents an essential methodical commodity. The same applies to the analysis of the rich repertory of non-linguistic vocal qualities and other bodily produced sounds researchers such as Fernando Poyatos (1976). Objects, theatrical and circus props, tales and dances, music and natural noises have also been extensively studied from a semiotic point of view, that is, according to their capacity to produce contractive meanings. The research skill involved in the production of successful verbal copies presupposes an advance level of "semiotic literacy" which provides both non trivial cognitive classes (what counts as information in a type of situation) and their labels (that is, admissible terms to be used as descriptors).

# VI
## From Rules of Performance to Rules of Description

The functional relations which exist between the pragmatic conditions of performance as they have been outlined in the third part of this essay and the classes of descriptors which are used to complete a verbal copy of a particular performance should now be obvious. In fact it would not be possible to determine *a priori* those classes of descriptors in the absence of a theoretical model of performance encompassing the whole situation with the audience and performers embedded in the socio-economic structure of a particular culture. The initial situation is an unstable relation characterized by a more or less confident expectation on the part of an audience. The performers have been credited in advance, so to speak, and their task will be to restore the equilibrium by meeting their commitments. Their currency is purely symbolical since it represents the meanings and values upon which the social system rests. This is why the classes of descriptors are intimately related to the maxim of relevance and the maxim of propriety, and their rhetorical arrangement by the maxim of communication which both must combine in order to achieve the effective manipulation of the audience's interest and bring it to a state of semiotic satiety. The verbal copy cannot merely produce lists of descriptors' labels but must reconstruct their dynamic relations and retrace the trajectory of the performance from its initial situation to its terminal state within the spatia-temporal frame which is dictated by cultural conventions.

This approach provides the student of performance with the theoretical and practical means to cope with cultural diversity since verbal copies are not meant to be the results of the blind application of a universal method, but rely on the prior elaboration of a descriptive matrix which is context-sensitive. However, the conceptual tools through which such as elaboration is possible belong to the metalanguage of semiotics without which performance researchers would probably be unable to free themselves from the taken-for-granted situation which our culture labels "the audience", and they would be restricted to produce "descriptions" which would be mostly redundant with respect to their feelings as an audience, that is, with respect to the effects of the cognitive manipulations engineered by the performers. This is why a description, in the usual uncritical sense of the term, cannot be the basis for a reconstruction of the performance "described", whereas a verbal copy, in the technical sense specified by Nowakowska, should be able to achieve such a goal.

*Paul Bouissac is Professor of French Language and Literature, Victoria College, University of Toronto.*

## REFERENCES

Bouissac, Paul, 1987, "The Marketing of Performance", in *Semiotics and Marketing*, Jean Umiker-Sebeok, ed., Berlin: Mouton de Gruyter, 391-406.

-----, 1990, "Incidents, accidents, failures: The Representation of Negative Experience in Public Entertainment", in *Beyond Goffman. Studies on Communication, Institution, and Social Interaction*, Stephen H. Riggins, ed., Berlin: Mouton de Gruyter, 409-443.

-----, 1991, "From Calculus to Language: The Case of Circus Equine Displays", *Semiotica* 85 (3-4), 291-317.

Eibl-Eibesfeldt, Irenaus, 1989, *Human Ethology*, New York: Aldine de Gruyter.

Ekman, Paul, 1982, "Methods for Measuring Facial Actions", in *Handbook of Methods in Nonverbal Behavior Research*, Klaus R. Scherer and Paul Ekman, eds., Cambridge: Cambridge University Press.

Goffman, Erving, 1974, *Frame Analysis. An Essay on the Organization of Experience*, New York: Harper and Row.

Grice, H. Paul, 1975, "Logic and Conversation", in *Syntax and Semantics. Speech Acts*, Peter Cole and Jerry L. Morgan, eds., New York: Academic Press, 41-58.

Hall, Edward T., 1969, *The Hidden Dimension Garden City*, New York: Anchor Books.

Laban, Rudolph, 1974, *Choreutics. The Language of Movement*, annotated and edited by Lisa Ullmann, Boston: Plays Inc.

Nowakowska, Maria, 1979, "Foundations of Formal Semiotics: Objects and their Verbal Copies" *Ars Semeiotica. International Journal of American Semiotics* Vol. 2 No. 2, 133-148.

Nowakowski, Maria, 1980, "An Empirical Approach to Foundations of Formal Semiotics", *Ars Semeiotica. International Journal of American Semiotics*, Vol. 3 No. 3, 313-349.

Poyatos, Fernando, 1976, *Man Beyond Words: Theory and Methodology of Nonverbal Communication*, Oswego, New York: NYCEC Monographs.

# Part Two

## *Mapping Semiotic Plots*

# Chapter 5

# Semiotics in a Peircean Light

Roberta Kevelson

## I
## Introduction:
## Frame First or Foto: A Chicken'n'Egg Problem

There is a gap in our understanding of Semiotics. This gap has been patched, painted over, repaired in various ways, but with each attempt to fill the opening it gets larger and larger. A solution: cover it over with something that becomes a virtual part of the wall but yet distinct from its original structure. But its material, appearance, and the way it is put together, seems to elude replication.

So we paste over this hole in the wall by hanging something in front of it which blocks it. Indeed, the decision to cover the missing piece of wall with something that will draw attention away from the gaping place brings with it its own problems:

If we think of the wall as an integral piece of an ideal structure that we call "the limits of human knowledge," this hole or settling crack that continually expands and opens, cries out for some super solution. Such a solution would be foregrounded against a structure of knowledge which seems clear, and that would be, as far as one can see, lacking in total completeness.

Still playing with this irreparable gap in this ideal wall of finite and completable human knowledge as was once imagined possible even into the late 19th century, let us conceive of a spark of genius emerging, as an answer to this, our holey wall: This answer, I suggest, is Semiotics. Semiotics is a theory of representation of what we may take at any given time, from any angle, with selected lens, filters, etc., of whatever is taken to be The Real... *as we see it.* As we *agree* to see it: as consensus.

I hesitate to carry the hole-in-the-wall analogy too far. But I think it is important to say that Semiotics — the "modern" version of Semiotics of the late 19th through this 20th century — came into being out of a context, which was, in effect, this unavoidable picture of a never-to-be-restored "completeness" in human knowledge. How to explain? How to devise further patch-ups? A new texture and fact of the wall may even come to symbolize the very background of the wall itself, the same ground which was initially to support it.

Thus out of the realization and acceptance that the once idealized notion of perfect human knowledge was becoming increasingly mythlike, a new view of human knowledge came to light. This new picture, called Semiotics, was not about *What* people may know. Rather, it focused on How we know, and How this How, or method of making knowledge grow, may serve in a purposeful manner. On its face Semiotics provided a new, integral structure. But in a deeper sense the covering of the gaps changed only its appearance.

The problem remained: Should Semiotics be directly applied to the imperfect wall, such that the hole would itself be visible as a central "object" of the semiotics picture? Or, should Semiotics be overlaid, occluding the hole and presented, or re-presented, as a piece of decoration, or a work of fine art, or craft, or trophy of the human hunt for new ideas? If Semiotics were to hang over the "hole" there are two alternatives as to how it should be hung: One, as suggested above, is to hang it so that the hole is part of the cover-up. The other alternative is to frame it.

To set a frame around Semiotics would give it an appearance of other wall-hangings upon the plane of human knowledge, along with Philosophy, with History, with Physics, with Law, etc. In this framed mode Semiotics could be part of a grouping. One might move the other areas of human inquiry into a kind of constellation of pieces of knowledge which, all together, constitute a sense of a whole. In this case the frame needs to be chosen very carefully, since it should be compatible with other members of its group. Thus by choosing the frame first one would be, in effect, setting a limit on the picture, on its boundaries, on its proper place and space in the overall geometrical scheme of topics of knowledge, especially with respect to the linearity of the modern university.

In fact, if one selected several kinds of frames and took shots of Semiotics from several perspectives, there could be a semiotics, if not for the millions, for almost every academic discipline in the modern world. E.g., one would have a properly framed view of a Semiotics of Art, of Law, of Biology, of History, of Semiotics (i.e., a Meta-semiotics montage). In this mode all the spaces, i.e., territories, of the specific academic disciplines would be respected and sustained. Semiotics would have the role of itinerant maiden aunt, as a visitor — even a useful guest — but rather outside the inner core of the discipline-classified family. Largely, the development of Semiotics over the past two and a half decades has been just this: Framed fotos taken from a variety of perspectives, with much skill and expertise.

This has resulted in a versatile version of a vague, general and fuzzy Semiotics, adroitly processed to enhance and fill out special areas of thought which constitute the block structure of the modern university.

But in so doing, in treating Semiotics as anyone's favorite guest, the Peircean concept of Semiotics remains as little understood today as it was some twenty-five years ago when the hole in the wall, the unfixable gap, became an intolerable eyesore, crying out with its wound-like appearance for concealment, for illusion, for decor.

The problem of how to justify a semiotics approach to broken ideals at first suggested the usual tactic, namely, to break down the whole, general concept of semiotics to parts and pieces.

Thus Old and New traditions of semiotics were distinguished: the old semiotics included all kinds of messages; verbal and nonverbal, instinctual, notational, apprehensible in all conceivable ways. The new semiotics was restricted to systems of communicable signs which were reducible to an infraverbal structure. Still too unwieldy, Semiotics was further broken down into lines of origin, e.g., to the Prague Linguistic Circle, to Saussurean linguistic influence, to several strains of ancient to modern philosophical threads of thought, to medical diagnostic practice, to alchemy, and not least, to the several ingenious ways that Peirce's theory of signs has come to be seen.

Of these several ways that Peirce's semiotics was regarded — and still is, from this fractured looking-glass of primarily philosophical cooptation — little or no attempt was made to show a full picture of Peirce's semiotics, and to integrate it with the "hole" or "zero-sign" with which it is correlated. In my work I have tried to do just this. In the following I will show Semiotics in this Peircean light.

## II
## The Real and the Virtual

For the moment we leave the knowledge gap or unfillable hole in the structure of human knowledge. We leave it, enhanced by the superimposed scheme of Peirce's semiotics. The theory of signs he offers lies *over* its referent problem, as a film-maker might superimpose one cell of film over another to create the notion of transparent effect, where the new idea overlays but does not cover up. This technique was used, as we know, by the early scribes of sacred texts who wrote upon the message they were editing in such a way that the referent text *with* its edited critique became a unified whole. This method of overwriting was the method of palimpsest scribing.

When Peirce invented what he called the Existential Graphs — sheets of paper which one was to imagine of infinite thickness — he proposed that these sheets, or graphs, could be "cut" so that each depth of a cut would reveal a "deeper" level of meaning of a proposition or statement. Its modes of connection and its implications could be disclosed in this manner, and in accordance with whether the method of reasoning used was of a deductive, inductive, or modal, i.e., probablistic or possibilistic kind.

Peirce uses this kind of palimpsestic, superimpositional overlay in another special context.  He uses it in connection with the idea of a representation as a map which so closely resembles its object — that which it stands for — that it would be indistinguishable from its object except that one would then cut a hole in this map or representation to allow for one's point of view.  I want to return to the representational "map" later in the chapter.

It is useful to know that a Peircean semiotics is the outgrowth of a route of inquiry in western thought which is not mainstream but is an alternative to mainstream inquiry.  Yet its historical path is of secondary interest, I think, to the key ideas by which it distinguishes itself from other ways of understanding.

By "understanding" I mean humankind's always tentative and provisional knowledge of the relationship between human interests and the rest of the world, and between human beings' interests with one another.  The former takes the route of the physical sciences, whereas the latter takes the form of inquiry into the institutions of human societies.  These are not sharply separable, however.  The great challenge to a Peircean semiotics is to find ways of linking these various areas of concern, these universes of discourse as I refer to them here.

The key ideas which are important to recognize and investigate — to open exploration into in this short chapter — are the following:  Representation; Interpretation; Evolution toward ever-greater complexity and dimensionality; Mediation; and Relation.

Mediation and Relation are inseparable from Representation, Interpretation, Evolution.  The whole of the semiotic process grows out of an acceptance that the minimal unit of completeness of significance or meaning is relational, and never atomistic or reducible to elemental singularity.  In ordinary vocabulary the smallest complete unit is a "we" and not an "I."

In the following section I will talk in more detail about these key ideas of Representation, Interpretation, and Evolution.  I will also discuss Peirce's concept of mediation as a relational device, not only for linking old with new information, but in symbolizing the nuclear structure of semiotics.  This nucleus is not the individual, *but is the relation between individuals*, even that which may stand for a minimal society of two.

In Peirce's world the Real is that which one understands by means of such signs and sign-functions that are our *ideas* of the actual world.  In other words, we can not ever know this actual world directly but only through the mediation of those signs or idea-systems which we, as people, create for our human use.  Many eminent semioticians will take issue with this last statement, and will hold that semiotic processes take place not only among human beings but at all levels of this universe we call our world.  I, in response, answer that these semiotic processes do occur throughout the world but only as we, who say so, identify them as such. It is we who speak from a position of semiotic inquiry, and so it is we who tag that we observe as this, or that, or other modes of being in the world.

Whatever we say we observe as a fact is the observation of those ideas which represent, in an indirect way, our judgments or speculations or imaginations about what we take as factive significant phenomena. All thought processes are sign-processes. Semiotics is that theory of sign-processes which we infer from having taken account of such processes and from our attempts to explain them in principled, repeatable, and stable ways. Such a theory, then, is a crystallization of assumptions which come out of the observation of a practice, or process, of significant interaction. At the same time, it must be emphasized, Peirce is not talking about ideas to which we merely attach names to. This is "nominalism," which characterizes almost all of western thought to date, Peirce argues.

Semiotics, from the Peircean perspective, differs from all nominalistic approaches to named or labelled tags for those phenomena we talk about primarily because Peirce's theory of signs is not about things as such. Rather, Peirce's semiotics is entirely focused on intellectual concepts. More explicitly, it focuses on the *development* of such concepts from one stage of their significance to evolved, further stages of significance.

Each stage of significance of any idea, or complex sign-system, is merely an artful stopping of the clock, of that whole continuum idea. In actuality the idea keeps moving and growing. Yet in order to refer to it, to tell about it, as we tell the time for example, we reify the process of the growing idea and speak of this process *as if* it were a thing. Ideas, or sign-processes — thoughts — are phenomena, but not things.

Therefore, Peirce's semiotic investigations deal with processes which may be subdivided into stages. It is a process which is capable of being analyzed into increments by adaptations from mathematics by semiotics. Mathematics is the model, *but not the method of Semiotics*. Pragmatism — his special Pragmatism (pragmaticism) — *is* such an adaptation of mathematical reasoning: Pragmatism *interprets* mathematics, in other words, and is therefore not *identical* with its interpretant or referent sign.

Since my objective here is to steer clear of technical jargon and attempt, instead, to introduce Peirce's semiotics in such a way that no prerequisite training, vocabulary, or specialized study is wanted, I will try to use the language of common sense. I distinguish this everyday common sense from that Critical Common Sense — British and Scottish Common Sense Philosophy — to which Peirce is deeply indebted.

Nevertheless it is important to present the core of Peirce's semiotics in his own words. We want to know how he speaks, and what these special terms mean in this context, just as we want to know how the actions of some one we know and care about are special to that person and are to be taken in that special way.

Only a taste of the unique Peirce is possible here.  But this still permits a useful introduction, not only to those terms mentioned above, but also to the way he subdivides the stages of semiotic processes into three:  Firstness, Secondness and Thirdness.  I will begin the next section with a discussion of these three categories, which Peirce did not invent but which in characteristic fashion he adapts to his special purposes.

There are three semiotic functions which correspond with these three categories.  These are:  the Icon, the Index, the Symbol.  Since we are not talking about things, but rather of stages of the phenomenal process of cultivating and growing thoughts, these three functions are always coexisting throughout a total semiotic process.  But depending on the inquirer's purpose at hand, one or the other or the third may dominate a particular stage of the process under observation.

In concise, and perhaps too brief a manner, the next section will attempt to clarify the meaning of the terms, Interpretation, Representation, and Mediation.  Also in this section the categories of Firstness, Secondness, Thirdness will be identified as Peirce conceived them.  Here, too, the three functions of Icon, Index and Symbol will be discussed, not with respect to things as either Icon or Index or Symbol, but, as mentioned above, as phases or stages in the development of an idea from the onset of a particular inquiry to the closing of that inquiry with the inquirer's temporary satisfaction. Again, no inquiry ever closes a topic permanently.  Rather, only the limits of the human imagination may seal inquiry on any topic.   Therefore, any semiotic process is in concept infinite and inexhaustible.

I will begin with the categories:  Firstness comes out of an infinite realm of the possible, out of the freedom of Pure Chance, of nondetermination, and of no causal authority.  One puts a frame around this semiotic inquiry only as a device, only as a means of distinguishing this inquiry from its ground: that "wall" upon which our inquiry is mounted.

Secondness anchors the inquiry into this experience, this here and now of the inquiry.   Secondness has all the characteristics of lived experience: conflict, opposition, struggle, drama, exchange, dispute, the very bones of relationships of person-to-person in human society.

Thirdness is the habit of use, the conventionalized, generalized smoothing-off of eccentricities of subjective sensibility and making a shared experience possible.  All language — verbal, notational, gestural — is symbolic and socialized.

# III
# A Gloss on Key Terms:
# Representation, Interpretation, Relation

Peirce says that Representation is a sign. All representations have three basic sign-functions. These three sign-functions are part of every phase of every stage of the development of the sign-meaning, from lesser to greater significance. More Significance, in Peirce's scheme, is equivalent with more Reality. Depending on the purpose of any particular inquiry into a semiotic process, any one of the three sign-functions may be focused upon, or be a dominant sign-function. These sign-functions are: Icon, Index, and Symbol. The focus may shift, in turn, from Icon to Index to Symbol. This moving forward from function to function parallels the process of developing thought: from Image, which is a spatial relation like maps, equations, graphics, etc., to conflictual or oppositional relations as in drama and in making distinctions, to conventionalized value-relation which is a codified member of any given system of human value.

In any of its three functions a representation does not necessarily bear a resemblance — a sensible or sense-perceptual likeness — to its referent idea/sign, or to actual things in the world. Nor does it replicate or duplicate its referent in a manner of "cloning" or of crystal-reproduction. Nor is it merely a transliteration, as from one language system to another, or one notational system to another. Rather, a representation has an *equivalent* meaning with its referent: it is a *verisimillitude*. In Peirce's terms, a representation or sign stands to someone, from someone, in place of something or some idea, which it brings into prominence — i.e., represents. But a representation is never identical with its referent or object. Even an apparent repetition of a word or a mark or a sound or a graphic design, for example, is never a mere copying of such mark; but it is a "mark of a mark". Each new mark carries forward new meaning. The meaning changes if for no other reason than the mark is a new time/space, or a new context and environment. Meaning, from the viewpoint of Peirce's semiotics, is context-sensitive.

Further, the initial sign of any inquiry does not stay put, is not constant. But it is carried along, as it were, with the dynamics of process so that the leading sign or principle accumulates meaning and transforms. With each new "appearance" of the initial "leading" sign, both that which precedes it and that which follows are being continually changed, so that meaning in any sense — affirming or negating of an initial idea — *increases in significance*.

Three stages comprise the shifts between each manifestation of an opening or leading sign of any inquiry/analysis. This triad refers at each stage to a basic linking of whatever is at each moment old or already known with that which is coming into existence as new information. In theory this process is infinitely divisible into new stages in the realization of meaning. Between each stopping place or point one may imagine an "interlude". This interlude allows for genuine novelty to enter into the picture, for new possibilities to occur, for choices to be made. These "interludes" are, according to Peirce, a kind of play, a *Pure Musement*, he calls it, where possibility and free choice as part of the process throughout, are connectives between known and new. Every interlude presents an opportunity for discovery and for the option of integrating the newly discovered with the established *thus far*.

To emphasize, every new possibility as well as every familiar fact or idea can only be referred to in an indirect way, i.e., by sign-processes which mediate between a now and then, a here and there, a present, a past, and a future. All signs are re-presentations, and never direct. Even instinctual impulses and feelings, in order to be of significance, are referred to through our ideas of them, i.e., through sign-processes.

If we would know feelings or instincts more fully we do so by a process of semiotics which dynamically transforms the referent sensible idea/sign and "grows" it into ever larger, more complex meaning. The three main stages of this transforming process, as mentioned, are the sign-functions of Icon, Index and Symbol.

The entire process of growing thought is also a relational process. The representation of a Before is linked to the representation of the Moment by an equivalent-making, interpretive process. The representative of the Moment moves forward toward some anticipated realization — a probability or a possibility — yet to occur. The process moves toward some future forecasted stage of each and every increment of every continuous act of inquiry. At every interlude there is a recurring Firstness: *a freedom and a nondetermined possibility for choice.*

Such relational processes can be understood as open-ended dialogic interactions between stages: between 1) stages in the development of a given sign process; 2) inquirer and process inquired into; 3) inquirer of here and now with that same inquirer of a different time, perspective, or purpose of inquiry; 4) two or more inquirers who elect to relate to one another as members of "community of inquirers" and 5) two or more complex idea systems or universes of discourse where each may be compared with a distinct and different language-system. Recall that it was mentioned above that equivalences between representations are the outcome of an interpretive process.

Just as relational links are between signs, between inquirers into sign processes (as in *metasemiotic* process), between aspects of a single inquirer and between different individual inquirers and/or separate sign-systems, so the interpretive process is also of a semiotic nature; equivalences are produced by interpretation.

Interpretation is sometimes by analogy and sometimes by supposition or imagined possibility. *Signs interpret other signs.* In fact, Peirce's entire emphasis is more on how *signs* interpret other signs, and less upon how *people* interpret signs. In other words, semiotics attempts to explain how one idea, *as idea*, can interpret another idea, so that the emphasis is not on the subjectivity of the human inquirer or semiotician but on the process, as conceivably objectively expressed, of how signs/ideas evolve out of themselves. Signs evolve as living existents, according to Peirce. They evolve in large part by adaptation to new and changing environment and circumstances.

The interpretive process is also triadic: Signs evolve from 1) Immediate Interpretant to 2) Dynamic Interpretant, to 3) Final Interpretant. Again, the 1, 2, 3... corresponds with Image, Struggle or dramatic conflict; and Accord or convention. Icon, Index, Symbol, are also equivalent with Sense, Struggle, Society. This is but a capsule version of Peirce's semiotics, and only a bare-bones chart of how to proceed further. According to Peirce, Pragmatism is the Method of the Theory of Signs. *The Method produces the Theory*, and not vice versa. Each time, a process of semiosis begins in freedom and closes with a judgment which is provisional only, final only until something like a "surprising fact" is noticed, *cannot be avoided*, as it seems to push itself into our attention. Then we must reconsider anew that which we have so far taken *as* the known, *as* the real, *As Is*.

Peirce's pragmatism operates by strategies that Peirce calls Pure Rhetoric. What he does here, as he does throughout his work, is to take a familiar concept and procedure and adapt it to a new purpose. So the traditional Rhetoric becomes, in the light of Peircean semiotics, a way of influencing the changing of behavior, conduct, or *acts of signs*. Signs act, just as there are Speech Acts, or acts of Law. These "acts" are such as to be consequential, to bring about effects or results in the world of human meaning.

Whatever has meaning, says Peirce, will make a difference in the world. Whatever does not make a difference, by contrast, is meaning-less.

As I noted earlier there are many semioticians today who assert that the process of semiotics is not restricted to human beings at all, but can be observed to occur everywhere, to "pervade" the universe. I must add that it is the action of *people* who represent such semiosis *as* semiosis. Without this concept the process may occur, but be unnoticed, uninterpreted, unrelated to other happenings in the world, and hence be without representation in terms of human meaning.

I remarked at the beginning of the chapter that the history of semiotics is, from my viewpoint, of secondary importance when compared with our grasp of its nodal ideas.  It is nevertheless important to touch upon its historic development.  But first I want to offer a few topics for semiotic workshops or research projects, or general discussion!

# IV
## Some Experiments and Projects to Play With

The following six short paragraphs suggest broad topics related to Peirce's Semiotics which a newcomer may wish to explore.  There is very little literature available in these topics but they are mentioned in Kevelson (see references).  The scope of possible projects on Semiotics in a Peircean light covers a wide range of Peirce's thought.

Here is a challenge:

1.) Models of Semiotic Processes

Peirce compares mathematical with philosophical *models* for the representation in semiotic analysis of the growth of thought.  The latter begins with verbalized concepts and is thus grounded in "nominalism", i.e., words and conventionalized definitions.  The former proceeds from an image, a spatial relation, and this becomes a Firstness or Iconic sign function in Peirce's schema.  Space relations, Peirce claims, are almost identical in actuality as they are in representation.  While Semiotics is not mathematical in its method of inquiry the mathematical model does provide the initial aspects of ideas; semiotic representations are verismillitudes of the mathematical image, which Gauss, for example, called *Abbildung*.

2.) Tools for Examining Signs

Peirce retrieves ancient imagistic notions of the idea as phenomenally visualizable.  His invention of a *pragmatico-semeiotical* explanation of the process of thought evolving coincides with the invention of the motion picture.  Its prototypes were: David Brewster's magic lantern, his kaleidoscope, in the area of Optics; also the 18th and 19th centuries' stereotypes — stereoscope and hyperscope — emerged around the time that Bentham introduced the *cenoscope* and *idioscope* as instruments for observing and tracking legal concepts.

3.) Superimpositions and Levels of Significance

Peirce also invented the Existential Graphs: These are sheets of paper that consist of infinite layers, each of which may be inscribed by code to stand for a development of thought according to Peirce's logic of relations and dilemmatic reasoning.  Each sheet represents an "argument" where an argument may be a continuum as extensive as is conceivably possible.  The "codes" are agreed to by members of the inquiring community, as is any jargon.  The encoded symbols are general ideas, i.e., topics adapted from the aristotelian topics by Peirce, and which each represent an "area" of thought,

i.e., a space.  Thus the particular mathematical model for Peirce is the noneuclidean topical geometry.  The "marks" upon these spaces/places/ represent the spatial relational beginnings of ideas or complex sign relations.
4.) The Film and Evolution of Thought
Peirce compares his Existential Graphs with the motion picture process. He had worked through the deductive and inductive modes of reasoning, the valid and the probabilistic modes of reasoning in large part, but had no time to complete the possible-istic modality which is, he claimed, the method of pragmatic reasoning that allows ideas to move and grow.
5.) Dilemmas as Alternatives
Peirce maintained that it is dilemmatic reasoning which best shows the evolution of ideas, as open-ended and increasingly complex.  Here the Real (or representation) and the Ideal (its "absolute" ideational referent) are nearly identical, as are actual and representational space almost indistinguishable from one another.
6.) On Willing the "Possible"
Peirce's semiotics and Schelling's leading aesthetic principle almost dovetail.  Peirce recognizes his affinity with Schelling through Royce. Schelling's thought: within the idea of the absolute there is virtually no difference between the actual and the possible (*Aesthetics* at p. 33).  In Pirandellan terms, "it is if you think it is."  And in the filmic world of cyberspace the virtual world is the communicable, sensible language: an image-based *representation as experience*.

# V
## On Semiotics as a Continuum

I will only offer among the chapter's selected references those sources, in addition to Peirce's own writings, which provide guidelines for further research into the paths Semiotics has travelled in the course of the history of Western ideas.

In the following I will briefly point to places in the lineage of Peircean semiotics where one may wish to explore further.  It is also important to call attention to the fact that interest in Peircean semiotics significantly developed in the sixth decade of this century, at a time when other developments which have been linked with his work also emerged.

For one, we want to note the emergence of a concern with signs and sign-systems which came out of the universities of Tartu and of Prague, between the 1920's and the 1930's, mostly with respect to functional linguistics and analysis of human cultures and institutions.

Around the 1950's the work of the famous linguist Ferdinand de Saussure began to be regarded as of great importance for its semiological insights.

Closely following Saussure were the works of the French Structuralists, Barthes, Kristeva, Greimas and others.

Roman Jakobson introduced Peirce around the world, and his student Charles Morris further provided links between American and European approaches to sign theory.

Thomas Sebeok, student of both Morris and Jakobson, actually provided through his own writings and through the enormous number of publications he edited, some of the earliest research tools in the post 1960's study of Semiotics throughout the world.   Thus Semiotic-based literature has grown from almost nothing except reference to medical semiotic diagnostic procedures to thousands of volumes on all conceivable semiotic topics.

This literature comes out of every continent in many languages, from viewpoints which now express concerns of almost every academic discipline.

Perhaps the most important early expositor of Peirce's approach to sign theory was the late Max Fisch.

I am grateful to them all, those I was fortunate enough to know personally and those who live for me and with me in their work, as does Charles Sanders Peirce.

While Peirce always acknowledged his indebtedness to mainstream western thought, e.g., Aristotelian traditional philosophy up to and through Descartes, and although he especially takes note of the great thinkers in all fields, he is wedded to none.   He breaks even with Kant during the last period of his life, especially on the Kantian distinction between inner and outer of Noumenon vs. Phenomenon in the realm of ideas.

Peirce is eclectic in appropriating what he needs from a vast array of specialists: e.g., from Bentham he adapts his "tools" for examining intellectual concepts.   From Boyle he makes use of the links between alchemy and modern chemistry.   Peirce sees his own thought as most closely connected with the work of Scottish and British Common Sense thinkers.   He especially sees his thought as an outgrowth of John Locke's *Essay Concerning Human Understanding*, and indirectly as evolving from the early work of the Stoics, on sign-relations in human knowledge.   Peirce is an exemplar of his own semiotic practice.   He adapts, reinterprets, re-presents, and, as if in dialogue and relation with his own referent sources, he sets about to create new meaning out of old.   Peirce integrates the key thought of the physical sciences, of the human sciences such as law, economics, linguistics, of the arts to some extent, of the mathematics to a large extent, into his own semiotics project.   He transforms the key concepts of his referents into metaphors — maps and models — for his pragmatics and his theory of signs. Peirce regards logic as an armature for forms of reasoning.   His own expanded logic is, he says, synonymous with all that he means by Semiotics. Different logics represent different kinds of reasoning, for different kinds of purposes. Logics do not prescribe. They describe how some special kind of reasoning may be represented. Whenever science makes a great discovery, a breakthrough in human invention, then logicians need to find a logic to represent that new process of reasoning.

Peirce held that the dilemmatic reasoning was that which most closely approximates his own understanding of semiotic processes: it is never fully conclusive, but is open-ended and provisional, and at bottom, *hypothetical.*

Finally, although it can be fairly admitted that semiosis is observable everywhere, it is only by means of semiotic inquiry that this omnipresent process can be described and re-presented. Thus the relation between semiotic inquirers, i.e., meta-semioticians, and the universe of semiotic phenomenal processes is one of reasoning *of a kind*, self-generating of meaning, and is *possibly infinite.*

## REFERENCES

Eco, Umberto, 1976/1979, *A Theory of Semiotics.* Bloomington: Indiana University Press.

Fisch, Max H., 1986, *Peirce, Semiotic and Pragmatism*, eds. K. Ketner and Ch. Kloesel, Bloomington: Indiana University Press.

Kevelson, Roberta, 1987, *Charles S. Peirce's Method of Methods*, Amsterdam: John Benjamins.

-----, 1990, *Peirce, Paradox, Praxis*, Amsterdam: Mouton.

-----, 1993, *Peirce's Esthetics of Freedom*, New York and Bern: Peter Lang.

-----, 1996, *Peirce, Science, Signs*, New York and Bern: Peter Lang.

-----, 1997, *Peirce's Pragmatism*, New York and Bern: Peter Lang.

-----, 1998, *Peirce and the Mark of the Gryphon*, New York: St. Martin's Press.

Merrell, Floyd, 1997, *Peirce, Signs, and Meaning*, Toronto: University of Toronto Press.

Peirce, Charles S., 1931-35, 1958, *Collected Papers*, 8 volumes, eds Ch. Hartshorne, P. Weiss, A. Burks, Cambridge: Harvard University Press.

Peirce, Charles S., 1968, manuscripts unpublished, 33 reels, microfilm edition, with R. Robins Annotated Catalog, Amherst: University of Massachusetts Press.

Sebeok, Thomas A., 1976, *Contributions to the Doctrine of Signs*, Bloomington: RCLSS with Lisse: Peter de Ridder Press.

# Chapter 6

# Music Theory and General Semiotics:
# A Creative Interaction

Robert S. Hatten*

## I

Music theory has a long and venerable history dating back to the Greeks. The first encounter with semiotic theory has been relatively recent, perhaps marked by Roman Jakobson's [n.a.] 1971, [n.a.] 1987) seminal essays relating musicology and linguistics. The interaction has since been mediated by a series of linguistic theories from Saussure to Chomsky (see Monelle 1992), suggested by the intriguing analogies between language and music as temporal, signifying auditory streams. But the more general semiotic theories of C. S. Peirce and A. J. Greimas have also played a significant role in American and European approaches to musical signification. In the present chapter I will first summarize important influences from linguistic and semiotic theories, and then propose ways in which music semiotics might in turn elucidate problems in general semiotics. Rather than take a strictly chronological or historical approach to music semiotics in the last quarter of this century, however, I will proceed theoretically with what I consider to be the important questions for which semiotic theory has helped provide answers.

## II
## What Music Theory Has Learned From Semiotics

From Ferdinand de Saussure (1916/1966) we learned that meaning is difference, yet the tendency to characterize musical meaning in purely structural terms led to an early focus on defining surface musical units (segmentation) based on similarity. The oppositional systems that support surface differences, however, were already a central part of music theory. To take the Western tradition as an example, the continuum of pitch frequency is discretely divided (often by highly sophisticated tuning systems) into octave cycles, which have been further organized into scales. Scales are actually hierarchically organized pitch systems; asymmetrical placement of half-steps in the major scale plays an essential role in determining unique functions for each scale degree. Scale-degree function, which enables us to determine a tonal center or key, is oppositionally defined on the one hand by the uniqueness of certain intervals (a single tritone and only two asymmetrically placed half-steps), and on the other hand by the systems of harmony and voice-leading that contextualize pitches as members of chords and parts of progressions. The temporal continuum is divided first into durations of sound vs. silence (the latter playing an often-overlooked functional role, as well). Equally spaced beats (in the central Western tradition) are organized into metric hierarchies, usually by simple multiples or subdivisions of beats, and the resulting measures enable us to speak of locational functions with respect to "event-classes" (Benjamin 1984) within the measure. A simple example of locational function is the opposition between first and last beats of a measure, which is interpreted, significantly for our embodied experience of much music, as *down*beat vs. *up*beat.

These systematic considerations precede actual composition, although of course they became established by years of usage in individual works. Saussure's opposition between *langue* and *parole* offers a model for that productive dialectic — between system and usage, in Hjelmslev's terminology — which was easily mapped to music in terms of the established systems of a musical style, as opposed to the more flexible organization of a musical work. Those compositions we value typically reinforce stylistic principles and the systematically defined categories and processes of a given period, while exhibiting creativity in their novel realization of possibilities implied but not laid out in advance by the style. The productive tension between the traditional weight of style and the innovative force of creative works suggests a dynamic basis for meaning and a potential source of change that will be addressed further below. Saussure concluded that language exists in everyday use as a stable system (synchronic), although the changes — either incremental or sudden — that have altered systems over time (diachronic) also deserve their own investigation. Since historical linguistics in the nineteenth century focused on the diachronic dimension, Saussure's promotion of the synchronic may be seen as an inevitable (and perhaps extreme) reaction to the theoretical neglect of stable systems underlying coherent communication.

The Saussurean distinction between the signifier and the signified has been criticized for its unmediated dualism between the physical vehicle of the sign and its immaterial meaning or content, as though the system were merely a code that prescribed fixed semantic reference to each unit (along the lines of Umberto Eco's [1976:36-40] s-code, or code-as-system). We will see how a Peircean conception provides the crucial mediation of an implied interpreter to explain semiosis.

Assuming that one could draw upon established music theory for the systematic oppositions of a style, how might one approach the unique meaning of a musical work? One approach, introduced early by Nicolas Ruwet (1972) and promulgated by Jean-Jacques Nattiez (1975), was based upon a fundamental observation about music — the extent to which it exploits repetition (equalled in language only by some forms of poetry and rhetoric). Drawing on one more of Saussure's distinctions, that between the *paradigmatic* and the *syntagmatic*, these music semiotic theorists sought an equally systematic analytical approach to the musical surface, segmenting units of musical discourse based on an objective, hence reproducible, hence scientific procedure. In language, those units which may be substituted for each other in a sentence are aligned along various paradigmatic axes (for example, all the proper names, nouns, or pronouns that may be used as the subject of a sentence with a given verb). In Ruwet's and Nattiez's "paradigmatic analysis" units were defined by repetition and displayed in columns of notated musical segments, with variation among segments in a column less significant than differences between columns. Nattiez, borrowing Kenneth Pike's terms, considered the former as *etic* and the latter, *emic*.

This type of analysis is modeled on the basic constituent analysis of the linguistic school associated with Leonard Bloomfield, which sought to explain language from the ground up by demonstrating how segments could first be isolated and then functionally labeled from the raw evidence of speech. Nattiez assumed that definition of units could precede contamination by prior assumptions as to their meaning, hence his controversial positing of a *neutral* level of analysis. Since meaning for the composer and the listener need not coincide, his analytical approach included subsequent levels of *poeitic* and *esthesic* analysis, corresponding more generally to the production and reception poles of musical organization and understanding. The opposition between these poles is familiar from literary theory, as well as from Jakobson's communication model for poetics. With respect to the latter, Nattiez's three levels would constitute focus on the message (neutral), the sender (poietic), and the receiver (esthesic), respectively.

Such objective "discovery procedures" (the goal of a "neutral," paradigmatic analysis of surface musical segments) had already been superceded by more generative approaches to underlying competency in linguistic theory (Chomsky 1957). Ruwet (1975) realized the importance of a more productive methodological dialectic between style and work, as exemplified by Charles Rosen's influential study, *The Classical Style* (1972), and further theorized by Leonard B. Meyer (1973, 1989). Indeed, the paradigmatic approach was criticized (Hatten 1980, 1982) for ignoring well-established stylistic knowledge (for which we need not pretend ignorance), and for failing to incorporate abductive or creative hypotheses in determining meaningful segments from the beginning of an analysis. While repetition, especially in less traditional styles such as Debussy's, can indeed be crucial in defining a thematic unit in the absence of sufficient stylistic cues, it is but one of many possible operations that might have bearing on delineating and selecting those "segments" most relevant to an analysis of musical meaning.   Finally, paradigmatic analyses often produced such a welter of detail through which successive poeitic and esthesic analyses would have to sort.   From a practical standpoint, one wonders why potential meaning was not considered from the start.

Moving away from a code-like approach to style, and toward a more generative, Chomsky-inspired mode of analysis (Keiler 1981; Lerdahl and Jackendoff 1983) were logical next steps within the formalist arena of music's structural functions.   Keiler's generative tree structures involved functional categories (akin to Chomsky's) in parsing a musical phrase.   Lerdahl and Jackendoff, on the other hand, incorporated a quasi-Schenkerian approach to reduction in tree structures whose nodes were simply the musical events at given time points.   Their generative analyses captured a temporal hierarchization based on sets of well-formed and preference rules, with a formalism whose appeal to experimental music psychologists was its clear prediction of cognitive organization by a competent listener.   The generative analytical system could be criticized, however, for overvaluing hierarchical organization on the basis of a single primal opposition, between instability and stability (or tension and release), to the neglect of other forms of musical function and meaning (Hatten 1990).

In Europe, where a musical hermeneutic tradition was inspired by 19th-century literary hermeneutics, various semiotic approaches included a more semantic dimension to interpretation (Stefani 1976, Jiránek 1985, and — from a Peircean perspective — Karbusicky 1986).   Eero Tarasti's influential *Myth and Music* (1978) introduced two important concepts from A. J. Greimas (1966), which were further amplified in Tarasti's *A Theory of Musical Semiotics* (1994; for discussion of the modalities, see 27-29, 38-43, 48-9, 60-63, and 70-73):

(1) modalities, expressed by the existential and modal verbs in French — *être, devenir* [being, becoming]; *vouloir, savoir,* [will, know — the *virtual* modalities] *pouvoir, devoir* [can, must — the *actual* modalities], and *faire, être* [do, be — the *real* modalities] — which suggest implied emotional attitudes or values that are interpretable in the music, whether or not one could speak of an implied persona (Cone 1974).   In his later work, Tarasti (1994:72) offers an important qualification:

When we say that modalization is a process that humanizes and anthropomorphizes music (unites it with the sphere of human values), we are not referring to any concrete, semantic content, which also can be attached to various levels of music.

(2) *isotopies, lexemes,* and *semes* — three levels of relatively synthetic stylistic meaning which Tarasti applies to 19th-century music, with special attention to Wagner's music dramas. Narrative analysis in *Myth and Music* is conceived as a syntagmatic fusion of Propp's analysis of the fairy tale and Lévi-Strauss's analysis of myth, each of which anticipate elements of Greimas's semiotic square. Tarasti (1994:73) sets forth a developmental model of narrativity in which *modalities* combine into *passions* (e.g., despair), and the ordering of passions may then suggest *narrativity* (assuming the appropriate engagement of temporal, spatial, and actorial categories).

Márta Grabócz (1986, 1996) further develops an approach inspired by Greimas's narrative theories and Tarasti's musical semes in her important *Morphologie des Oeuvres pour Piano de Liszt*. Drawing, as did Tarasti, on Boris Asafiev's (1930/ 1977) intonation theory to characterize types of themes, she includes generic formations inspired by modes — pastoral, religious, heroic — as well as formal genres — scherzo, march, recitative.

The concept of *seme* is perhaps related to that of topic in the work of Leonard Ratner (1980) on the Classical style (see below). *Isotopy*, a term Greimas borrowed from physics, is a bit more complicated to grasp. Eero Tarasti's glossary (1994: 304) offers the following definition, modeled on Greimas's:

*Isotopy*: a set of semantic categories whose redundancy guarantees the coherence of a sign-complex and makes possible the uniform reading of any text. In this sense, semes are (semantic) categories of *style*, which may combine into lexemes (the rough equivalent of words in language), whereas isotopies might appear to refer to consistent complexes of semes that lend coherence to a given *work*. Tarasti (1994: 7-10), however, expands the concept of isotopy to embrace five means by which we interpret the coherence of a work, drawing upon style categories:

(1) deep structures, such as Schenker's *Ursatz* or Greimas's semiotic square, which move from achronic to temporal unfolding as we analyze the dynamic structuring of a work,

(2) thematic coherence, in the sense of Rudolph Réti's (1951) Schoenberg-inspired approach to organic thematic relationships,

(3) musical genres, ranging from the formal to the topical,

(4) musical texture, functioning as a "milieu, a musical landscape in which the theme-actant moves and acts" (10), and

(5) text strategies, including thematic transformations that fulfill narrative/dramatic roles in an overall plot structure that leads to "achievement or unfulfillment of the action, to perfectivity or imperfectivity (in Greimas's terms)" (10).

Márta Grabócz (1996:117-121) utilizes another term drawn from Greimas, the *classeme*, which Greimas uses for contextual semes that recur in the discourse and guarantee the isotopy. Classemes, which Grabócz roughly equates with Asafiev's intonations, form a syntagmatic chain that cohere as an isotopy. For examples, the heroic isotopy might involve such classemes as "agitato," "march," "recitative," and "grandiose triumph," as well as such semes as "military fanfare." Other isotopies found often in Liszt include "grief," the "pastoral," the "religious," and the "pantheist," the latter formed by a combination of those classemes supporting pastoral and religious isotopies (122). Whereas a work generally has a single isotopy, the possibility of two or more provides for interesting narrative trajectories. Liszt's Piano Sonata in B minor includes six: the "quest," "pastoral-amorous," "heroic," "macabre struggle," "religious," and "pantheist" isotopies (123).

The first book-length music semiotic study in the United States to examine similar semantic categories is Kofi Agawu's *Playing with Signs* (1991). Agawu explains music meaning in Haydn, Mozart, and Beethoven by synthesizing topical analysis as derived from Ratner (1980:9-30) with Schenkerian analysis of voice-leading trajectories, embraced by a beginning-middle-end model of temporal functions. Topics in Ratner's sense range from the incorporation of generic types (minuet, march) or styles (Sturm und Drang, learned style) as contrastive textural units within a larger work (for an outline and critique, see Hatten 1994:74-5). Agawu presents a useful overview of semiotic theories (10-16), but he draws primarily on Roman Jakobson's (1971:704-5) distinction between *introversive* and *extroversive* semiosis, relating Schenkerian analysis to the former and topical analysis to the latter. Whereas Jakobson felt that music was primarily introversive, Agawu makes a strong case for the importance of the mutual interaction with extroversive semiosis, which is productively achieved in what he calls a "region of play" between the two. Thus, the analyst should attempt to combine structuralist and referentialist accounts.

Agawu's topical labels, or the semes and classemes of Tarasti and Grabócz, might be criticized as being on the one hand too loosely applied — the opposite of the problem encountered in the paradigmatic analysis of early Ruwet and Nattiez — and on the other, barely interpreted (Hatten 1992). With respect to the first problem, one wonders what underlying system supports the identification and discrimination of various topics or classemes. Are these "intonations" simply supported by the habitual association of types of music with types of function? As to the latter issue, how should one interpret a given topic's contribution to expressive meaning? Agawu stops after assigning (introversive) beginning, middle, or end functions, with the extroversive component merely residing in the label itself. Grabócz's and

Tarasti's analyses go further, indicating how classemes are bundled into isotopies, and drawing upon Greimas's narrative theory to suggest how dramas or narratives might be constructed by successions of isotopies. But beyond the labeling, what constitutes meaning in a given context? How, in other words, do we go beyond denotation to capture connotation, beyond labeling to open up an interpretation, and beyond formalism to embrace the hermeneutic?

Hatten (1994) attempts to provide answers to these questions, beginning with an oppositional framework for structuring topics (as well as other, less synthetic musical categories), and continuing with a theory of expressive genres and tropes to address the creative interpretation of topics (and other correlations) within a work. The framework of oppositions is organized according to the principle of *markedness* first enunciated for language (Trubetzkoy 1939/1969; see also Jakobson 1971 and Shapiro 1976, 1983) and since applied widely to a range cultural semiotic systems. If musical meaning is difference, then markedness theory predicts that stylistic oppositions are asymmetrical, with the marked term having with a narrower range of content than the unmarked term. Markedness oppositions in musical structure *correlate* with oppositions in various planes of meaning, from the functional meanings of musical "syntax" — including voice leading, harmonic progression, and the like — to the "semantic" levels of so-called extramusical meaning — including expressive states, dramatic trajectories, narrativity, allegorical interpretation, and the like. Correlations are types in the style; they appear as tokens in the musical work (the type-token distinction is drawn from Peirce [1931, 1960]). Tokens of a type have features that are "typical" — but not always "invariant," as Wittengenstein (1933-35/1960) demonstrated — and other features that are variable. One way styles acquire new correlations is by foregrounding variable features with new oppositions.

*Interpretations* go beyond the general style meanings of correlations to more specific meanings appropriate to the contexts of use in a work. Contexts include the thematic strategies of a work, its expressive genre (as negotiated with formal genre), tropological figurations (musical metaphor, irony, shift in level of discourse), and intertextuality. Because markedness is the underlying principle, strategic markedness can help explain the relatively original oppositions created within the work. Indeed, markedness regulates the degree of precision with which meaning can be ascribed. For examples, the opposition between minor and major is correlated with a rather general opposition, "tragic vs. non-tragic," for the Classical style; oppositions among pastoral, heroic, and comic or *buffa* further articulate the semantic field of the "non-tragic". But markedness can also track the growth process by which the variable features of tokens develop significance (as marked oppositions).

The Peircean sign categories (icon, index, symbol), first invoked for music theory by Wilson Coker (1972), have been investigated more fully by Vladimir Karbusicky (1986:39-107) and Raymond Monelle (1992:193-219), while also influencing Nattiez (1990:5-6, 21-25), Hatten (1994:257-62), and Tarasti (1994: 54-57). The varieties of Peircean interpretant have been investigated by William Dougherty, with special application to the semiosis of art song (1993).

The work of David Lidov (1987, 1993) on musical gesture illustrates the distinction often drawn between physical gesture and more abstract or formal musical logic. Lidov (1987:71) notes how the gesture, originating as icon and index, is sublimated into symbol as it becomes a sign functioning in a formal system. But the index has priority over the icon in his originary semiotics, since the indexical is most particular yet least articulate, and directly expressive in a physical sense (1987:73). The iconic is already once-removed, in that articulate shapes are interpreted as "the isomorph or trace of some object or force not immediately in contact with it" (1987:73). The symbol is fully articulated within a system, and involves "formal relations" such as "the developmental calculi of fragmentation, inversion, transposition, et cetera, which can be but need not be subordinated to images of feeling" (1987:74). But one might counter that even in its emergent symbolic role, gesture maintains its potency and immediacy through both the dynamics of physical performance, and through the logic of thematic structure (Hatten 1997:2). With respect to the latter, one can observe in Schubert, as well as Beethoven, a concern for development of the gestural attributes of gesturally conceived motives (Hatten 1993).

Interestingly, Roland Barthes (1975/1985) saw embodied gesture as an alternative to the formal sterility of semiologies of discrete structure for music. For him, music was "a field of signifying and not a system of signs" because "the referent is the body" and "the body passes into music without any relay but the signifier" (1985:311). His "figures of the body" (1985:307) are attractive metaphors of compelling force, and Barthes does not deny that a semiology is capable of treating the "system of notes, scales, tones, chords, and rhythms" (1985:312). Nevertheless, Barthes' rhetoric, inspired by the physicality of effective performances of Schumann's piano music, presumes that semiotics is incapable of accommodating the gestural as well as the more formal. David Lidov (1993) further establishes gesture within the realm of the semiotic by defining gesture as movement that is marked as meaningful. One might develop this insight beyond the marked opposition of gesture to movement and consider the oppositional structuring of cultural gestural types. The musicologist Wye Allanbrook, in her study of Mozart operas (1983), offers a stylistic inventory of dance meters, their accentual properties, and their implied tempos (hence, the background gestural fields from which musical gestures emerge, and with which motivic-rhythmic gestures can interact) for the Classical style. Current interest in musical performance (reviewed in Hatten 1996) offers another avenue for exploring the particularity of gestural semiosis in conjunction with stylistic constraints on a performer's interpretation. Finally, the gestural pedagogy of Alexandra Pierce (1994), with its integration of bodily and analytical interpretation, affords the music semiotician a rich field for further theorizing about musical meaning.

The past decade has seen an increased interest in musical meaning and interpretation from a variety of ideological and other perspectives, a trend that has been dubbed the New Musicology, but whose presuppositions are increasingly those of postmodernism — as, for example, Lawrence Kramer's Classical Music and Postmodern Knowledge (1995). Semiotic theory is faced with competition from numerous constituencies, many of which prefer to dismiss semiotics as an outdated form of structuralism (an incomplete view perhaps attributable to an association with Nattiez's paradigmatic analyses). Yet various cultural-semiotic approaches (for example, feminist "readings") risk deflecting attention from the meaning and aesthetic value of the work of music and instead appropriating it as evidence for a particular (generally flawed) bias in the culture from which the work emerged. Another issue arises from increasingly relaxed standards for claims of musical meaning. As Eco (1990) pondered, are there any limits to interpretation? These issues are addressed in Hatten (forthcoming), an essay which begins with an examination of hermeneutic theory, its roots in the nineteenth century (Schleiermacher), its appropriation by musicology and music theory, and ways in which hermeneutics might be fruitfully grounded in semiotics.

# III
## What Music Semiotics Might Offer to General Semiotic Theory

As coda to this condensed overview of music semiotics, I will speculate on areas in which music semiotic investigation may contribute to a more general semiotic inquiry. The first of these is temporality. Music has means of shaping time (J. Kramer 1988, Epstein 1995) that far exceed those of poetry or sophisticated narrative techniques. Even without such linguistic means as tense, music has the capacity to play with temporal perspective, and to set up the various frames and levels of discourse that are required for narrative structure (i.e., to give the impression of a "telling" rather than merely a "portrayal" of a sequence of events), and hence for manipulating the temporal sequence, as well as the expressive significance, of the events in a dramatic "plot" (Hatten 1997). Although narrativity in this sense may be rare in music, schemes of pattern and expectation are quite common, and many styles have a depth of hierarchical organization that enriches or enlarges our perceptual/cognitive, and hence semiotic, capacities. Thus, the exploration of music's temporal organization and strategies may offer a window on the brain's vast potential for semiotic organization of perceptual information.

Another area of immense potential is the intersection between music as formal or abstract patterning and music as performed (or embodied) gesture. Without some of the complexities of linguistic reference to obscure this interaction, yet with a more developed abstraction of its basic materials than is found in dance, music can be a unique laboratory for studying ways in which meaning arises from the synthesis of bodily and mental processing. In turn, the age-old problem of body-mind dualism may be more helpfully formulated, if not resolved. Music affords a model of creativity that draws upon the gestural as expressive motivation for the structural, and structural as logical or systematic motivation for creating and developing the gestural. Their interaction and negotiation in the gestation of a musical work may provide insights into more general semiotic issues pertaining to the creative process.

Because of music's well-developed analytical systems, and the tendency of artistic styles to change faster than language, music offers a unique laboratory for the investigation of growth and change in semiotic systems. Elsewhere (Hatten 1982) I have distinguished growth and change in terms of a theoretical concept of style (growth serving to enlarge a style, and change involving radical hierarchical reformulation, if not complete displacement, of a style). Certain extreme twentieth-century styles, where one cannot speak with assurance of stylistic competency, or in every case find a community of shared stylistic values, may challenge our more general intuitions concerning the function of semiotic systems. The plurality of potential styles within a given musical work (already a feature of Mozart's operas) may provide insight into modes of dialogism and multi- voicedness as propounded for the novel by Bakhtin (1935/1981). Issues of voice in music have been shown to be especially significant in opera, as well as in programmatic music (Abbate 1991), and the discovery of various kinds of subjectivity in music may suggest further possibilities in studies of other communication systems.

Theorists have drawn upon literary and cognitive conceptions of metaphor and other tropes in their efforts to understand particularly creative combinations and figurations of musical meaning. While this borrowing has been somewhat one-sided, the distinctive character of troping in music (which lacks the means of predication presumed in linguistic metaphor) may offer insight into the more general principles underlying this form of semiotic creativity.

That language is a universal of all human cultures needs little explanation. But why should it be the case that every culture has music? Among the various rationales — ranging from the culturally regulative embodiment of mythic or spiritual truths to the personally therapeutic expression of emotion, from the rhythmic underpinning and social solidarity of work songs to the cognitive development of the individual attributable to music as play — the greatest obstacle to tackling this issue has been the absence of a grounded theory of musical meaning. It is ironic that at the very time music theory and musicology has begun to address this lacuna, American schools are cutting music programs in response to budget crises — as though music were a dispensable luxury, or merely the commodity that it has become in the mass media's creation of an "entertainment industry". Perhaps the greatest return on the investments of semiotic theory that music semioticians can offer is a stronger case for music itself as one of the most complex and meaningful of semiotic systems — one that is essential to human life.

*Robert S. Hatten is Professor of Music and Music Theory at The Pennsylvania State University.*

## REFERENCES

Abbate, Carolyn, 1991, *Unsung Voices: Opera and Musical Narrative in the Nineteenth Century*. Princeton: Princeton University Press.

Agawu, V. Kofi, 1991, *Playing with Signs: A Semiotic Interpretation of Classic Music*. Princeton: Princeton University Press.

Allanbrook, Wendy, 1983, *Rhythmic Gesture in Mozart*. Chicago: The University of Chicago Press.

Asafiev, Boris V., 1930/1977, *Musical Form as a Process [Muzykal'naja forma kak process]*. 3 vols., trans. with commentary by J. R. Tull. Unpub. Ph.D. diss., Ohio State University.

Bakhtin, Mikhail, 1935/1981, *The Dialogic Imagination: Four Essays* by M. M. Bakhtin, Michael Holquist, ed., Caryl Emerson, trans. Austin: The University of Texas Press.

Barthes, Roland, 1975/1980, Rasch. In *The Responsibility of Forms: Critical Essays on Music, Art, and Representation*, trans. Richard Howard. Berkeley: University of California Press, 299-312.

Benjamin, William E., 1984, A Theory of Musical Meter. *Music Perception* 1:4, 355-413.

Chomsky, Noam, 1957, *Syntactic Structures*. The Hague: Mouton.

Cone, Edward T., 1974, *The Composer's Voice*. Berkley: University of California Press.

Coker, Wilson, 1972, *Music and Meaning: A Theoretical Introduction to Musical Aesthetics*. New York: Free Press.

Dougherty, William P., 1993, The Play of Interpretants:  A Peircean Approach to Beethoven's Lieder.  In *The Peirce Seminar Papers:  An Annual of Semiotic Analysis* 1, 67-95.

Eco, Umberto, 1976, *A Theory of Semiotics*. Advances in Semiotics, Thomas A. Sebeok, gen. ed., Bloomington: Indiana University Press.

-----, 1990, *The Limits of Interpretation*. Bloomington:  Indiana University Press.

Epstein, David, 1995, *Shaping Time: Music, the Brain, and Performance*. New York: Schirmer Books.

Grabócz, Márta, 1996, *Morphologie des oeuvres pour piano de Liszt: Influence du Programme sur l'Évolution des Formes Instrumentales*. 2nd ed., Paris:  Éditions Kimé, 1st ed., Budapest:  MTA Zenetudományi Intézet, 1986.

Greimas, Algirdas Julien, 1967, *Sémantique structurale:  Recherche de méthode*. Paris: Larousse.

Greimas, A. J. and Joseph Courtès, 1979, *Sémiotique: Dictionnaire raisonné de la théorie du langage*. Paris:  Hachette.

Hatten, Robert, 1980, Nattiez's Semiology of Music: Flaws in the New Science. *Semiotica* 31:1/2, 139-155.

-----, 1982, Toward a Semiotic Model of Style in Music:  Epistemological and Methodological Bases. Unpub. Ph.D. diss., Indiana University.

-----, 1990, The Splintered Paradigm:  A Semiotic Critique of Recent Approaches to Music Cognition. Review article: Lerdahl and Jackendoff, *A Generative Theory of Tonal Music; Serafine, Music as Cognition*; and Sloboda, The Musical Mind. *Semiotica* 81:1/2, 145-78.

-----, 1992, Review of Agawu, *Playing with Signs* (1991), and Nattiez, *Music and Discourse* (1990). *Music Theory Spectrum* 14:1, 88-98.

-----, 1993, Schubert the progressive:  The Role of Resonance and Gesture in the Piano Sonata in A, D. 959. *Intégral* 7, 38-81.

-----, 1994, *Musical Meaning in Beethoven: Markedness, Correlation, and Interpretation*.  Advances in Semiotics, Thomas A. Sebeok, gen. ed. Bloomington: Indiana University Press.

-----, 1996, Review-article, *The Practice of Performance* (1995), John Rink, ed. Indiana Theory Review 17:1 (Spring, 1996), 87-117.

-----, 1997, Music and Tense.  In *Semiotics around the World:  Synthesis in Diversity.  Proceedings of the Fifth Congress of the International*

*Association for Semiotic Studies*, Berkeley, 1994, ed. Irmengard Rauch and Gerald F. Carr. Berlin, New York: Mouton de Gruyter, 1997, 627-30.

Hatten, Robert, 1997-8, Embodying Sound: The Role of Semiotics. Lecture 2 in the online series *Musical Gesture*, ed. Paul Bouissac. Toronto: Cyber Semiotic Institute.

Hatten, Robert, forthcoming. Grounding Interpretation: A Semiotic Framework for Musical Hermeneutics," to appear in the *American Journal of Semiotics*.

Jakobson, Roman, 1960, Concluding Statement: Linguistics and Poetics. In *Style in Language*, ed. Thomas A. Sebeok. Cambridge, Mass.: The M.I.T. Press, 350-77.

-----, [n.a.] 1971, Language in Relation to Other Communication Systems. In *Selected Writings*, vol. 2. The Hague: Mouton, 697-708.

-----, [n.a., c. 1930?] 1987, Musicology and Linguistics. In *Language in Literature*, Krystyna Pomorska and Stephen Rudy, eds. Cambridge, Mass.: Harvard University Press, 41-6.

Jiránek, Jaroslav, 1985, *Zu Grundfragen der musikalische Semiotik*. Berlin: Neue Musik.

Karbusicky, Vladimir, 1986, *Grundriss der musikalischen Semantik*. Darmstadt: Wissenschaftliche Buchgesellschaft.

Keiler, Allan R., 1977, The Syntax of Prolongation, part 1. In *Theory Only* 3, 3-27.

-----, 1981, Two Views of Musical Semiotics: Some Properties of the Design and Syntax of Tonal Music. In *The Sign in Music and Literature*, ed. Wendy Steiner. Austin: The University of Texas Press.

Kramer, Jonathan, 1988, *The Time of Music: New Meanings, New Temporalities, New Listening Strategies*. New York: Schirmer Books.

Lerdahl, Fred, and Ray Jackendoff, 1983, *A Generative Theory of Tonal Music*. Cambridge, Mass.: The M.I.T. Press.

Lidov, David, 1987, Mind and Body in Music. *Semiotica* 66:1/3, 69-97.

-----, 1993, The Discourse of Gesture. Unpub. paper delivered to the Semiotic Society of America, St. Louis.

Meyer, Leonard B., 1973, *Explaining Music*. Chicago: The University of Chicago Press.

-----, 1989, *Style and Music*. Philadelphia: University of Pennsylvania Press.

Monelle, Raymond, 1992, *Linguistics and Semiotics in Music*. Contemporary Music Studies 5, Chur, Switzerland: Harwood Academic Publishers.

Nattiez, Jean-Jacques, 1975, *Fondements d'une sémiologie de la musique*, 10/18, série 'esthétique' dirigée par Mikel Dufrenne, Paris: Union générale d'éditions.

-----, 1990, *Music and Discourse: Toward a Semiology of Music,* trans. Carolyn Abbate. Princeton: Princeton University Press.

Peirce, Charles Sanders, 1931/1960, *Collected Papers of Charles Sanders Peirce*, vols. 1-6, Charles Hartshorne and Paul Weiss, eds.; vols. 7-8, Arthur W. Burks, ed. Cambridge: Harvard University Press.

Pierce, Alexandra, 1994, Developing Schenkerian Hearing and Performing, *Intégral* 8, 51-123.

Ratner, Leonard, 1980, *Classic Music: Expression, Form, and Style.* New York: Schirmer Books.

Réti, Rudolph, 1951, *The Thematic Process in Music.* New York: Macmillan.

Rosen, Charles, 1972, *The Classical Style: Haydn, Mozart, Beethoven.* New York: Norton.

Ruwet, Nicolas, 1972, *Langage, musique, poésie.* Paris: Seuil.

-----, 1975, Théorie et méthodes dans les études musicales. *Musique en jeu* 17, 11-36.

de Saussure, Ferdinand, 1916/1966, *Course in General Linguistics.* Charles Bally and Albert Sechehaye, eds., Wade Baskin, trans. New York: McGraw-Hill.

Shapiro, Michael, 1976, *Asymmetry: An Inquiry into the Linguistic Structure of Poetry.* Amsterdam: North Holland.

-----, 1983, *The Sense of Grammar.* Bloomington: Indiana University Press.

Tarasti, Eero, 1978, *Myth and Music: A Semiotic Approach to the Aesthetics of Myth in Music, Especially that of Wagner, Sibelius, and Stravinsky.* Acta Musicologica Fennica 11, Helsinki: Suomen Musikkitieteellinen Seura.

-----, 1994, *A Theory of Musical Semiotics.* Advances in Semiotics, Thomas A. Sebeok, gen. ed., Bloomington: Indiana University Press.

Trubetzkoy, N. B., 1939/1969, *Principles of Phonology*, trans. Christine A. M. Baltaxe. Berkeley: University of California Press.

Wittgenstein, Ludwig, 1933-35/1960, *The Blue and Brown Books.* New York: Harper & Row.

# Chapter 7

# Semiotics and Language:
# The Work of Roman Jakobson[1]

Linda R. Waugh*

## I

There are many connections between work on language (in such fields as linguistics, literary studies, anthropology, psychology, sociology) and work in the general field of semiotics. But there is, perhaps, no other scholar of language who has taken as thorough-going a semiotic perspective on language as Roman Jakobson. He was one of the major linguists, literary theorists (poeticians), and semioticians of this century. Moreover, he was a "major 'catalyst' in the contemporary 'semiotic reaction'" (Eco 1977:41). This is due to the fact that many of the basic assumptions of modern semiotic research have been defined and/or furthered by Jakobson's work. For him, language is a system of signs used for communication, and thus the study of language (linguistics, broadly defined) is but a subpart of semiotics, the study of any semiotic system. Signification is everywhere and the major principle which unifies sign systems is that they exist for the generation of messages (instances of *parole*) through which communication takes place. Thus, linguistics is the study of communication by any verbal message and is included in semiotics, the study of communication by any message, which in its turn is part of a larger study of communication, involving social anthropology, sociology, and economics (Jakobson 1969). Now, some linguistic messages have an aesthetic, poetic function. Thus, according to Jakobson, poetics, the study of communication by poetic messages, is a subpart of linguistics, which encompasses the study of messages with any function.

Language, for Jakobson, is the human semiotic system *par excellence*, the phylogenetic and ontogenetic basis for all other semiotic systems and thus the starting point for any valid semiotic analysis. It is important, moreover, to confront language with other sign systems in order to discover what the specific properties of language are and to avoid "the imprudent application of the special characteristics of language to other semiotic systems" (Jakobson 1975a:214). In particular, attention should be paid to what differentiates sign systems: e.g., intentional communication vs. unintended communication (Jakobson 1969:661ff).

# II
## Language as a System of Signs

Jakobson defined language as a structured system of signs. He argued —
against the theory of Ferdinand de Saussure — that since language is an
interpersonal (intersubjective) means of communcation, *langue* and *parole*
(code and message in "modern, less ambiguous terminology", see Jakobson
1971b:718) must be seen as mutually dependent and thus functionally and
structurally linked as for any semiotic system. Moreover, any state of a
language presents a dynamic synchrony: changes in progress are manifested
as stylistically or socially marked variants (subcodes) — for example, older
vs. newer ways of speaking. In this way, he insisted on the inclusion of time
(and space, in geographical and social dialects) as an element of synchronic
structure (Jakobson/Pomorska 1980:56-90). Thus, he declared the Saussurian
dichotomy of internal-external (conditions on language structure) to be
invalid: anything which is pertinent to semiotic structure is by definition
internal.

The central element of language structure is the linguistic sign, defined as
a "*referral* (*renvoi*) (following the famous *aliquid stat pro aliquo*)" (Jakobson
1975a:215), a referral from *signans* to *signatum* and vice versa, and
secondarily a referral from one sign to another. Jakobson insisted on the
indissoluble dualism of the linguistic sign: "speech sounds must be
consistently analyzed with regard to meaning and meaning in its turn analyzed
with reference to sound form" (1949b:50). His work in this area began with
an examination of the function of sound in poetry (Jakobson 1921a, 1923),
and indeed sound proved to be the laboratory in which he explored the nature
of the linguistic sign throughout his life. For Jakobson the sound
(phonologial) system of any language (or any analogous semiotic system) is
a structural whole, dominated by general laws; sound is not a thing in itself
but a functional element: it serves signification (Jakobson 1949b:50ff,
1962a:631ff, 1962b:280ff). The primordial properties of sound are the
distinctive features, those minimal sound elements which serve to distinguish
larger signs (e.g., words) from each other (Jakobson/Fant/Halle 1952:1ff,
Jakobson/Halle 1956:13ff). This means that the distinctive features (and the
phoneme, a bundle of distinctive features) are signs, whose *signatum* is
"(mere) otherness" or pure differentiation: they are pure "signs of signs",
unlike all other types of signs, which have some content. Thus, language
exhibits two very different types of signs. And Jakobson claimed that it and
the genetic code — see 1968b, 1969:678ff, 1974 — are the only systems to
have this kind of structure. Language is a completely semiotic system: "an
important structural particularity of language is that at no stage of resolving

higher units into their component parts does one encounter informationally pointless fragments" (1963:283).

According to Jakobson, language is a pure system of signs, and not only sound, but also grammar and syntax, must thus be subjected to a semantic analysis; the study of meaning cannot be excluded from linguistics, nor from other semiotic systems such as music and non-representational painting (see Jakobson 1932b, 1964/1967, 1968a, 1975a:212ff). That is, any formal analysis of signs necessitates a concomitant semantic analysis, whether the object of study be phonological elements, morphological systems, syntactic structures, formal aspects of texts, discursive structure of poems, and so forth. Concomitantly, no semantic analysis can be done without close attention to form — e.g., the meaning/interpretation of a sentence or of a whole text depends crucially on how that meaning is interrelated with the formal elements.

All linguistic signs are simultaneously wholes composed of parts and themselves parts included in larger wholes (Jakobson 1963:280ff). Hierarchy, then, is the fundamental structural principle: language is a part-whole hierarchy of signs from the smallest (distinctive features) through phonemes, syllables, morphemes, words, phrases, clauses, sentences, to the largest (discourses and texts). Signs lower in the hierarchy are incorporated into the larger signs through two types of combination: simultaneous (e.g., distinctive features in the phoneme) and sequential (e.g., phonemes in the syllable). Up to the level of the word, signs are encoded as wholes — thus the combinations are prefabricated — whereas above the word level specific rules of combination (syntactic matrices, syntactic structures) govern how phrases, clauses and sentences are formed. Discourses and texts arise from only very generalized, and optional, rules of combination and thus allow the most freedom to be creative. That is, there is an ascending scale of freedom in the ability of speakers to create and addressees to understand new signs. In other words, many signs are codified as such, but others are only evidenced as messages. Semiotic creativity, then, is associated with semiotic structure.

# III
## Signs and Relational Structure

What was for Jakobson the most important property of signs (and thus the dominant topic and methodological device underlying his research) was invariance: any sign is defined by invariant properties, those constant characteristics of the sign that differentiate it from the other elements in the system of which it is a part. In this way, within a language he was able to unify seemingly diverse signs; across languages too, he also insisted on the importance of universal invariants (language universals), again establishing the equivalence of diverse sounds.  In addition, he correlated invariance with contextual variation: any sign evidences variation as it enters specific contexts.  Contextual variants are not equal, but hierarchized: some are more basic, others more marginal.  Invariance and variation apply to the *signans* (e.g., variation across phonemes) and the *signatum* (e.g., the semantic properties of the case and verbal systems of Russian [1932a, 1936a]).  In semantics, by incorporating invariance (context-independent meaning, general meaning) and variation (context-specific meaning, polysemy), he gave the basis for a rigorous semantics — whether of lexical items, syntactic constructions, morphological categories, or phonological entities.  Moreover, by insisting that reference (extension) is linguistic since it is implicated in contextual variation (Jakobson 1973:315ff), he helped pave the way for the integration of pragmatics as a fundamental part of linguistics.

Invariance for Jakobson was always invariance in relationship (equivalence); and the primary type of relation in language is that of binary opposition (1959b:264ff), whether it be phonological (e.g., the distinctive feature nasal vs. oral in *m* vs. *b*), grammatical (e.g., the difference between singular and plural), or lexical (e.g., spatial vocabulary pairs like *near-far, here-there, high-low*).  But such binarism for him was always based on an asymmetry in the relationship between a marked (focused or weighted) and an unmarked (neutral) term (Jakobson/Pomorska 1980:93ff): e.g., marked nasal vs. unmarked oral, marked plural vs. unmarked singular, marked *near* vs. unmarked *far*).  Jakobson immediately saw the relevance of markedness for semiotics: "I think that it will become important not only for linguistics, but also for ethnology and the history of culture, and that correlations encountered in the history of culture, such as life/death, liberty/oppression, sin/virtue, holidays/workdays, etc., can always be reduced to the relation a/not a; the relevant thing is to establish what constitutes the marked set for each period, group, people, and so on" (1975b:163 [written in 1930]; cf. Jakobson/Waugh 1979:93ff and Jakobson/Pomorska 1980:95ff, Waugh 1982).

Jakobson's analysis of the relational and binary nature of signs also brought him to further theoretical work on the nature of the zero sign: the absence of a form can be meaningful only if it is in relation to a corresponding overt form (1939, 1940).  Such zero signs are crucial to language as well as to all other semiotic systems.

# IV
## Signs and Multifunctionality

While distinctive features are the most fundamental properties of sound, the speech sound is actually a complex sign made up of a variety of signs each with its own particular function.  Speech sounds are totally defined by a variety of feature types: distinctive features differentiate between words which are different in meaning (see Jakobson 1966b:705ff, Jakobson/Waugh 1979:29ff, Waugh 1987), whereas redundant features are relevant for perception because they serve to support and enhance the distinctive features (Jakosbon/Fant/Halle 1952:4ff, Jakobson/Waugh 1979:39-41). Configurative features show the unity or the boundaries of meaningful units like words and phrases, expressive/stylistic features inform about the placement of vocabulary items in a special subset of the lexicon and/or about the subjective attitude of the speaker, physiognomic features inform about the age, sex, geographical and ethnic origin, social class, education, kinesthetic type, personality, and so forth of the speaker (Jakobson/Waugh 1979, Waugh 1987). All of these feature types together represent the entire makeup of a sound (its "shape"). Thus, there is nothing which is pure sound, which does not combine function and sound essence. Hence, the Saussurian distinction between form and substance is invalid: both the phonic essence and its structural organization are semiotic artifacts (Jakobson 1949a:423, Jakobson/Waugh 1979:33ff, 48ff). Consequently, the oppositions traditionally made between linguistic and non-linguistic, abstract and concrete, functional and non-functional, (phon)emic and (phon)etic are inappropriate (see also Lévi-Strauss 1972/1973:22, Waugh 1984:1255-56).

# V
# Functions of Language

For Jakobson, the *raison d'être* for language, as for any semiotic system, is communication. While for many, the purpose of communication is referential, for Jakobson (and the Prague structuralists) "reference is not the only, nor even the primary, goal of communcation" (Caton 1987:231). Language is rather a system of sytems suited to various communcative goals, which in turn are correlated with the act of communication in which language is used. In his famous article, "Linguistics and Poetics", Jakobson defined the six primary factors of any speech event (1960: 21-22, based in part on Saussure 1916, Bühler 1934, and on communication theory, see Shannon and Weaver 1949): 1) speaker, 2) adressee, 3) context (including the thing referred to), 4) message (*parole*), 5) code (*langue*), 6) contact (medium) of communication. In conjunction with these, Jakobson then defined (1960:22-27; cf. 1976:113-115) the "functions of language" in terms of a focus (*Einstellung*) in the message on one of the factors: 1) emotive function (focus on the speaker) — e.g., intonation showing anger; 2) conative function (focus on the addressee) — e.g., imperatives and vocatives; 3) referential function (focus on the context) — e.g., realism; 4) poetic function (focus on the message) — e.g., poetry; 5) metalingual function (focus on the code) —

e.g., definitions of words; and 6) phatic function (focus on the contact) — e.g., "hello, do you hear me?". While these functions are the result of a predominance of focus within the message itself on one of the factors, they can also occur in other contexts, but not as the predominant one: e.g., a referential message may carry expressive information and may serve as a conative appeal. In like fashion, "the poetic function is not the sole function of verbal art but only its dominant, determining function, whereas in all other verbal activities it acts as a subsidiary, accessory constiutuent" (Jakobson 1960:356). It nevertheless remains true that given their focus on the message itself, poetic texts are the most semioticized and semantically the richest of all texts: as signs, they are cut off from reference (they deepen the fundamental dichotomy of signs and objects) and refer back to the poetic text itself (Waugh 1980).

# VI
## Metaphor and Metonymy

In 1956, Jakobson published his famous "Two Aspects of Language", where he analyzed the relation between communicative processes and properties of linguistic structure, by redefining the "axes" of language first propounded by Kruszewski (see Jakobson 1967) and later simplified by Saussure (1916) as associative (paradigmatic in later terminology)/syntagmatic. On the one hand Jakobson distinguished the two operations used for encoding (production) and decoding (comprehension): selection (substitution) for encoding and combination (also called contexture) for decoding. On the other hand, he contrasted two types of relations in language structure: similarity (all types of equivalence) and contiguity (temporal and spatial neighborhood). Thus, linguistic items belong to classes or types which share properties and they always appear in a context. Jakobson extensively used similarity vs. contiguity and the corresponding tropes, metaphor (based on similarity) vs. metonymy (founded on contiguity) in his work on poetics and semiotics (especially cinema) (1921a, 1921b, 1932b, 1933, 1935, 1936b, 1937). But in 1956, he shows that the tension between contiguity and similarity permeates the whole of language and that in particular the two structural relations underlie the two operations: i.e., the elements in a selection set are normally associated by similarity, and those in combination by contiguity (pp. 241ff). Thus, the operations by which speakers and addressees encode or decode messages are linked to the means by which the elements of the message are related to each other.

Moreover, the similarity vs. contiguity dichotomy was also used by Jakobson to deepen the definition of, in particular, the poetic function: in poetry, where focus on the message is dominant, equivalence (similarity) relations are used to build the combination rather than only to underpin statically the elements of the selection set. "In the poetic function, the relation of equivalence is projected from the axis of selection to the axis of combination" (Jakobson 1960:27): i.e., in the operation of combination, equivalence relations are more crucial when the poetic function is predominant than when it is not. According to this projection principle, parallelisms between equivalent units help to structure the poetic text; tropes built on similarity, such as metaphor, are more likely to be found in poetry, whereas metonymy is more characteristic of prose. In the latter, especially in ordinary prose, focus is on some other facet of the speech event and contiguity is the essential constructional principle. Literary prose, on the other hand, is a mixture of the referential with the poetic, and in general various types of prose have more or less of the poetic, i.e., the metaphorical, as an important (but not the predominant) structuring principle. Jakobson also used similarity vs. contiguity to characterize various artistic schools (e.g., symbolism, based on similarity, vs. realism, based on contiguity), the structure of dreams, the principles underlying magic rites, personality types, and so forth (1956:254ff, Jakobson/Pomorska 1980:125-35). With one stroke, he defined a fundamental semiotic polarity of language, texts, culture, and human thought (cognition) in general.

# VII
## Grammar

The close relation betwen code and message, which is effective both in the nature and in the operation of language, also underlies shifters (1957:131ff), those elements whose general meaning in the code can only be specified by taking into acount their use in messages, because the codal meaning includes information about particular elements of the speech event. For example, pronouns designate speaker (*I*) and addressee (*you*). Thus, language encodes pragmatic factors of the context of utterance, a further proof of its context-sensitivity: linguistics, and perforce semiotics, necessarily includes syntax, semantics, and pragmatics (Jakobson 1969: 655ff, 1970b:697ff).

Grammatical categories (both morphological and syntactic), for Jakobson, are defined as those which are obligatorily present in the construction of acceptable messages (1959a:492ff, 1959b:264ff). They are thus an important factor in shaping messages, even though speakers may be unaware of their workings, whereas particular lexical categories (e.g., words referring to space) are optional. Through this view of grammar, Jakobson provided a semantic and operational approach to the relation between language and cognition: grammatical categorizations provide the necessary patterns of thought.

# VIII
## The Influence of Charles Sanders Peirce

Jakobson's coordinate concern with function and structure can also be linked with his discovery in the early 1950's of the "drafts ... of epochal significance" (Jakobson 1966a:346) of Charles Sanders Peirce (published as 1931-35). He characterized Peirce as "the most inventive and the most universal of American thinkers" (1966a:345) who "in this country has been for me the most powerful source of inspiration" (1971e:v). The Peircean ideas which recur most often are those concerning the three sign types: icon, index, and symbol, and their combinations (e.g., Jakobson 1966a:347ff, 1969:661, 1970b:699ff). He redefined them through two binary relations, the already established similarity-contiguity, and the new factual-imputed. He then added a fourth term to the sign types, namely the artifice (imputed simliarity), which he correlated with his work on similarity relations in poetry. The index (factual contiguity) underlies his work on shifters and deictic categories. The icon (factual similarity) and the symbol (imputed contiguity) were particulary influential and impelled Jakobson to a more profound analysis of the non-arbitrariness of the lingustic sign (1966a) and to a rejection of the Saussurian principle of arbitrariness as too absolute (although, in 1971a, Jakobson showed that Saussure himself recognized non-arbitrariness in his work on anagrams). For example, Jakobson established a set of close parallels between various morphological and syntactic categories and their formal expression; a grammatical category such as the plural is iconic since it always has a form which is longer and/or more complex than the singular, due to its meaning (Jakobson 1966a:352). And in *The Sound Shape of Language* (Jakobson/Waugh 1979:181ff), a new dichotomy was defined, namely, mediacy vs. immediacy: an indirect relation between sound and meaning (double articulation) vs. a direct rleation between sound and meaning (see also Waugh 1987). Immediacy is exemplified by phenomena such as sound symbolism, synesthesia, glossolalia, and mythic, poetic and magical uses of sound (Jakobson/Waugh 1979:181ff), in all of which sound has a direct — and often iconic — relation to meaning. This dichtomy was also related to the hemispheres of the brain (left vs. right respectively) in Jakobson 1980 (166ff).

Jakobson was also inspired by Peirce's notion that the essence of a sign is its interpretation, i.e., its translation by some further sign. Henceforth, he defined the *signatum* as that which is "interpretable" or, better, "translatable" (Jakobson 1959b:261, 1977:251) by a potentially unlimited series of signs. He characterized the Peircean approach as "the only sound basis for a strictly linguistic semantics" (1976:118), and insisted that a widened definition of translation — as the interpretation of one sign by another — was an essential aspect of semiotic activity: intralingual translation (paraphrasing), interlingual (translation proper) and intersemiotic (transmutation from one semiotic system to another) (Jakobson 1959b:261).

## IX
## Literary Poetics

As a founding member of the Prague Linguistic Circle of the 1920's and 1930's, and as a leader in the Russian formalist movement in the 1910's, Jakobson had participated in movements that consciously juxtaposed poetry to other aesthetic uses of semiotic systems (music, painting, film) and that also focused on the conventionality of literature as a system of signs. Like language as a whole, literature is subject to synchronic laws and to diachronic formation and transformation; it is also interdependent with all other historico-cultural phenomena, which, according to him, must be taken into account for a more integrative — that is, a more semiotic — approach to literary data. His first work on the sound system of language was embedded in his work on the sound structure of poetry (1921a, 1923): for him the ultimate question about a system of sounds and the use of that system for versification was its signifying value as a sign phenomenon in correlation with other poetic, literary, and broader semiotic systems (see 1971c, 1979).

One of Jakobson's most important semiotic papers of the 1930's (1936b) analyzed the sharp rift between Czech versification of the Gothic and Hussite periods. In it he details the radically different attitudes toward language and the sign in general during the Middle Ages and the Reformation and illustrates the repercussions these opposed semiotic orientations had not only on the metrical systems in question, but also on the chief religious and social controversy of the period, the celebration of divine communion. This study is an example of a semiotic approach toward different historical series — literary, social and religious — that is full of numerous insights relevant for contemporary semiotic inquiry.

Jakobson's works on versification, collected in volume 5 of his *Selected Writings* (1979), display a thorough-going semiotic orientation, in that for him the ultimate question about a system of versification was its signifying value as a sign phenomenon in correlation with other poetic, literary, and broader semiotic systems.

## X
## Poetic Mythology

A central focus of Jakobson's literary studies of the 1930's was the question of the symbolic systems of individual poets, the set of themes and devices specifying their oeuvre as uniquely their own, and the correlated question of the "myth of the poet" (see Jakobson/Pomorksa 1980: 136-151), a concept Jakobson introduced to breach the gap between the biography of a writer and his or her literary output. For example, Jakobson succeeded (1931) in demonstrating the invariant unit of Majakovskij's symbolic system despite seemingly irreconcilable stylistic, generic, and diachronic variations; he studied (1935) Pasternak's symbolic system and his artistic devices and their evolutionary and generational place, against the background of his output in both poetry and prose; and, in one of his most suggestive semiotic studies of the Prague period (1937), he isolated a central mytheme pervading Pushkin's work, the myth of the destructive statue, which is persuasively linked to the poet's own tragic demise. The essay is also one of the few works that discusses in a semiotically coherent way sculpture as a sign system and its translation into literary signs, and represents "one of the first examples of the analysis of semantic structures at work within a text: rest and movement, death and life, living and still matter" (Eco 1986:404).

# XI
# Grammar of Poetry

A central focus of Jakobson's late work was the "poetry of grammar and grammar of poetry" (see Jakobson 1961, 1968a, 1981a:157ff, and Jakobson/Pomorska 1980:110-124), a unique field of inquiry transecting the disciplines of linguistics, poetics, and semiotics. He sought to demonstrate through painstaking anlysis the signifying functions that grammatical categories may carry in poetic texts, either through their foregrounding and correlation with semantic units proper or through their pervasive role in the structuration of poetic messages, which, he argued, could not be entirely without semantic import, whether consciously perceived by the poet or the reader.

Jakobson's most famous analysis of this sort, co-authored with Claude Lévi-Strauss, concerns one of Baudelaire's sonnets, "*Les Chats*" (1962). It sparked a remarkable debate (see in particular Delacroix and Geerts 1980) about the issue of structuralism, linguistic imperialism, the question of the hierarchy and potential significance of formal units, authorial intention or reader response. Of Jakobson's last works on the grammar of poetry, a particularly resonant study from a semiotic point of view is 1981b about a succinct and enigmatic outburst supposedly uttered by Turgenev and examined by Jakobson from the phonological, morphological, grammatical, semantic, poetic, social, sexual, alimentary and culinary points of view and amply illustrates Jakobson's voraciousness in the maximal exploration of the manifold levels of the concrete speech act as a semiotic given with immense powers of referral.

# XII
## Studies of Other Semiotic Systems

Jakobson also studied other semiotic systems. In a study of music (1932b), he insisted on the concept of system, on the hierarchical relation of elements rather than their absolute values, on opposition as a tool for musical analysis, and (in 1970b:701ff, 1975a:215ff) on the nature of interal and mutual referral as a carrier of meaning in music and other systems dependent on the artifice. In a pioneering essay on film (1933), Jakobson insisted that sound and silence, like the visual elements in film, are semiotic and not mere imitative (mimetic) facts, used to convey information and not merely to reproduce real stimuli.

From his earliest days as a member of the Russian avant-garde, Jakobson was intrigued by the differences and common semiotic properties of auditory and visual signs in the arts. His central theoretical text on this question (1964/1967) differentiates signs that use space as a medium and are thus based on simultaneity, as opposed to those that unfold in time and rely on successivity. The connection of vision with iconicity and indexicality and of the auditory realm with symbolism is related in turn to his earlier work (1956) on aphasic disturbances: the cardinal division between visual and auditory signs is, in his view (1980), linked to differences in the way the brain perceives and processes them.

Jakobson's late works on "grammar of poetry" often invoke a parallel between the role of grammar in poetry and that of geometrical construction in pictorial art (see 1970c). This work opens up new perspectives for a coherent study of visual and verbal art in their interrelation. An ingenious foray into gestural signs (1970a) examines the interrelation of naturalness and conventionality: although expressed in opposite ways in different cultures, yes and no gestures share the same binary, antithetical character.

# XIII
## Jakobson's Legacy in Semiotics

Despite the fact that only one of Jakobson's articles explicitly includes the term semiotics (1975a — which is a major contribution to the historiography of semiotics), that most of his earlier work in semiotics was written in Czech (see Galan 1985, which highlights his Czech semiotic work of the 1930's; see also Jakobson/Pomorska 1980:152-157), and that much of his later work is couched in terms of linguistics or poetics, Jakobson's work has been extraordinarily influential on the development of modern semiotics. This is due in part to the direct influence of some of his most famous studies: "Two aspects of language" (1956), which brought together selection/combination, similarity/contiguity, metaphor/metonymy and fostered the extension of these concepts to larger semiotic inquiry; and "Linguistics and Poetics" (1960), which delineated the functions of language and a semiotically-oriented aesthetics (poetic function) and which "has profoundly influenced the development of semiotic studies all over the world" (Eco 1986:404). Other components of the conceptual capital of modern semiotics — e.g., distinctive features (sometimes renamed pertinent features), redundancy, opposition, markedness, binarism, invariance, parallelism — have either originated in or been abetted by Jakobson's linguistic work. Moreover, many of his studies on specific semiotic systems have been of importance — for example, his 1933 paper on film, which "contains virtually all the elements of the semiotic theories of film born in the early sixties" (Eco 1986:404 — see Metz 1968, 1971).

Jakobson's work has also had an impact on recent semiotic research due to his role in the development of the discipline as a whole. At an early stage, the Prague School and especially Prague structuralism, helped to define the fundamental principles of much of modern semiotics (see Hawkes 1977, Galan 1985). The Prague Circle theses of 1929 (co-written by Jakobson) have been taken as the birthdate of structuralism and it was Jakobson himself who coined the term (see 1971b:711). While there are many definitions of structuralism, not all of which are compatible in their details with Jakobson's, his work, and that of his Prague colleagues, has been extremely influential in defining and setting the goals for structural analysis, and thus, in the long run, of semiotics (see Hawkes 1977 for an explicit paring of structuralism and semiotics). But Prague, and Jakobson, are equally well known for a functional approach to sign systems, and their holistic, goal-oriented view of language has opened the door to functionalist approaches in linguistics as well as in semiotics and has abetted developments in discourse and textual analysis and pragmatics.

Jakobson was also responsible for discovering the work of Charles Sanders Peirce and the relevance of Peirce's work for linguistics, and since it was he above all who led in the "marriage" of linguistics (and Praguean functional-structuralism) with the work of Peirce, he may be credited ultimately with introducing Peirce to many semioticians.

Literary theory, too, which in its turn has had an enormous influence on semiotics, has been fostered by Jakobson's work (especially 1960, 1968a, Jakobson/Lévi-Strauss 1962, and Jakobson/Jones 1970), which have been "translated, paraphrased, genuflected to, attacked" (McLean 1983:18), and there have been some imaginative applications of Jakobson's literary approach by literary scholars (see Brooke-Rose 1976, Lodge 1977, 1986, Osterwalder 1978, see also Göttner/Jacobs 1978). His approach to literary analysis was also enthusiastically developed in France, from where it gained international recognition, which then led to the flowering of interest in literary theory not only in France and Europe, but also in the U.S. Semiotics in its turn was launched in Europe in part because of interest in literary poetics, especially since many semioticians were also literary theorists who knew Jakobson's work or were conversant with the explosion in literary theory.

An important indirect influence of Jakobson's theories has been the work of Lévi-Strauss, who has said that it was through Jakobson that he "received the revelation of structural linguistics" (1976:xi) and who has used many Jakobsonian themes in his own work. Given Jakobson's impact on Lévi-Strauss, many researchers in a variety of domains are "deeply indebted to Roman Jakobson ... even though the filiation is somewhat indirect" (Leach 1983: 10).

Thus, both Jakobson's work and structuralism broadly conceived are a major part of the intellectual history of current semiotics and have assured that the issue of language is central to thinking about the nature of semiotic inquiry.

*Linda Waugh is Professor of Linguistics, Romance Studies and Comparative Literature at Cornell University.*

## NOTES

1. This chapter is based on Waugh and Rudy in press, which also draws on Waugh and Monville-Burston 1990. I would like to thank both of my co-authors for the many insights they have contributed to my thinking about Jakobson's work.

## REFERENCES

Brooke-Rose, Christine, 1976, *A Structural Analysis of Pound's Usura Canto. Jakobson's Method Extended and Applied to Free Verse.* The Hague-Paris: Mouton.

Bühler, Karl, 1934, *Sprachtheorie.* Jena: Fischer.

Caton, Steven, 1987, Contributions of Roman Jakobson, *Annual Review of Current Anthropology* 16:223-260.

Delacroix, Maurice and Walter Geerts (eds.), 1980, *"Les Chats" de Baudelaire: Une confrontation de méthodes.* Namur: Presses Universitaires de Namur/Presses Universitaires de France.

Eco, Umberto, 1977, The Influence of Roman Jakobson on the Development of Semiotics, *Roman Jakobson: Echoes of his Scholarship*, ed. by D.

Armstrong and C. H. van Schooneveld, 39-58. Lisse: Peter de Ridder Press.

Eco, Umberto, 1986, "Jakobson, Roman (1896-1982)," *Encyclopedic Dictionary of Semiotics*, ed. by T. Sebeok, Tome I, 402-408. Berlin: Mouton de Gruyter.

Galan, Frantisek W., 1985, *Historic Structures: The Prague School Project, 1928-1946*. Austin: University of Texas Press.

Göttner, Heide/Joachim Jacobs, 1978, *Der logische Bau von Literaturtheorien*. München: Wilhelm Fink.

Hawkes, Terence, 1977, *Structuralism and Semiotics*. Berkeley: University of California Press.

Jakobson, Roman, 1921a, *Novejsaja russkaja poezija. Nabrosok pervyj. Victor Xlebnikov*. Prague: Politika. Eng. partial transl., "Modern Russian Poetry: Velimir Khlebnikov", in *Major Soviet Writers: Essays in Criticism*, ed. by E. J. Brown. New York: Oxford University Press, 1973.

-----, 1921b, On Realism in Art, Cf. Jakobson 1981a, 723-731 (Russ. orig.) and 1987, 19-27 (Eng. transl.).

-----, 1923, *O cesskom stixe - preimuscestvenno v sopostavlenii s russkim*. Cf. Jakobson 1979, 3-121.

-----, 1931, On a Generation that Squandered its Poets, in *Major Soviet Writers: Essays in Criticism*, ed. by E. J. Brown, 7-32. New York-London: Oxford University Press, 1973; repr. in 1985a, 111-132 (Russ. orig.) and 1987, 273-300 (Eng. transl.)

-----, 1932a, Structure of the Russian Verb, Cf. Jakobson 1971d, 3-15 (Ger. orig.) and 1984a, 1-14 (Eng. transl.).

-----, 1971d, Musicology and Linguistics, 1932b. Cf. Jakobson, 551-553 (Ger. orig.) and 1987, 455-457 (Eng. transl.).

-----, 1933, Is the Film in Decline?, Cf. Jakobson 1981a, 732-739 (Eng. transl.).

-----, 1935, Marginal Notes on the Prose of the Poet Pasternak, Cf. Jakobson 1979, 416-432 (Ger. orig.) and 1987, 301-317 (Eng. transl.).

-----, 1936a, Contributions to the General Theory of Case: General Meanings of the Russian Cases, Cf. Jakobson 1971d, 23-71 (Ger. orig.), and 1984, 59-103 and 1990, 332-375 (Eng. transl.).

-----, 1936b, Remarks on the Poetry of the Hussite Era, (Czech orig.). Cf. Jakobson 1985a, 704-737 (Eng. transl.).

-----, 1937 The State in Pushkin's Poetic Mythology, (Czech orig.). Cf. Jakobson 1979, 237-280 (Eng. transl.).

-----, 1939, Zero Sign, Cf. Jakobson 1971d, 211-219 (French orig.) and 1984, 151-160 (Eng. transl.).

-----, 1940, *Das Nullzeichen*, 12-14. Cf. Jakobson 1971d, 220-222.

Jakobson, Roman, 1949a, On the Identification of Phonemic Entities, Cf. Jakobson 1971c, 418-425.

-----, 1949b, Notes on General Linguistics: Its Present State and Crucial Problems, Cf. Jakobson 1990, 49-55.

-----, 1956, Two Aspects of Language and Two Types of Aphasic Disturbances, Cf. Jakobson 1971d, 239-259 and 1990, 115-133.

-----, 1957, *Shifters, Verbal Categories, and the Russian Verb*, Cf. Jakobson 1971d, 130-147.

-----, 1959a, Boas' View of Grammatical Meaning, Cf. Jakobson 1971d, 489-496 and 1990, 324-331.

-----, 1959b, On Linguistic Aspects of Translation, Cf. Jakobson 1971d, 260-266.

-----, 1960, Linguistics and Poetics, in *Style in Language*, ed. T. Sebeok, 350-377. Cambridge, Mass.:MIT Press. Cf. Jakobson 1981a, 18-51.

-----, 1961, Poetry of Grammar and Grammar of Poetry, Cf. Jakobson 1981a, 63-86 (Russ. orig.) and 1987, 121-144 (Eng. transl.) [see also 1968a].

-----, 1962a, Retrospect, in Jakobson 1971c, 631-658.

-----, 1962b, *Zur Struktur des Phonems*, in Jakobson 1971c, 280-310.

-----, 1963, Parts and Wholes in Language, Cf. Jakobson 1971d, 280-284 and 1990, 110-114.

-----, 1964, On Visual and Auditory Signs, 216-220 and About the Relation Between Visual and Auditory Signs, 1967. Cf. Jakobson 1987, 466-473 (revised, combined version).

-----, 1966a, Quest for the Essence of Language, Cf. Jakobson 1971d, 345-359 and 1990, 407-421.

-----, 1966b, The Role of Phonic Elements in Speech Perception, Cf. Jakobson 1971c, 705-717.

-----, 1967, Kruszewski's Part in the Development of Linguistic Science, Cf. Jakobson 1971d, 429-449 (Polish orig.), 449-450 (Eng. summary).

-----, 1968a, Poetry of Grammar and Grammar of Poetry, (abridged and reworked version of 1961). Cf. Jakobson 1981a, 87-97.

-----, 1968b, *Vivre et parler - un débat entre François Jacob, Roman Jakobson, Claude Lévi-Strauss, et Philippe l'Héritier. Les lettres françaises*, no. 1221, 3-7, No. 1222, 4-5.

-----, 1969, Linguistics in its Relation to Other Sciences. Reprinted in Jakobson 1971d, 655-696 and 1990, 451-488, and published in *Main Trends in the Science of Language*. New York: Harper and Row 1974.

-----, 1970a, Motor Signs for 'Yes' and 'No', (Russ. orig.). Cf. Jakobson 1987, 474-478 (Eng. transl.).

-----, 1970b, Language in Relation to Other Communication Systems, Cf. Jakobson 1971d, 697-708.

Jakobson, Roman, 1970c, On the Verbal Art of William Blake and Other Poet-Painters, 3-23. Cf. Jakobson 1981a, 322-344.

-----, 1971a, *La première lettre de F. de Saussure à A. Meillet sur les anagrammes*, Cf. Jakobson 1985b, 237-247.

-----, 1971b, Retrospect, in Jakobson 1971d, 711-724.

-----, 1971d, *Selected Writings*, Vol. 1: *Phonological Studies*. 2nd, expanded ed. The Hague-Paris: Mouton (1st ed.:1962)

-----, 1971d, *Selected Writings*, Vol. 2: *Word and Language*. The Hague-Paris: Mouton.

-----, 1971e, Acknowledgements and Dedications, in Jakobson 1971d, v-viii.

-----, *Aspects of the Theories of Roman Jakobson*, ed. by M. van Ballaer. Katholieke Universiteit te Leuven: Fakulteit der Wijsbegeerte en Lettern 1973. Partial reprinting in Jakobson 1990, 315-323.

-----, 1974, Life and Language (review of F. Jacobs, The logic of life: a history of heredity), *Linguistics* 138, 97-103.

-----, 1975a, A Glance at the Development of Semiotics, (Fr. orig.). Cf. Jakobson 1985b, 199-218 (Eng. transl.).

-----, 1975b, *N. S. Trubetzkoy's Letters and Notes*, ed. R. Jakobson. The Hague-Paris: Mouton.

-----, 1976, Metalanguage as a Linguistic Problem, Cf. Jakobson 1985b, 113-121.

-----, 1977, A few Remarks on Peirce, Pathfinder in the Science of Language, Cf. Jakobson 1985b, 248-253.

-----, 1979, *Selected Writings*, Vol. 5: *On Verse, its Masters and Explorers*, eds. S. Rudy and M. Taylor. The Hague-Paris: Mouton.

-----, 1980, Brain and Language: Cerebral Hemispheres and Linguistic Structure in Mutual Light, Cf. Jakobson 1985b, 163-180 and 1990, 498-513.

-----, 1981c, *Selected Writings*, Vol. 3: *Poetry of Grammar and Grammar of Poetry*, ed. S. Rudy. The Hague-Paris-New York: Mouton.

-----, 1981b, Supraconscious Turgenev, in Jakobson 1981a, 707-711 (Russ. orig.) and 1987, 262-266 (Eng. transl.).

-----, 1984, *Russian and Slavic Grammar: Studies, 1931-1981*, ed. by L. Waugh and M. Halle. Berlin-New York: Mouton.

-----, 1985a, *Selected Writings*, Vol. 7: *Contributions to Comparative Mythology. Studies in Linguistics and Philology*, 1972-1982, ed. by S. Rudy. Berlin-New York-Amsterdam: Mouton.

-----, 1985b, *Verbal Art, Verbal Sign, Verbal Time*, eds. K. Pomorska and S. Rudy. Minneapolis: University of Minnesota Press.

-----, 1987, *Language in Literature*, eds. K. Pomorska and S. Rudy. Cambridge, Mass.: Harvard University Press.

Jakobson, Roman, 1990, *On Language*, eds. L. R. Waugh and M. Monville-Burston. Cambridge, Mass.: Harvard University Press.

Jakobson, Roman/C. Gunnar M. Fant/Morris Halle, 1952, *Preliminaries to Speech Analysis*. Cf. Cambridge: M. I.T. Press 1963 (revised ed.) Cf. Jakobson 1988a, 583-654.

Jakobson, Roman/Morris Halle, 1956, *Fundamentals of Language*. The Hague: Mouton (2nd, revised ed: 1971). Cf. Jakobson 1971d, 464-504.

Jakobson, Roman/Lawrence G. Jones, 1970, *Shakespeare's Verbal Art in 'Th'Expence of Spirit,* Cf. Jakobson 1981c, 284-303.

Jakobson, Roman/Claude Lévi-Strauss, 1962, *'Les chats' de Charles Baudelaire,* Cf. Jakobson 1981c, 447-464.

Jakobson, Roman/Krystyna Pomorska, 1980, *Dialogues*. Paris: Flammarion. Cf. Cambridge: Cambridge University Press 1983 (Eng. transl.).

Jakobson, Roman/Linda R. Waugh, 1979, *The Sound Shape of Language*, Cf. Berlin: Mouton de Gruyter, 1986 (2nd ed.). Cf. Jakobson 1988a, 1-315.

Leach, Edmund, 1983, Roman Jakobson and Social Anthropology, in *A Tribute to Roman Jakobson*, 1896-1982, 10-17. Berlin: Mouton.

Lévi-Strauss, Claude, 1972, Structuralism and Ecology, *Barnard Alumnae* (Spring), 6-14. Cf. *Social Science Information* 12.1, 1973, 7-23.

-----, 1976, Préface, to Jakobson 1976, 7-18.

Lodge, David, 1977, *Modes of Modern Writing: Metaphor, Metonymy and the Typology of Modern Literature*. Ithaca, New York: Cornell University Press.

-----, 1986, *Working with Structuralism*. London: Routledge and Kegan Paul.

McLean, Hugh. 1983, A Linguist Among Poets. In *Roman Jakobson: What He Taught Us. International Journal of Slavic Linguistics and Poetics* 27, supplement, 7-19.

Metz, Christian, 1986, *Essais sur la signification au cinéma*. Paris: Klincksieck. (Oxford-New York: Oxford University Press 1974, Eng. transl.).

-----, 1971, *Langage et cinéma*. Paris: Larousse. (New York: Norton 1974, Eng. transl.).

Osterwalder, Hans., 1978, *T. S. Eliot: Between Metaphor and Metonymy: a Study of his Essays and Plays in Terms of Roman Jakobson's Typology*. Bern: A. Francke 1978.

Peirce, Charles Sanders, *Collected Papers of Charles Sanders Peirce*, Vol. I - VI, eds. Ch. Hartshorne and P. Weiss. Cambridge, Mass.: Harvard University Press 1931-1935.

Pomorska, Krystyna et al eds., 1987, *On the Generation of the 1890's: Jakobson, Troubetzkoy, Majakovskij*. Berlin: Mouton.

Prague Linguistic Circle, 1929, "Thèses présentées au Premier Congrès des philologues slaves," *Travaux du Cercle linguistique de Prague* 1, 5-29. Cf. *The Prague School: Selected Writings*, 1929-1946, ed. by P. Steiner, 3-31 (Eng. transl.) Austin: University of Texas Press, 1982.

Saussure, Ferdinand de, 1916, *Cours de linguistique générale.* Paris: Payot (2nd, revised edition, 1922).

Shannon, C. E. and W. Weaver, 1949, *The Mathematical Theory of Communication.* Urbana: University of Ill. Press.

Waugh, Linda R., 1985c, The Poetic Function and the Nature of Language. *Poetics Today* 2.1a, 1980, 57-82. Repr. in Jakobson, 143-168.

-----, 1982, Marked and Unmarked: a Choice Betwen Unequals in Semiotic Structure". *Semiotica* 38.3-4, 299-318.

-----, 1984, The Relevance of Research into the Sound Shape of Language for Semiotic Studies, in *Semiotics Unfolding*, ed. by T. Borbé, 1255-1262. Berlin: Mouton.

-----, 1987, On the Sound Shape of Language: Mediacy and Immediacy. In *Pomorska* et al, 157-173. Cf. Jakobson/Waugh 1979 (1987), 255-271 and Jakobson 1988a, 255-271.

Waugh, Linda R./Monique Monville-Burston, 1990, Introduction: The Life, Work, and Influence of Roman Jakobson. In Jakobson, 1-45.

Waugh, Linda R./Stephen Rudy, Jakobson and Structuralism, in *Semiotics: a Handbook on the Sign-Theoretic Foundations of Nature and Culture*, eds. R. Posner, K. Robering, T. Sebeok. Berlin/New York: Walter de Gruyter, in press.

# Chapter 8

# Semiotics and History

William Pencak*

## I
## Summary

**1. Introduction.** Peircean semiotics permits historians to resolve the mind/ body, culture/nature, fact/interpretation dichotomies which have plagued their discipline by allowing *a measure* of freedom for people to construct the past and interpret the future within the limits of contemporary social reality. This freedom increases during periods of chaos, change, and revolution which thrust forth new ways of interpreting and shaping the world.Semiotics also permits historians to become more aware of what they have always been doing — selecting "signs" (facts, data) to serve as symbols of an underlying reality. Eric Voegelin worked out a Peircean semiotics of history on a grand scale. At the same time, history can provide the material for semioticians to make their method relevant to real human problems.

**2. Founding Fathers.** Semiotic history, which constructs the past both with respect for real events but also self-consciously with regard to the concerns of the present, has been practiced since the days of Herodotus and Thucydides. It stands opposed to the idea that historical events stand alone and are only to be explained by a unique context, since we can only understand the past by recognizing equivalent symbolizations which cut across time. Also, semiotics contests the idea that history and people are merely the "products" of "forces" such as race and class, while granting that such factors do play some role in understanding history. Other scholars who have developed semiotic history are Giambattista Vico, Charles Peirce, John Lukacs, Thomas Kuhn, Eugen Rosenstock-Huessy, Carl Becker, Walter Benjamin, and Michel Foucault.

**3. Current Practitioners.** At least five main areas are currently being studied by semiotic historians, who are uncovering practices and ways of thought previously hidden from history, and reevaluating well-known discourses which have maintained power in the past. They are thereby recreating a new history of greater relevance to all the world's people: a) Microhistory — looking at events like a 1722 French massacre of cats (Robert Darnton) or the popular punishment of moral offenders known as rough music (Natalie Zemon Davis) to reveal what ordinary people believe; b)

Construction of "Others" and post-colonial studies — examining how the identity of colonizers is shaped by the very stereotypes they attribute to conquered nations and races in order to subjugate them (Edward Said, Gayatri Spivak); c) Opening the public sphere — how methods of reading, writing, publishing, and communicating through public and private meetings outside the official limits  of church and state shaped the Enlightenment and the development of modern participatory politics (Jürgen Habermas, Marshall McLuhan); d) The Body and Sexuality — how certain forms of sexuality have been repressed to maintain order, self-denial, and a privileged patriarchy (Peter Brown, John Boswell); e) Political Power — how symbols (ceremonies, flags, parades, national myths) maintain and undermine governments (Benedict Anderson, Eric Hobsbawm).

**Key words:** Objectivity/subjectivity, mind/body, nature/culture, fact/interpretation, freedom/determinism, relativism, history, microhistory, "Others", revolution, public sphere, sexuality, the body, political symbolism.

# II
# Introduction

When Winfried Nöth published the revised version of his *Handbook of Semiotics*, he devoted only one short paragraph to the semiotics of history (Nöth 1990: 330). It consisted mostly of bibliographic references to works by semioticians which debate the nature of history (e.g. Finlay-Pelinski 1982; Haidu 1982; see also Cohen 1986).  These debates signalled a crisis of confidence among professional historians.  Scholars who had simply assumed that they could at least try to be objective and interpret the real world found themselves under assault from postmodernists who denied both the validity and intelligibility of the world of western civilization. Historians were told by deconstructionists and literary theorists that reality was in the mind of the beholder, that the evidence, data, or "signs" (mistakenly known as "facts") only pointed to other signs in infinite regress, and that no real knowledge was possible (Toews 1987; Harlan et al. 1989).

Although semioitics has sometimes been classed with deconstruction, it is really its antidote.  Since Nöth's work has appeared history and semiotics have begun to appreciate that each can remove the tarnish from the other's reputation.  Building on a pioneering session at the 1987 American Historical Association annual meeting (described in Williams 1988), a special issue of *Semiotica*  (Williams and Pencak 1991) showcased the work of practicing historians who incorporated semiotic methodology into the writing of history.  Also in 1991, in *The History Workshop,* Raphael Samuel argued that "semiotics is a wonderful tool, and a splendid provocation to historical reflection and research" (1991/92: 245). James Hoopes, in the *American Historical Review* (1993: 1554) focused on the semiotic of Charles Peirce in particular as the way to affirm both objectivity *and* relativism: "The meaning of the sign is determined partly by its real relation to the object," but also partly "by what the human being makes of the sign in a subsequent thought." Other historians following the Peircean line include Pencak (1993, 1996), Williams (1985, 1991), and Munslow (1997: 86-87).

Peirce thus provides the basis for reconciling two false dichotomies that have plagued historians as well as philosophers: Is humanity shaped by nature or culture? Does the mind dominate the body or vice-versa? He therefore allows for *a measure* (within the constraints of real social conditions) of human freedom to interpret the past and thus shape the future. At the same time, he insists that neither knowledge nor history are arbitrary, but that understanding and change are achieved by communities of interpreters who follow certain rules which "work" — that is, assure the survival and success of the community in question by interpreting reality until their disruption compels their reassessment. In short, while we cannot definitively know everything, we can provisionally understand many things if we are cognizant of the interpretive perspective we are using (Wilson 1968; Pencak 1991; Brent 1993). If semiotics can remove the *vs.* which has traditionally separated rather than linked "mind" and "matter," historians can in turn redeem semioticians from dwelling on trivial examples such as stop signs and smoke signals to illustrate their basic points. It is vital that semioticians retread basic theoretical ground less and address pressing human concerns more — who has power and how it is wielded through codes and symbols; what symbols hold human communities together or separate them — to demonstrate why semiotics should be taken seriously by a humanity that suffers and loves. As Williams writes "the human *Umwelt* [total environment] presents us with a continuum of past, present, and future in which continuity and change, convention and invention, commingle, and of which the ultimate source of unity is *time*" (1985:274). Thus, concludes John Deely in *Basics of Semiotics* (1990:118) "penetrating the traditional field of historiographical study from an explicitly semiotic point of view, is one of the most essential advances in the developing understanding of semiotics today." Every sign and interpretation has an (often unacknowledged) historical dimension.

If explicit reflection on semiotics and history as disciplines has only occurred in the last two decades of the twentieth century, historians have been thinking semiotically since they began to write history. They have realized that singular events and individuals must be interpreted as signs of greater historical processes, and that making history is a process in which human agency interacts with natural and social constraints. If these points seem obvious, we should reflect on two contrary assumptions of many modern historians: that historical events are unique and can only be explained by the specific context which produces them ("historicism" or "positivism") and that people are the "products" of socio-economic conditions (Marxism, racism, and world-views asserting the inevitable triumph of liberal democracy). Determinist historians deny that communities of interpreters construct historical writing and thus history itself.

Thus, we may postulate that an implicitly semiotic approach to historical inquiry is as old as historical consciousness itself. The thinker who explained this was Eric Voegelin (1970; 1974; see Pencak 1993:109-129 for more detail and a bibliography). He examined in depth how different civilizations developed comparable systems of symbols (originally "compacted" as myths) to express fundamental human experiences of nature (interpreted today through the natural sciences and technology), the soul (psychology), the social order (government and the social sciences), and the transcendent (religion). He maintained that these were the basic constituents of humanity, and that adequate symbolizations interpreting human existence had to take them all into account. The Biblical Hebrews and ancient Greeks first formulated "history" as a process in which human beings could take responsibility for their own fate in an open-ended universe: "history" emerged to oppose the "cosmos" which the ancient empires believed embodied the gods' fixed plans for humanity (Voegelin 1956/1957). Voegelin (1952, 1968) had only scorn for modern intellectuals, and the murderous ideologues who followed them, who created "dream worlds" or "perfect societies" which fixed humanity's evolving quest for meaning in dogmatic formulations about the perfect social order, the perfect race, or the perfect explanation. Heavily influenced by Peirce, whose writings he studied as a young man, Voegelin (1928:32-41; 51-52) praised his predecessor for having reopened the human soul and restored the means of thinking seriously and freely about a world "closed" by the positivists, Marxists, and Social Darwinists.

An overview of the relation of semiotic to history therefore contains two parts: first, a sprint over more than two thousand years to glean insights from historians who thought like semioticians before the concept was coined; second, an examination of how historians in the late twentieth century who employ semiotic methodology (although not always semiotic terminology — no discipline is as gun-shy of jargon as history) are at the forefront of historical study and point the way to an even more exciting historiographical future.

# III
# Founding Fathers

Although Herodotus and Thucydides are usually contrasted as representatives of the anecdotal and analytic styles of history, they shared a common notion of history as a field in which human beings and their societies appeared as signs of moral principles and laws by which civilizations rose and fell. Herodotus (c. 430 B.C.E.; see Pencak 1994 for an analysis) saw history as a struggle between the forces of freedom and slavery, signified at different times and places by different individuals and nations. (He especially considered respectful treatment of women a sign of a free and admirable society.) If he gloried in Greece's, and especially Athens', espousal of liberty in his own time, his *Histories* are filled with Greeks who sacrificed freedom and justice in the pursuit of wealth and power. He ends with a tale of how the Persians, too, once cherished their liberty and respected that of others before they were bitten by the imperial bug. By refusing to fix either Greeks or non-Greeks as the permanent repository of freedom, and showing a broad appreciation for the achievements of different races, sexes, and social systems, Herodotus, literally, freed the world in the face of xenophobic Greeks and their close-minded successors for all posterity, although of course he could not prevent backsliding into ideological dogmatism.

Thucydides' *The Peloponnesian War* examines the signs of great civilizations — Athens and Sparta — based on contrasting principles of personal liberty and communal responsibility. Each produces sterling exemplars such as Pericles and Archidamus, but then Thucydides shows how prominent figures who signify public morality deteriorate along with their societies under protracted conditions of war and strife. Great civilizations destroy themselves because they cannot help but carry to extremes the very principles which caused them to rise — Athenian expansionism and the austere Spartans' refusal to tolerate difference. Thucydides consciously selects incidents and people to demonstrate this deterioration: he constructs "the war" itself from at least three major wars and the uneasy truces which separated them. He also states that when he did not know the content of an important speech, he wrote what was called for by the situation. (Thucydides c. 400 B.C.E.: Book 1:22-24; Finley 1942:73-77; Pencak 1993:237-258). This does not mean Thucydides was dishonest, any more than the Biblical historians so eloquently defended by Halpern (1988): rather, he presented data intermingled with interpretation — although not in the form modern historians now adopt — to show the real choices people face at different points in their history. The fact that Thucydides does not end his book with Athens' final debacle is not best explained as the result of an incomplete manuscript or his refusal to face an unbearable reality. Rather, it is most appropriate that a Persian general conducting operations in Greece, about to invade Greek cities in Asia, repeats the sacrifice to Artemis with which the Greeks initiated the invasion of Asia in the Trojan War. Common signifiers denote a common humanity among Greeks and "barbarians." Thucydides thus brings us back to the beginning of his work, where he argues that similar struggles will occur throughout history. Great powers with different ideologies and followed by strings of allies and dependencies will clash; therefore "The Peloponnesian War" is a sign of "the great war" for all time (Thucydides c. 430 B. C. E.: Book 1, 22-24).

In contrast to the complex judgments of the Greeks, historical writing in the ancient Roman world and Christian Middle Ages looked at history simplistically as the struggle of good vs. evil. Virtuous Romans and Christians confronted evil barbarians and infidels successfully; degenerate Romans and Christians suffered defeat at their hands (Haskins 1927: ch. 8; Plumb 1970; Voegelin 1975:3-34). Humans were not given the opportunity to shape their destiny, but only to conform to or reject the true path. The magnificent exceptions to this retreat from historical semiosis are the great Icelandic sagas — *Njal's, Grettir's, Egil's, Laxdaela, and Eyrbyggja* — written for the most part in the thirteenth century as the Icelandic republic degenerated into aristocracy and anarchy before taking refuge under the protection of the Norwegian monarchy its citizens had originally fled. The sagas present historical figures as signs to permit us to weigh the strengths and weaknesses of different religions, forms of government, personality types, and systems of law in a sophisticated fashion worthy of the best Greek thinkers (Pencak 1995).

The pre-modern precursor of semiotic history is generally considered to be Giambattista Vico, whose *New Science* (1744) contains the germs of much semiotic thought. Vico maintains that humans are primarily poetic and creative beings, and that science and political institutions spring from creative transformations in the use of language. People shape their own history, although they do it according to discernable patterns: every society has burial, marriage, and religious practices, and all civilizations pass through definable stages of growth and decline, from the religious to the heroic to the human followed by decay and repetition of the cycle. Each stage is identifiable by a different type of society, language, law, reason, writing, and conception of human nature. Nevertheless, although similar to the "morphology" of history sketched by Oswald Spengler in *The Decline of the West* (1926/1928), Vico allows for human agency and progress. In the Hebrew and Christian worlds each new cycle was able, through a divinely conveyed continuity with and sense of the past — that is, a sense of its own evolving history — to incorporate historically acquired knowledge and move humanity to a higher level (see White 1978:197-218 for a concise explanation of Vico).

Charles Sanders Peirce, the pioneer theorist of modern semiotics, also developed a semiotic of history, for the most part in his writings on the history of science, but also in several short essays, most notably "Evolutionary Love" (1893a; see Pencak 1993:17-84). Making "an onslaught upon the doctrine of necessity," Peirce held that the universe incorporated both "necessity" and "spontaneity." History did not evolve, it erupted in cataclysms where a habit of thought which ceased to work was overthrown by another "sure to be widely disparate from the first" (Peirce 1892a: 150). At moments of crisis, men whom he termed "monstrous births" (1901:872-875) — Peirce wrote illustrative essays on Napoleon (c.1893b) and the fourteenth-century revolutionary Rienzi (c.1892b) as well as the more familiar pieces on great men of science (1892a) could emerge and make a genuine historical difference. Such great men become the keys to determining the structure of history, the "firsts" who oppose the "seconds" of chaos and revolution. They form part of Peirce's community of truth-seekers: *to the extent that* they actually pursue their visions and are not diverted by the lures of power and wealth, they will provide the basis for a further evolution of thought and society. The Peircean "third" is the community's judgment and working out of their ideas in the "routine" period which follows the time of troubles — a cycle of twenty to forty years when "a universal movement or struggle of thought, action or feeling, absorbs men's attention and suppresses other tendencies" (Peirce 1901:872-875).

Peirce's historical theories anticipate those of Henri Bergson's *Two Sources of Religion and Morality* and *Creative Evolution* (1911; 1935) and Thomas Kuhn's *The Structure of Scientific Revolutions* (1962, rev. 1970) which showed how science evolves through paradigm shifts, successive world views such as the Ptolemaic, Newtonian, and Einsteinian, none of which was either definitively true or logically evolving out of the previous system. Rather, due to changes in questions scientists ask and the inability of the existing paradigm to answer them, discontinuous shifts in the construction of knowledge occur.

John Lukacs, in *Historical Consciousness* (1968, rev. 1985) has argued persuasively that since modern science is based on Einsteinian relativity and Heisenberg's uncertainty principle, historians who think scientific history deals only with provable facts are blindly following a theory deemed obsolete by scientists themselves. He agrees with Heisenberg that "the breakdown of the mechanical concept of causality" has established "the principal importance of potentialities and tendencies.... Not the essence of 'factors' but their relationship counts." Thus the Cartesian dualism separating mind and matter, history and the historian, "falls away." Historical events, like scientific "facts," depend for their existence on their relationship to the inquirer: "instead of the cold and falsely antiseptic remoteness of observation we need the warmth and penetration of personal interest" for history to exist. Lukacs insists that "this is no longer the solitary longing of a humanist, a poetic exhortation": it is science itself. In the twentieth century, there are so many documents, many of which are neither read nor written by those whose signature they bear, that "it is not the documents that make history ... rather, it is history that made the documents" (Lukacs 1968, rev. 1985:278-287; 337).

A much-neglected but profound thinker who applied Peirce's semiotic (via William James) to the grand sweep of history was Eugen Rosenstock-Huessy. He maintained that like it or not, humankind had to respond to great, unpredictable revolutions which "are eccentric, they exaggerate, they are brutal and cruel. But the life of the rest of the world is regenerated by their outbreak." With each revolutionary advance — secular monarchy introduced by the Protestant Reformation, the gentry parliament by the English Civil War, democratic individualism by the French Revolution, and economic planning by Bolshevik Russia — came a panoply of myths, institutions, personality types, ideas, ceremonies, a new calendar, and new heroes — and villains. While revolutionaries and future supporters of each cause elevated the partial truths for which they proselytized as the solution to humanity's problems, the world in practice has borrowed from each great revolution. All their principles have been retained in the collective memory of humanity and fought and interacted with each other in unpredictable ways. Hence, Rosenstock-Huessy replaced Descartes' dictum: "I think, therefore I am," with "I respond although I will be changed" as the fount of knowledge (Rosenstock-Huessy 1938:24, 125, 151, 477, 490, 625-627; 1970:1-19).

No one more eloquently demonstrated how new historical perspectives arose out of revolution than Walter Benjamin (c. 1940). If Peirce argued that we reason to relieve doubt, Benjamin tells us that both the making and writing of meaningful history occurs "in a state of emergency" as "the tradition of the oppressed teaches us." In a vital sense, we only become aware of a historical event when we "seize hold of a memory as it flashes up at a moment of danger." It is the task of the historian to keep history from "becoming a tool of the ruling classes. In every era the attempt must be made anew to wrest tradition away from a conformism that is about to overpower it," Benjamin wrote in his brief "Theses on the Philosophy of History." Otherwise, "even the dead will not be safe" from slander and oblivion. Benjamin's historian is akin to Peirce's scientist, uncovering lost discourses of the oppressed and questioning those by which the powerful maintain their rule.

Another seminal semiotic historian was Carl Becker, who taught us that "Everyman [Is] His Own Historian" (1932a; see Pencak 1993:85-108 for an analysis). We do not, and cannot, discover "the truth" about the past, but must write narratives that accord with our own needs: "the past is a kind of screen on which we project our vision of the future." Becker prefers to call "facts" "affirmations," "representations," "symbols," or even "illusions" (1926:329, 330, 337). What the historian can do is map the "climate of opinion" of a different era expressed through a "code" — "magic words ... unobtrusive words with uncertain meanings that are permitted to slip off the tongue without fear and without research; words which, having from constant repetition lost their metaphysical significance, are unconsciously mistaken for objective realities." God, Heaven, grace, and salvation were magic words for the Christian centuries; for the eighteenth, "the words without which no enlightened person could reach a restful conclusion were nature, natural law, first cause, reason, sentiment, humanity, [and] perfectibility" (1932b:47). "Chance, accident ... relativity, process, adjustment, function, and complex" have become the code words for a twentieth century that regards humanity as "carelessly thrown up between two ice ages by the same forces that rust iron and ripen corn" (1932b: 12-16).

Becker's climates of opinion easily translate into the "discourses" or "epistemes" of Michel Foucault (1961; 1967; 1969; 1971; 1980; for an analysis see Pencak 1997). Denying that we can definitively know historical causes and effects — and that those causes and effects we select are signs of historians' political agendas — Foucault insists we can only, like archeologists and genealogists, map the discourses of different eras which exhibit striking discontinuities. All discourses are dialogues between the powerful and *supposedly* powerless — since the powerful are dependent on those they dominate for both sustenance and identity. In apparently free, modern, liberal societies, "capillaries" of power create new structures of repression. Prisons, schools, insane asylums, and bureaucracies now try to force internal assent to the social order rather than merely "disciplining and punishing" deviants. Historical spontaneity and freedom arises in gaps, spaces, and interstices between institutions. Foucault calls these spaces of freedom "heterotopias" to distinguish them from the next wave of would-be hegemonic Utopias — Bohemian Paris or gay San Francisco as opposed to the Communist Internationale or the Moral Majority, for instance. Michel de Certeau, one of Foucault's most important interpreters, has termed him the great explorer of the "zones" science and rationality have "left as their remainder or unintelligible underside," a retriever of "object[s] *lost* by history." Foucault leads history to the realm of "margins, limits, silences, and semiosis, where what is said signifies what is repressed" (1988:39-40; see also 1986).

# IV
## Contemporary Practitioners

De Certeau's agenda was being executed even before he set it.  Historians began unearthing past discourses in Becker's day, notably Herbert Butterfield on *The Whig Interpretation of History* (1931), and E. M. W. Tillyard (1943) and Basil Willey (1934) on early modern British views of the world.  Arthur Lovejoy (1933) and Richard Koebner (1961) respectively explored shifting meanings of the great chain of being and empire.  In recent times, Daniel Rodgers has done the same for republicanism (1992) and other key words which constitute the vocabulary of politics in the modern United States (1987).   Michael Kammen (1978; 1986) has traced how "the American Revolution" and "the Constitution" have also been reconstructed again and again over the past two centuries. Norbert Elias has traced *The Civilizing Process* (1978) in Europe, whereas John Kasson has looked at *Rudeness and Civility in Nineteenth Century America* (1990).   Michael Walzer (1985) reveals the persistence of the invocation of the Biblical Exodus from Egypt by revolutionary movements in modern times. Marcel Mauss (1967) delineated the changing historical significance of gifts, Johan Huizinga (1950) of play, and Francis Nicholson (1955) of good behavior.

Building on the anthropologist Clifford Geertz's notion of "thick description," especially his painstaking analysis of all the cultural implications of the Balinese cock-fight (1973: esp. 412-453), by the late 1970s the *Annales* school of historians (e. g. Braudel 1972/1973; LeRoy Ladurie 1978) began to augment their detailed research into economic life and social structure with the study of *mentalités*, or world-views, especially  of early modern Europe. Microhistory,the intensive examination of obscure communities, events, and individuals who emerge for the most part in legal records, could illuminate the history of the "lost peoples of Europe."   Three scholarly journals *Annales*, *Past and Present*, and *Quaderni Storici* (see Muir and Ruggiero 1990, 1991, and 1994 for topical collections from the last of these on crime, sexuality, and microhistory) are internationally famous for microhistory. Natalie Zemon Davis (1975, 1983, 1987), Carlo Ginzburg (1980, 1990, 1991), Robert Darnton (1984, 1990), and E. P. Thompson (1993) were among the pioneers of a history that revealed the significance of popular rituals like rough music (crowd punishment of moral deviants or outsiders), the massacre of cats, or the persecution of witches. An underground, hitherto almost unknown world of neo-pagan practices and popular culture was decoded, widening the scope of history beyond both traditional political and social themes.

Accompanying this extension of "history from the bottom up" was a new way of reading texts produced by the elite.  Much attention has especially focused on constructions of "otherness," especially in "encounters" — no longer "discoveries" — between Europeans and the peoples of Asia, Africa, and the Americans during the Age of Exploration. Tzvetan Todorov (1984), Stephen Greenblatt (1990, 1991), and Anthony Grafton (1992), among many others, have carefully analyzed the language of documents designed to justify taking possession of new lands by branding the inhabitants as inferior. Winthrop Jordan (1968), Edward Said (1978), and Alden Vaughan (1994) have been especially astute in showing how African slaves, Orientals, and Amerindians, respectively, who were stereotyped in terms of vices the Europeans both practiced and feared themselves, were vital to the construction of the European self-image. Gannanath Obeyesekere (1992) and Gayatri Spivak (1987, 1990) have followed them, spearheading post-colonial or subaltern studies, the decoding of western imperialism from the perspective of the colonized (see Ashcroft, Griffiths, and Tiffin 1995). Eric Hobsbawm has brought dignity to "bandits" he has redefined as "primitive rebels" (1965; 1969).

The history of reading and literacy also frutifully complicate the meaning of texts hitherto interpreted primarily by explaining just what was on the printed page or "influences" of authors upon each other or movements. Interacting audiences, authors, publishing milieus, and political and economic contexts are all now elements in explaining that multifaceted entity known as the "text." Canadians Harold Innis (1951) and Marshall McLuhan (1962; 1964) — famous for the catchy oversimplification "the medium is the message" — are the frequently unacknowledged predecessors of a more scholarly movement that began with Elizabeth Eisenstein (1979). It theoretically culminated in Jürgen Habermas' idea that a public sphere emerged in the early modern period (seventeenth century England, eighteenth century France and America) where literate citizens without official government standing began to participate in political affairs (1989). Of numerous works following in their aftermath, Richard D. Brown (1989) and Michael Warner (1990) have delineated how a public sphere dominated by the government and clergy in colonial America grew due to expansion of publication and proliferation of voluntary associations. Robert Darnton (1993; Darnton and Roche 1989) has shown the importance of the writers' market for shaping the French Revolution. James Smith Allen (1981; 1991) has linked reading habits of the nineteenth-century French bourgeoisie to their political proclivities. R. Jackson Wilson (1989), on the other hand, shows how career opportunities for men of letters shaped the output of leading American writers. Dena Goodman (1994) has noted how eighteenth century salons empowered women.

Studies of women, gender, the body, and sexuality have been a major part of the new semiotic history. Much like post-colonial studies, they have shown how the public triumph of patriarchy, self-restraint, and heterosexuality in the modern west has been achieved through suppression of alternatives. Joan Landes (1988) notes that the increasing democratization of society for white men in revolutionary France deprived women of the limited rights they had enjoyed in the public sphere of the *ancien regime*. Carroll Smith-Rosenberg (1985) and Linda Kerber (1997) have done the same for the early nineteenth century United States. Conversely, Ann Firor Scott (1984) has shown how women's roles in American reform movements have been suppressed in histories written largely by males.

Gender history is now also being enhanced by history studies of how human bodies are constructed and judged. Londa Scheibinger (1989, 1993) has shown how the supposedly neutral language of early modern science was heavily gendered and implied the subordination of the female to the male, the "passive" to the "active." Peter Brown (1988), in his study of the role of repressed sexuality in early Christianity, explicitly acknowledges Foucault's influence. John Boswell (1980, 1994), Jonathan Goldberg (1992, 1994), and Alan Bray (1995) have unearthed the presence of hidden practices and discourses of same-sex love in early modern Europe, as have George Chauncey (1994), Jonathan Ned Katz (1995), and Lillian Faderman (1991) for the early twentieth century United States.

The panoply of political symbolism especially invites semiotic studies. Benedict Anderson in *Imagined Communities* (1983) and Eric Hobsbawm and Terence Ranger in *Inventing Tradition* (1983) demonstrate that the modern nation and its supposed heritage are in fact recent, deliberate constructions facilitated by elite manipulation of symbols. Maurice Agulhon (1989) and Lynn Hunt (1992) have explored the symbols of French nationhood, Lester Olson (1991) and Wilbur Zelinsky (1988) of American. Susan Davis (1986), Simon Newman (1997), and David Waldstreicher (1997) have recently turned their attention to parades and civic rituals as creators of early American nationalism. David Cannandine and Simon Price (1987) look at the cermonial foundations of traditional societies. Jean Starobinski (1987) and Ronald Paulson (1983) have shown how works of art contribute to and reflect revolutionary change.

If semiotics claims to be the method of methods, history claims to be the discipline of disciplines. Good history is good sociology, good economics, etc. employing the perspective of change over time. A sampling of articles in recent collections on semiotics and history appearing in *Semiotica* (Williams and Pencak, 1991) and *The American Journal of Semiotics* (Pencak, 1998), demonstrates how history itself is being reshaped in a multitude of ways by scholars with semiotic inclinations uncovering and explaining disparaged or lost discourses. Alternatively, they apply new scrutiny to dominant discourses which have been insufficiently examined: ethnic stereotyping in nineteenth-century American theatre (James Dormon); the various uses of the terms "genocide" and "holocaust" (Gregory Goekjian); the meaning of colors and decorations in large letters in medieval illuminated manuscripts (Edward Gorsuch); how certain symbols were selected for certain words when western languages had to be translated into Japanese (Douglas Howland); reasons behind multiple interpretations of Salem witchcraft (Ross Pudaloff); how a black educator redirected racist language against whites in the nineteenth-century South to obtain facilities for a "separate but equal" black college (Beth Raps); changing notions of God during the Cold War (Mary Miles); justifications for using ordinary popular speech as "the" language of early modern Italy (Santa Casciani); the persistence of alchemy into nineteenth-century Britain as seen by J.M.W. Turner's coded use of colors (Jason Kelly); the idealization of body building in modern America (Hartmut Heep) and the denigration of women's bodies through the language used to describe menstruation (Meta Mazaj); toys as cultural symbols of changing gender roles and parent/child relations (Gary Cross); manipulation of stereotypes by modern politicians (Catherine Lugg); definition of radio waves as occupying "space" to permit government regulation (David Zeeman); the construction of Indian national identity through nineteenth-century travel narratives (Kumkum Chatterjee). Given this extraordinary range of topics, we can only conclude with Brooke Williams, who initiated the formal scholarly rapprochement of semiotics and history in the 1980s:

> The semiotic solution thus provides history (and no longer simply intellectual history) with an integral model of human experience that situates, as it overcomes, the false options of previous paradigms, and therefore points toward a convergence of history and philosophy in the decades ahead. At the same time the newer paradigm works for history as it does for semiotics, precisely by a shift in perspective that reveals the centrality of history in the truly transdisciplinary perspective opened by the sign (Williams 1991:412).

*William Pencak is Professor of History at The Pennsylvania State University.*

## REFERENCES

Agulhon, Maurice, 1981, *Marianne into Battle: Republican Imagery and Symbolism in France, 1789-1880.* trans. Janet Lloyd. Cambridge: Cambridge University Press.

Allen, James Smith, 1981, *Popular French Romanticism: Writers, Readers, and Books in the Nineteenth Century*. Syracuse: Syracuse University Press.

-----, 1991, *In the Public Eye: A History of Reading in Modern France, 1800-1940*. Princeton: Princeton University Press.

Anderson, Benedict, 1983, *Imagined Communities: Reflections on the Origin and Spread of Nationalism*. London: Verso.

Ashcroft, Bill, Griffiths, Gareth, and Tiffin, Helen, eds. (1995). *The Post-Colonial Studies Reader*. New York: Routledge.

Becker, Carl, 1926, What is the Historical Fact? Paper read at the 41st annual meeting of the American Historical Association and published as What are historical facts?, *Western Political Quarterly*, 1955, 327-240.

-----, 1932a, Everyman His own Historian. *American Historical Review*, 37, 221-236.

-----, 1932b, *The Heavenly City of the Eighteenth Century Philosophers*. New Haven: Yale University Press.

Benjamin, Walter, c. 1940, Theses on the Philosophy of History. trans. Harry Zohn in *Illuminations*. New York: Schocken Books, 1969, 253-264.

Bergson, Henri, 1911, *Creative Evolution*, trans. A. Mitchell. New York: D. C. Holt.

-----, 1935, *The Two Sources of Religion and Morality*. trans. R. Audra and C. Brereton, New York: D. C. Holt.

Boswell, John, 1980, *Christianity, Social Tolerance, and Homosexuality*. Chicago: University of Chicago Press.

-----, 1994, *Same-Sex Unions in Pre-Modern Europe*. New York: Villard.

Braudel, Fernard, 1972/1973, *The Mediterranean and the Mediterranean World in the Age of Philip II*. trans. Sian Reynolds. New York: Harper and Row.

Bray, Alan, 1995, *Homosexuality in Renaissance England*, 2d. ed. New York: Columbia University Press.

Brent, Joseph, 1993, *Charles Sanders Peirce: A Life*. Bloomington: Indiana University Press.

Brown, Richard D., 1989, *Knowledge is Power: The Diffusion of Information in Early America, 1700-1865*. New York: Oxford University Press.

Brown, Peter, 1988, *The Body and Society: Men, Women, and Sexual Renunciation in Early Chrsitianity*. New York: Columbia University Press.

Butterfield, Herbert, 1931, *The Whig Interpretation of History*. London: G. Bell and Sons.

Cannandine, David, and Price, Simon, eds., 1987, *Rituals of Royalty: Power and Ceremonial in Traditional Societies*. Cambridge: Cambridge: University Press.

Certeau, Michel de, 1986, *Heterologies, Discourses on the Other*. trans. Brian Massumi. Minneapolis: University of Minnesota Press.

-----, 1988, *The Writing of History*. trans. Tom Conley. New York: Columbia University Press.

Chauncey, George, 1994, *Gay New York: Gender, Urban Culture, and the Making of a Gay Male World, 1890-1940*. New York: Basic Books.

Cohen, Sande, 1986, *Historical Culture: On the Recording of an Academic Discipline*. Berkeley: University of California Press.

Darnton, Robert, 1984, *The Great Cat Massacre and Other Episodes in French Cultural History*. New York: Basic Books.

-----, 1990, *The Kiss of Lamourette, Reflections on Cultural History*. New York: Norton.

-----, 1993, *The Forbidden Best-Sellers of Pre-Revolutionary France*. New York: Norton.

Darnton, Robert, and Roche, Daniel, eds., 1989, *Revolution in Print: The Press in France, 1775-1800*. Berkeley: University of California Press.

Davis, Natalie Zemon, 1975, *Society and Culture in Early Modern France*. Stanford: Stanford University Press.

-----, 1983, *The Return of Martin Guerre*. Harvard: Harvard University Press.

-----, 1987, *Fiction in the Archives: Pardon Tales and Their Tellers in Sixteenth-Century France*. Stanford: Stanford University Press.

Davis, Susan G., 1986, *Parades and Power: Street Theater in Nineteenth Century Philadelphia*. Philadelphia: Temple University Press.

Deely, John, 1990, *Basics of Semiotics*. Bloomington: Indiana University Press.

Eisenstein, Elizabeth, 1979, *The Printing Press as an Agent of Change: Communication and Cultural Transformation in Early Modern Europe*. New York: Cambridge University Press.

Elias, Norbert, 1978, *The Civilizing Process*. trans. E. Jephcott. New York: Urizen.

Faderman, Lillian, 1991, *Odd Girls and Twilight Lovers: A History of Lesbian Life in the Twentieth Century*. New York: Columbia University Press.

Finlay-Pelinski, Marike, 1982, Semiotics or History: From Content Analysis to Contextualized Discursive Praxis. *Semiotica* 40 (3/4), 229-66.

Finley, John H., Jr., 1942, *Thucydides*. Cambridge: Harvard University Press.

Foucault, Michel, 1961, *Madness and Civilization: A History of Insanity in the Age of Reason*. trans. Richard Howard. New York: Mentor, 1967.

-----, 1967, Of Other Spaces, lecture translated in *Diacritics*, 16 (1), 1986, 22-27.

Foucault, Michel, 1969, *The Archeaology of Knowledge*. trans. A. M. Sheridan-Smith. New York: Harper and Row, 1972.

-----, 1971, Nietzsche, Genealogy, and History. trans. Paul Rabinow. In *The Foucault Reader*. New York: Pantheon. 1984.

-----, 1980, *Power/Knowledge. Selected Interviews: 1972-1977*. New York: Pantheon.

Geertz, Clifford, 1973, *The Interpretation of Cultures: Selected Essays*. New York: Basic Books.

Ginzburg, Carlo, 1980, *The Cheese and the Worms: The Cosmos of a Sixteenth-Century Miller*. trans. John and Anne Tedeschi. Baltimore: Johns Hopkins University Press.

-----, 1990, *Myths, Emblems, Clues*. trans. John and Anne Tedeschi. London: Hutchinson Radius.

-----, 1991, *Ecstasies: Deciphering the Witches' Sabbath*. trans. Raymond Rosenthal. New York: Pantheon.

Goldberg, Jonathan, 1992, *Sodometries: Renaissance Texts, Modern Sexualities*. Stanford: Stanford University Press.

-----, ed., 1994, *Queering the Renassance*. Durham. Duke University Press.

Goodman, Dena, 1994, *The Republic of Letters: A Cultural History of the French Enlightenment*. Ithaca: Cornell University Press.

Grafton, Anthony, 1992, *New Worlds, Ancient Texts: The Power of Tradition and the Shock of Discovery*. with April Shepard and Nancy Siriasi. Cambridge: Belknap Press of Harvard University.

Greenblatt, Stephen, 1990, *Learning to Curse: Essays on Early Modern Culture*. New York: Routledge.

-----, 1991, *Marvelous Possessions: The Wonder of the New World*. Oxford: Clarendon Press.

Habermas, Jürgen, 1989, *The Structural Transformation of the Public Sphere*. trans. Thomas Burger. Cambridge: MIT Press.

Haidu, Peter, 1982, Semiotics and History. *Semiotica* 40 (3/4), 187-228.

Halpern, Baruch, 1988, *The First Historians: The Hebrew Bible and History*. San Francisco. Harper and Row.

Harlan, David, et al., 1989, *American Historical Review*. Forum — entire issue 94 (3).

Haskins, Charles Homer, 1927, *The Renaissance of the Twelfth Century*. Cambridge: Harvard University Press.

Herodotus, c.430 B.C.E., *The Histories*. trans. Aubrey de Selincourt. Baltimore: Penguin, 1954.

Hobsbawm, Eric, 1965, *Primitive Rebels*. New York: Norton.

-----, 1969, *Bandits*. New York: Delacorte.

Hobsbawm, Eric, and Ranger, Terence, eds., 1983, *The Invention of Tradition.* Cambridge: Cambridge University Press.

Hoopes, James, 1993, Objectivity *and* Relativism Affirmed: Historical Knowledge and the Philosophy of Charles S. Peirce. *American Historical Review* 98(5), 1545-1555.

Huizinga, Johan, 1950, *Homo Ludens,* trans. R. F. C. Hull. New York: Roy.

Hunt, Lynn, 1992, *The Family Romance of the French Revolution.* Berkeley: University of California Press.

Innis, Harold, 1951, *The Bias of Communications.* Toronto: University of Toronto Press.

Kammen, Michael, 1978, *A Season of Youth: The American Revolution and the Historical Imagination.* New York: Knopf.

-----, 1986, *A Machine that Would Go of Itself: The Constitution in American Culture.* New York: Knopf.

Katz, Jonathan Ned, 1995, *The Invention of Heterosexuality.* New York: Dutton.

Jordan, Winthrop D., 1968, *White Over Black: American Attitudes Toward the Negro, 1550-1812.* Chapel Hill: University of North Carolina Press.

Kasson, John, 1990, *Rudeness and Civility in Nineteenth Century America.* New York: Hill and Wang.

Kerber, Linda, 1997, *Toward an Intellectual History of Women.* Chapel Hill: University of North Carolina Press.

Koebner, Richard, 1961, *Empire.* Cambridge: Cambridge University Press.

Kuhn, Thomas, 1962, rev. 1970, *The Structure of Scientific Revolutions.* Chicago: University of Chicago Press.

Landes, Joan, 1988, *Women and the Public Sphere in the Age of the French Revolution.* Ithaca: Cornell University Press.

LeRoy Ladurie, Emmanuel, 1978, *Montaillou: The Promised Land of Error.* trans. Barbara Bray. New York: Braziller.

Lovejoy, Arthur, 1933, *The Great Chain of Being: Studies in the History of an Idea.* Cambridge: Harvard University Press, 1964.

Lukacs, John, 1968, 1985, *Historical Consciousness: The Remembered Past.* 2d. ed. New Brunswick: Transaction Books.

Mauss, Marcel, 1967, *The Gift: Forms and Functions of Exchange in Archaic Societies.* trans. Ian Cunnison. New York: Norton.

McLuhan, Marshall, 1962, *The Gutenberg Galaxy: The Making of Typographic Man.* Toronto: University of Toronto Press.

McLuhan, Marshall, 1964, *Understanding Media: The Extensions of Man.* New York: McGraw-Hill.

Muir, Edward, and Ruggiero, Guido, eds., 1990, *Sex and Gender in Historical Perspective.* Baltimore: Johns Hopkins University Press.

Muir, Edward, 1991, *Microhistory and the Lost Peoples of Europe*. Baltimore: Johns Hopkins University Press.

-----, 1994, *History from Crime*. Baltimore: Johns Hopkins University Press.

Munslow, Alun, 1997, Authority and Reality in the Representation of the Past. *Rethinking History* 1(1), 75-87.

Newman, Simon, 1997, *Parades and the Politics of the Street: Festive Culture in the Early American Republic*. Philadelphia: University of Pennsylvania Press.

Nicholson, Francis, 1955, *Good Behaviour, Being a Study of Certain Types of Civility*. Garden City: Doubleday.

Nöth, Winfried, 1990, rev. ed., *Handbook of Semiotics*. Bloomington: Indiana University Press.

Obeyesekere, Gananath, 1992, *The Apotheosis of Captain Cook: European Mythmaking in the Pacific*. Princeton: Princeton University Press.

Olson, Lester C., 1991, *Emblems of American Community in the Revolutionary Era*. Washington: The Smithsonian Institution Press.

Paulson, Ronald, 1983, *Representations of Revolution (1789-1820)*. New Haven: Yale University Press.

Peirce, Charles S., 1892a, Lectures on the history of science commonly known as "Lowell Institute Lectures." In Carolyn Eisele, ed., *Historical Perspectives on Peirce's Logic of Science*. Berlin: Mouton de Gruyter, 1985, 139-285.

-----, c.1892b, Rienzi, last of the tribunes. In Carolyn Eisele, ed., *Historical Perspectives on Peirce's Logic of Science*. Berlin: Mouton de Gruyter, 1985, 550-554.

-----, 1893a, Evolutionary Love. In Charles Hartshorne and Paul Weiss, eds., *Collected Papers of Charles Sanders Peirce*, vol. 6, Cambridge: Harvard University Press, 1931-35, paragraphs 290-314.

-----, c.1893b, Napoleon, ms. 1319, microfilm edition of the Charles S. Peirce papers, originals at Houghton Library, Harvard University. Catalogued in Richard S. Robin, *Annotated Catalogue of the Papers of Charles S. Peirce*. Amherst: University of Massachusetts Press, 1967.

Peirce, Charles S., c. 1901, Great Men of the Nineteenth Century. In Carolyn Eisele, ed., *Historical Perspectives on Peirce's Logic of Science*. Berlin: Mouton de Gruyter, 1985, 872-876.

Pencak, William, 1991, Charles S. Peirce, Historian and Semiotician. *Semiotica* 83 (3/4): 311-332.

Pencak, William, 1993, *History, Signing In: Studies in History and Semiotics*. New York: Peter Lang.

Pencak, William, 1994, Herodotus and Fukuyama: The Beginning and End(?) of History. Roberta Kevelson, ed. *Codes and Customs: Millennial Perspectives*. New York: Peter Lang, 225-243.

-----, 1995, *The Conflict of Law and Justice in the Icelandic Sagas*. Amsterdam: Rodopi.

-----, ed. 1996, *Worldmaking*. New York: Peter Lang.

-----, 1997, Foucault Stoned: Reconsidering Insanity, and History. *Rethinking History* 1 (1), 34-55.

-----, ed. 1998, *American Journal of Semiotics*, special issue, history and semiotics, 14 (3/4). Publication delayed of 1995 issue.

Plumb, J. H., 1970, *The Death of the Past*. Boston: Houghton Mifflin.

Rodgers, Daniel T., 1987, *Contested Truths: Keywords in American Politics Since Independence*. New York: Basic Books.

-----, 1992, Republicanism: the Career of a Concept. *Journal of American History* 79 (1), 11-38.

Rosenstock-Huessy, Eugen, 1938, *Out of Revolution: Autobiography of Western Man*. Norwich: Argos Books, 1969 reprint.

-----, 1970, Farewell to Descartes. In *I Am An Impure Thinker*. Norwich: Argos Books, 1-19.

Said, Edward, 1978, *Orientalism*. New York: Pantheon.

Samuel, Raphael, 1991, Reading the Signs. *History Workshop* 32, 88-109.

-----, 1992, Reading the Signs II: Fact-grubbers and Mind-readers. *History Workshop* 33, 220-251.

Scott, Ann Firor, 1984, *Making the Invisible Woman Visible*. Champaign-Urbana: University of Illinois Press.

Schiebinger, Londa, 1989, *The Mind Has No Sex? Women in the Origins of Modern Science*. Cambridge: Harvard University Press.

-----, 1993, *Nature's Body: Gender in the Making of Modern Science*. Boston: Beacon Press.

Smith-Rosenberg, Carroll, 1985, *Disorderly Conduct: Visions of Gender in Victorian America*. New York: Knopf.

Spengler, Oswald, 1926/1928, *The Decline of the West*. trans. Charles F. Atkinson. New York Knopf.

Spivak, Gayatri, 1987, *In Other Worlds: Essays in Cultural Politics*. New York: Methuen.

-----, 1990, *The Post-Colonial Critic*. ed. Sarah Harasyn. New York: Routledge.

Starobinski, Jean, 1987, *The Invention of Liberty, 1700-1789*. New York: Rizzoli.

Thucydides, c.400 B.C.E, *The Peloponnesian War*, trans. Rex Warner. Harmondsworth: Penguin, 1954.

Thompson, E. P., 1993, *Customs in Common: Studies in Traditional Popular Culture*. New York: The New Press.

Tillyard, E. M. W., 1943, *The Elizabethan World Picture*. New York: Macmillan.

Todorov, Tzvetan, 1984, *The Conquest of America: The Question of the Other*. trans. Richard Howard. New York: Pantheon.

Toews, John, 1987, Intellectual History after the Linguistic Turn: The Autonomy of Meaning and the Irreducibility of Experience. *American Historical Review* 82 (4), 879-907.

Vaughan, Alden T., 1994, *Roots of American Racism*. New York: Oxford University Press.

Vico, Giambattista, 1744, *The New Science*. 3d. ed., trans. Thomas G. Bergin and Max H. Fisch. Ithaca. Cornell University Press, 1948.

Voegelin, Eric, 1928, *Über die Form des Amerikanischen Geistes*. Tubingen: Mohr.

-----, 1952, *The New Science of Politics*. Chicago: University of Chicago Press.

-----, 1956/1957, *Order in History,* vols. 1-3. Baton Rouge: Louisiana State University Press.

-----, 1968, *Science, Politics, and Gnosticism*. Chicago: Henry Regnery.

-----, 1970, Equivalences of Experience and Symbolizations in History. *Eternita è Storia*. Florence: Valecchi, 215-234.

-----, 1974, Reason: the Classic Experience. *Southern Review* 10:238-264.

-----, 1975, *From Enlightenment to Revolution*, John Hallowell, ed. Durham: Duke University Press.

Waldstreicher, David, 1997, *In The Midst of Perpetual Fetes: The Making of American Nationalism, 1776-1820*. Chapel Hill: University of North Carolina Press.

Walzer, Michael, 1985, *Exodus and Revolution*. New York: Basic Books.

Warner, Michael, 1990, *The Letters of the Republic: Publishing and the Public Sphere in Eighteenth Century America*. Cambridge: Harvard University Press.

White, Hayden, 1978, *Tropics of Discourse: Essays in Cultural Criticism*. Baltimore: Johns Hopkins University Press.

Willey, Basil, 1934, *The Seventeenth Century Background*. London: Chatto and Windus.

Williams, Brooke, 1985, What has History to do with Semiotic? *Semiotica* 54 (3/4), 267-333.

Williams, Brooke, 1988, Opening Dialogue between the Discipline of History and Semiotics, in Thomas A. Sebeok and Jean Umiker-Sebeok, eds. *The Semiotic Web 1987*. Berlin: Mouton de Gruyter.

-----, 1991, History and semiotics in the 1990s. *Semiotica* 83 (3/4), 385-417.

Williams, Brooke, and Pencak, William, eds., 1991, *Semiotica*; special issue history and semitoics, 83 (3/4).

Wilson, R. Jackson, 1968, *In Quest of Community: Social Philosophy in the United States, 1860-1920*. New York: Wiley.

-----, 1989, *Figures of Speech: American Writers and the Literary Marketplace, from Benjamin Franklin to Emily Dickinson*. New York: Knopf.

Zelinsky, Wilbur, 1988, *Nation into State: The Shifting Symbolic Foundations of American Nationalism*. Chapel Hill: University of North Carolina Press.

# Part Three

## The Visible Sign

# Chapter 9

## Marking Marks
### or
## The Semiotic Theater of Dr. Pearce Explains Visual Semiotics to Kathy Bishop

Steven Skaggs*

Kathy Bishop fiddled with the electrode leads trailing like dreadlocks down her back. As instructed, she entered in the room labelled Semiotic Theater in understated grey Palatino caps. It was a circular room with grey carpet, beige walls, a white noise ambience and domed ceiling that reminded her of a planetarium. Dr. Pearce was dressed in jeans and a red sweater. She stood beside a black leather recliner in the center of the room.

"Welcome, Kathy. Glad to see the electroding process went smoothly. Occasionally, we have to redo some of them if the connections are weak. Despite improvements in nano-biotechnology, glial cells within the cerebellum seem to have a mind of their own, if you'll excuse the pun."

"The light in here is dim, Doctor, it took me a moment to realize it was you."

"Yes, we try to lessen the anxiety as much as we can although we understand that you may have butterflies. Just make yourself comfortable." She extended a hand toward the lounge chair.

When Kathy had positioned herself comfortably in the chair, an assistant appeared and began threading the cables through an elliptical opening in the back of the chair and jacking them to a set of connecting lines. The thick bundle of connecting lines reminded her of a shock of wheat. They were gripped by an o-ring harness at floor level before continuing beneath the carpet. She knew the computer occupied the storey beneath her. As Dr. Pearce helped the assistant with the connections, she continued, "As you know, Kathy, this experience is simply a demo version to give you a sense of the kind of experiment we are doing. We will run it for all the media now that the project is public. But when you write your story, be sure to convey that this is not virtual reality. There is nothing virtual about it. It will be your reality in as complete a sense as the term can be used. As you know from your briefing, the experience will last only 1.5 seconds in our time, although you will be experiencing a more protracted time scale on your end. After the experience, we will talk about the process of developing this ability.

But for now, simply relax and listen to some quiet music. Brahms?, oh yes, we remember you prefer Faure. Here is a Nocturne..."

"Dusk.  A small cabin in the woods.  The room is as you've always known it.  The room in which you were born.  You have returned to collect the few remaining artifacts that your mother has left upon her death.  A bed. A bureau.  A small night table supporting a few books.  You take off your coat and lay it upon the bed.  Sunlight carrying the spiked shadows of stripped maples builds in intensity, painting a shadow-play upon the window's sheer curtains.  A beam finds its way through the place where the pulled curtains fail to meet, rakes across the bureau striking a framed photograph. It is as if the photograph, having been hidden in the shadows, now steps to center stage.  It is a photograph of your mother in her youth.  She smiles broadly.  You can just recall that smile, the full lips, the black hair.  For a moment you are held between two visions:  that of your mother as you earliest knew her, and that of the 80 year old woman wasting in a hospital bed.  You shiver, pull your coat over your shoulders until the chill passes.

"It is the handwriting you first notice.  A paper protruding slightly from the back of the photograph.  The handwriting is that of your mother's.  The forms rise and fall in great breast-like swells, the loops of the ascenders full and graceful.  At the end of each paragraph the last trailing stroke pulls in a back-arching curve as if looking after the rest of the writing, making a period unnecessary, though one appears unfailingly placed in the center of the loop. The writing has been made with liquid ink flowing freely from a nibbed pen, making the writing at once old-fashioned and very personal.  You can sense just where the writing picked up pace, just where pressure was applied, and at the closing sentence, how your mother was finishing with a sense of conviction.

The letter reads:

> *Henry, I know that you are feeling many conflicting emotions as you read this. My life was a long and successful one. Do not feel sorrow for me but the happiness that comes from a game well played. As you read this note, you wonder how it is possible that it could have been secluded in this photograph for all these years only to be discovered now. Henry this experience you are having is a result of an experiment. Indeed, you will write of this experience in your own words and in your own handwriting so that other people can live it vicariously. Your life is in some ways nothing but a similar transcription: a kind of transcription of the signs you have seen. Their lives, too, are transcriptions to those around them, those who do or who have loved them, or who have contacted them in any way.*

*Your memories of me are placed just now in your mind. Your knowledge of this place is just enough for you to make sense of what you see and find here. Do not feel that this gives you less power or makes your life less rewarding or even less your own. You have enough to make sense, and that is all you need. It is all any of us or any of them can ever pretend to own.*

*And finally, Henry, remember that I have always and will always love you as you have me even though the bond is necessarily one constructed by others for our pleasure, our pain, and we be but the tools for them to understand their own transcriptions.*

*Your Mother, Jean*

The second measure of Faure's Nocturne was sounding Dr. Pearce was standing in the same position as before but her arm had seemed to have jerked as in the kind of stop action that a strobe light produces.

Dr. Pearce and the assistant approached the chair and began disconnecting.

"Good God", Kathy said at last, "I was a middle aged man. How...how did you do that?"

"Relax, listen to the rest of the Faure while we disconnect, then we'll go around the corner to the pub and I'll tell you all about it over lunch. Are you ok? Would you like some water?"

Inside The Acorn, the Stones had replaced Faure. It had a revitalizing effect on Kathy. Dr. Pearce chose a booth in the back corner far enough from the loudspeakers so that conversation was easy. Kathy remembered her note pad. Dr. Pearce carried a black briefcase which she slid onto the bench first, propping it against the wall, motioning at the same time for a waiter to bring a pitcher of beer. The pitcher arrived, and as Dr. Pearce paid the waiter, Kathy filled the mugs.

Kathy reached for hers. "A toast to the Semiotic Theater". The mugs touched. She hoped the cold brew would help her collect her thoughts. "I hardly even know what questions to ask. Perhaps you can begin by giving some background, and I will be able to respond to that."

"Yes, a good strategy, Kathy. I will try to explain the nature of the problem first and then we can go on to our semiotic model of visual experience."

"From your background reading, you know that semiotics is concerned with understanding the characteristics of signs and understanding sign action, or semiosis. The reason for this interest is that all experience can be thought of as the by-product of such an exchange of signs. You will recall that Charles Sanders Peirce formulated a model of semiotic action in which a sign mediated between the thing that it represented, called the sign's object, and an interpretive or inferential effect, called the interpretant. That interpretant, in turn, could become the sign leading to subsequent inferences, and so on in a kind of chain reaction of sign exchange. Meanwhile, Ferdinand de Saussure formulated a model of the sign that considered signification to be a bonding of signifier and signified in a kind of marriage of form and content. Throughout 20th century, but especially peaking in the latter half of the century, these semiotic tools provided insight into a large array of disciplines, from literature to anthropology to architecture to film studies.

"But for those of us working in the visual modes, the semiotics of Peirce, which was grounded in logic, and that of the Continental semiologists which was grounded in linguistics, offered only crude tools.  Perhaps the word 'crude' is not accurate.  The tools were exquisite, actually, far superior than the general kinds of mere descriptions that had served before them, but the new semiotic concepts did not always fit the visual world as snugly as the world of language or the world of logic.  The visual world is messy.  The problem is that in the visual world, the object of study — the visual sign vehicle — is not easily incised — so easily objectified.  Neither is it easy to fit visual communication into a code system like a language, although that has been tried.

"In any event, important attempts were made to tame the beast:  Barthes, Moles, Saint-Martin, Sonneson, Kress, Williamson and the others on your reading list.  I trust you have made yourself at least passingly acquainted with their points of view.  Irrespective of their important contributions, by the end of the century, their work considered collectively, seemed to demonstrate the difficulty of dealing with the visual world from a semiotic perspective.  It was something of a crisis in semiotics because in each of these cases the semiotic model was being strained to cover familiar visual phenomenon.  As Kuhn had pointed out in mid-century, when a paradigm begins to be stretched to the breaking point in order to explain observations, the paradigm itself is called into question.  Perhaps there were fundamental problems with the whole notion of the primacy of sign exchange in explaining visual experience.

"When we put together the proposal for a cyber-experience, what became the Semiotic Theater, we looked at perception theories, psychological theories, and neurological data of course.  In spite of its historical problems, we eventually settled upon semiotics as our foundational structure.  It alone offered a chance to make out of the cold input data, a single, coherent, interpretive act.  But we had to grope our way toward a workable model.  We realized what we would be making certain kinds of signs, making marks in the imagination so to speak, and these marks would be interpreted in ways we would predict.  Well, to be honest, these marks would be produced in ways that we would not simply predict but completely control.  We don't like to stress that aspect of our work, but to be certain that we were understanding the process completely we had to be able to produce particular, specific and predicted experiences.

"Before long, we had run up against the difficulties of implementing a visual semiotic model. It was actually John, my assistant, who first suggested we begin reading aesthetics. His idea was that, in a way, we were creating a particular experiential artifact — a kind of art making — and that a background in aesthetics might open some doors. So we turned to aesthetics for our basic research for this project.

"We discovered that aesthetic theories over the ages can be lumped into four families[1]. There are offshoots, of course, and permutations, but these four lines of thought constitute the major body of work running all the way back to the Greeks."

"Plato thought of art as an imitation of nature, and certainly this imitative quality is something that is important in many artworks. We see this when we hear people say that a painting looks like it's real. There is often something compelling about seeing a painting or image that portrays something else with a certain exactitude. The illusion itself is enchanting. There is no question that the portrayal, or imitative, aspect of art continues to be important. Yet, to say that all art must portray or imitate seems difficult to defend, and certainly that is not all that art seems to do. Many of us appreciate abstract art which has no clear subject matter other than the very paint it's made of. And in any event, there seem to be other factors at work in the aesthetic experience beyond that of mere imitation.

"A second type of aesthetic theory sees artwork as a special kind of expression, in which the emotions are, presumably, passed or conveyed from artist to viewer. The romanticists were largely concerned with expression of emotion. Tolstoy thought of it as a 'contagion of feeling'. Collingwood in England and Croce in Italy, developed similar theories that were somewhat more sophisticated. Each of these 'modified expressionist' theories saw two kinds of parallel experiences in viewing art. One was a categorization process that was conceptual or intellectual; the other was an appeal by the surface form to the intuition or imagination of the viewer. These processes, one conscious and one unconscious, the former relying somewhat on knowledge, the latter innately triggered, constituted together the aesthetic experience. The intuitive aspect, being triggered by certain formal properties, made the aesthetic experience transcendental in the sense that it carried one away from 'normal' experiences and caused the viewer to enter into a more intimate communication with the object of attention. But what is that intuitive act, and what is its trigger? If it is something in the form of the artwork, is there a key to be found in studying form alone?"

"Formalism, the third line of aesthetic inquiry, was espoused in Kant's *Critique of Aesthetic Judgement* in which he proposed two kinds of beauty: Free beauty which is produced by form alone, and dependent beauty which depends upon the consideration to which the object is directed. In the latter, something is beautiful when it is for a good cause or when it is for a good cause or when it relates to other pleasurable aspects that are known by the viewer. But in free beauty, the form is sufficient, in and of itself, to excite the aesthetic sensibility. For instance, in music, the beautiful is produced by form alone unfettered from relationships or reference to further ends. Of course, this begs the question of how it could be possible for people to disagree about a piece of music. You enjoyed the Faure, but you also enjoyed the Stones a moment ago even though the forms of those two pieces were very different. It is not easy to see what qualities Nocturne #3 and 'satisfaction' share. So you can see that a view of aesthetics based entirely on form is difficult to defend.

"In some theories, such as that of Langer, an attempt is made to reconcile expression and form by claiming that some forms 'symbolize' feeling. In other words, art employs forms that correspond to formal features of emotion, so that there is a kind of mapping of perceived form onto a kind of emotional form. This is a kind of resemblance of features across emotional and proportional terrain and a correspondence between them causes a kind of resonance. In the most extreme of these theories, Manfred Clynes claimed to have isolated specific categories of form, each linked to a specific emotion. In these hybrid theories of art we have attempts to combine features of the principle lines of inquiry which by themselves are inadequate."

"A fourth aesthetic theory sees art as making a kind of claim toward truth. In this kind of theory, the artist makes assertions or statements about the way the world is. But the artist's manner of doing this is entirely metaphorical. So in these theories, understanding the metaphor becomes especially important. In the most sophisticated of such theories, language must be thought of as not a strict denotation of word to concept, but instead a 'speech act', standing as a whole, for a concept. The speech act is a kind of idiomatic utterance that points toward its concept even when the particular words employed in another context may not denote the same thing at all. Searle sees metaphor as an indirect speech act: a kind of speech act cluster in which properties of one speech act are shared by another speech act like a Venn diagram in which someone recognizing the overlap gains a new awareness. Art is like that in that it is a speech act that can be taken metaphorically to refer to something greater than and different than itself. Goodman goes further to point out quite explicitly the difference between the extreme metaphorization of art and the direct denotation found in the nonaesthetic experience. Art does not describe, he says, it exemplifies. It provides a launching pad for further relations. It does not condense meaning toward a locus, on the contrary, art is able to be continuously unpacked by the viewer, offering always more connotational references. Art may be a kind of truth, but it is a truth in which the receiver participates."

The waiter arrived. Kathy ordered cream of broccoli soup, Dr. Pearce a hamburger well done and fully dressed. Mugs were refilled they resumed.

Kathy raised an eyebrow. "Ok, I think I follow the general lines of these aesthetic theories. But did you really find them to be of service in explaining the visual experience?"

"Kathy, I gotta tell you that at this stage we were more confused than ever. Here we were trying to shed light on semiotic ideas by following an aesthetics path, and the aesthetic theories were proving at least as unwieldy as the semiotic ones. They covered a broad range of territory, and not only that, they even contradicted one another. For instance, notice how speech act is in some ways the opposite of imitation: imitation depicts and describes, points to a single referent; metaphorical speech acts exemplify, reach out to a host of potential connotations.

"Another problem is how to deal with this concept of the immediate, innate, sensibility or perception of form which so many thinkers have considered to be essential to aesthetic experience: how to reconcile it with the aspects of aesthetic experience, such as metaphor, that seem to demand careful conscious consideration and which rely on a knowledge base? And underlying all these questions is the question of what separates aesthetic experience from other types of experience, which for our purposes was a question of great importance."

"We were thrashing these problems out when we came across Eco's study of medieval concepts of art and beauty. In particular, two frameworks struck us as being helpful."

"The first was that put forth by Witelo in the 13th century [2]. Witelo held that there were two types of visual perception. In one type there is the grasp of visible forms through intuition alone. In the second, perception occurs through intuition but this time it is combined with preceding knowledge. Witelo claims that aesthetic perception is of the second type. Here we see the splitting of perception into immediate and dynamic aspects. An immediate perception might be today called unconscious. But perception in which one becomes aware of the perceiving is something a little special. It becomes active in the sense of bringing into play more cognitive areas. This is something that we would find helpful to retain. By using this kind of bifurcated structure, Witelo felt he could explain why certain forms seemed immediately pleasing: principles of rhythm, size, color, etc. were directly 'understood' by intuition; but he could also account for the relativity of taste: people liked different things because they filtered these immediate perceptions through past experiences. Because each person's experiences are unique, there will always be differences in taste. Witelo said, 'each person makes his own estimate of beauty according to his own custom'[3]."

Kathy looked up from her notewriting. "That's a remarkable thing to say in pre-Renaissance Europe."

"Indeed. Witelo made another important contribution. He pointed out the importance of environmental conditions surrounding the perception. Someone's experience will be affected by the distance to the object, its size, movement, and such things as the angle at which it is seen. We noted that few of the thinkers in the intervening centuries had paused to remark on the importance of those kinds of fundamental things."

"The second medieval system that was of interest was that of Aquinas. He spoke of four proportions. First was the importance of matter to form: In *Comm. de Anima* he said, 'If matter is not disposed to receive the form, the form disappears'[4]. The second proportion is that of essence to existence. The third is the proportion of a thing's suitability to be experienced by a subject — the relation of the knower to the known. The fourth is the proportion of the adequacy to itself and to its function. 'Every craftsman aims to produce the best work he can, not in a simple manner, but by reference to an end'."[5]

Kathy nodded, sipping her beer, "These four proportions are wrapped in the classical concepts of essence and substance — potentiality and actuality, right?"

"Absolutely, Kathy. And that ancient concept still proves useful. For instance, the material that something is formed in is very important to how well it communicates. In other words, the characters of handwriting might be thought of as idealized forms, but they cannot exist apart from the pen and ink. Their material manifestation is crucial to their conveyance. Try writing with a stick in mud and one quickly realizes why cuneiform writing evolved into a very different form than cursive. The second proportion speaks of the essential idea and how well it is expressed. Considered from the receiver's side, it could just as well be referring to the adequacy for a given speech-act to metaphorically link with a concept. The third proportion, the suitability of a thing to be experienced by a subject speaks to the necessity for the audience to have a proper grounding in knowledge for the message. A message will be lost otherwise. And the fourth, the adequacy of something to its function, seems to harken right back to Witelo's notion of the importance of he environmental conditions of use. A notion of practicality, this."

Kathy nodded. "Yes, and I can see how some of these very early concepts begin to relate to some of the later ones."

"Precisely. So we were brimming with concepts from centuries past when we came across research by the psychologist Mihaly Csikszentmihalyi."

Kathy squinted: "What's that name again?"

"It is pronounced 'chick-sent-me-high'. Hand me your notebook and I'll spell it for you."

Dr. Pearce wrote on the top margin of the page, then returned the notepad.

"So anyway, Csikszentmihalyi and his colleague Robinson tried to get to the bottom of the aesthetic experience by conducting an experiment with art collectors and curators. They found a cluster of 'dimensions', or 'challenges' of aesthetic interpretation: perceptual — the strange and compelling attraction to the object; emotional — the ability of the object to provoke strong feelings; intellectual — how the object fits int a category, style, historical period; communicative — the entering into a kind of discourse with the object and then through the object to the artist. Csikszentmihalyi makes the important point that one must separate the structure of the aesthetic experience (that is, the quality of the experience itself) from the content of the experience (the particular route that is taken in thought). Structure is a centering of attention, clarity, wholeness, and freedom; content is characterized by dealing with the challenges: the perceptive, emotional, intellectual and communicative dimensions. The former is ubiquitous — he avoids saying universal but clearly implies it — the latter is not universal but varies greatly from person to person and experience to experience."

Just then the waiter returned, placing a steaming bowl of hot soup in front of Kathy and an enormous burger on an elliptical platter so large it necessitated rearranging the table on Dr. Pearce's side. The conversation drifted to lighter topics over lunch, one of which was Kathy's interest in calligraphy, which seemed to interest Dr. Pearce greatly.

Kathy was amazed at how quickly Dr. Pearce devoured the sandwich. She was not yet to the bottom of her bowl of soup when Dr. Pearce pushed his over to the bus girl who removed it. Dr. Pearce asked for several fresh napkins, and when they came, she used the top two to wipe clean the area in front of her. By now, Kathy's soup had also been removed. Seeing that Kathy was ready once more to take notes, Dr. Pearce continued.

"We noticed that the aesthetic experience, whatever it was, seemed to be a patchwork of several kinds of phenomena. We noticed too, that Csikszentmihaly was echoing the ideas of Witelo in that he saw a bifurcation of the experience into a subjective, almost ineffable, state but one that also carried with it a cognitive and describable component. What seemed to separate the aesthetic experience from mundane experience was not so much something inherently different in it, but that it was a kind of heightened 'meta-experience', a change of level one might say. If that be the case, then there would be a way in which our cyber-experience could be, in a sense, the aesthetic experience of the viewer, and that the content of the experience would stay at or be similar to, normal mundane experience."

"The trigger to the hyper state might be certain aspects of form, or conditions in which the form was perceived (as Witelo observed). We could there fore present conditions that were heightened and the attention to form could be strengthened. Put another way, conversely, making from unusual [6] is a technique for transforming mundane into heightened experience, as is changing the circumstances of viewing. For instance, a museum's environment changes the conditions of experience, as does a church, as does a grave site."

"With this background, we thought we could see some compatibilities of ideas through history. We thought we could begin to see ways in which h these various conceptions could be grouped."

"Now you might want to make a list of these, Kathy because this became the operational structure for us and the basis for our subsequent thinking about visual semiotic interactions. There are four classes. The first is a class we called *Concrete*. Under that class are the historical concepts of imitation, speech act (when it is direct and denotational), essence to existence, and communicative traits. Things that are visually concrete share the tendency to be denotative, descriptive, specific, resemblance — oriented, identification based, incisive, articulate manifest."

"The second class is that of *Attitude*, or *Tone*. Under this fall the historical notions of expression, association, dependent beauty, exemplification, idiomatic utterance, intuition when coupled with preceding knowledge, suitability to be experienced by subject, emotionality, and intellectuality in the sense of being cognitively processed. These attitudinal or tonal traits are connotative, stylistic, associational, metaphorical, have manifold references. They spin attention and reference away from the particular perceived object toward more generalized or indirect relationships."

"The third class is that of *Form*, considered only in and of itself. Here we have the historical concepts of free beauty and also intuition when acting immediately, sensitivity to form, expression, formal shapes, colors, geometry and other descriptive qualities, and their capabilities for attention-attraction. The class is dominated by physical and spatial compostitional components, the arrangement, the topographical order of the sign."

"The fourth class is that of *Practice*. Here one finds such things those things that Witelo and Aquinas first isolated: such entities as the environmental context, the conditions for viewing, matter to form, adequacy of itself to its function. Practice is the physical grounding necessary for the perception of the visual thing. Practice involves all the aspects that lead to the ability of a sign to function as a token of its ideal self."

"So, Kathy, to sum up this part of the explanation, our survey of aesthetics allowed us to see a pattern in the way visual experience is handled, a pattern that semiotics must complement, explain and extend. The pattern was only emerging, but at least we could see that the contributions of all these amazing thinkers over the centuries could be assembled into an ordered system. We don't claim that it is the *only* way to order these ideas, but it is one that allowed us considerable insight when coupled with certain semiotic themes."

"Kathy, the next part of the explanation is best accompanied by some visual aids. I've prepared some diagrams for you that will guide our explanation."

Dr. Pearce reached to the side and clicked open the briefcase. She withdrew a sheaf of papers which she held in her lap. She lifted one of the papers to the table top.

"The four classes — concrete, attitude, form and practice — are labeled in these diagrams with their initials: C, A, F, and P. First, we want to consider the classes according to the concepts of expression and content (figure 1). In Saussurian semiotics, these concepts play an important role. The sign is considered to be the bonding of a signifying expression and its signified content. You'll recall from your background reading that Hjelmslev elaborated this model effectively, but don't be confused by this notion of 'form': it is quite different from our use of the term. In our model, concrete and attitude are components of content. Form and practice are components of expression."

"This next diagram illustrates how the four classes can be distinguished by their 'tendencies' (figure 2). Concrete tends to be denotative and specific, while attitude tends to be connotative. Form tends to concern figurative aspects and practice tends to involve ground, in the sense that figure and ground are used in perception. Form is concerned with all those figural features, the materiality or geometry of the sign vehicle while practice can be though of as the conditions under which form becomes possible."

"The four classes can also be situated in reference to each other according to a matrix as the next diagram illustrates (figure 3). Here, Kathy, you see a kind of web comprised of semiotic concepts. Concrete and attitude are related by both being primarily semantic interactions. Form and practice are related by being syntactic in nature. Concrete and practice share iconicity, or resemblance to the objects they represent, while attitude and form both operate symbolically.

"But there is more. There are certain qualities that bind groups of classes (figure 4). For each of these attributes, one class is a 'favorite child', two are complaisant, and one is excluded. For example, three of the classes have a pragmatic dimension in the sense of Charles Morris, that there is a concern with how the sign's meaning relates to the receiver. The concrete class is heavily pragmatic, but pragmatic concerns involve the attitude and practice classes too.  However, pragmatics has nothing to do with form.  Form is highly indexic, in that it speaks of the means by which it was made.  Practice and attitude also involve index, but concrete signs have nothing of indexicality in them.   Attitude is highly cognitive in that the indirectness that is the hallmark of attitude or tone is an engagement of all the references the receiver can muster.  Concrete and form are two other classes that involve significant cognition, but practice is not related to cognition.  Practice is highly involved with perception, or the requirements of the percept.   Perceptive aspects operate in the concrete sign and the formal sign as well, but are absent in the attitudinal class.

"What we weave here, Kathy, is a network in which a sign is placed within this web of functions and by being cognizant of the *functional web*, as we call it, we can begin to control the experience itself."

"The next diagram illustrates the entire functional web (figure 5).  As a by-product of this, Kathy, we noticed how the Cartesian 'mind-body' problem can be reconciled, as Peirce realized, through the sign.  To see this, we rotate the diagram 45 degrees like this... (figure 6).  Now, the upper third becomes mind, the lower third becomes matter or body and the middle third is the sign proper."

"Yes, but if I see the central third as being the sign proper, don't I get a dyadic model instead of Peirce's triadic one?"

"Good observation, Kathy.  Two things to keep in mind.  First, the last thing we cared about was choosing sides in a semiotic war between dyadic and triadic.  We were looking for something that would help us explain visual signs and we're going to demonstrate that in a moment.  So we weren't interested in starting from or staying with a semiotic tradition although we recognized the tremendous contributions of each.  The second thing to realize is that although this structure can be made to look quite Saussurian, it does so only by neglecting the perceptive and cognitive dimensions.  When these dimensions are included as a unified thing complementing the formal sign vehicle and its concrete object, determined by and determining them, they begin to function, in tandem, very much like Peirce's interpretant."

Dr. Pearce picked up a fresh napkin.

"Watch.  Suppose I label the four corners of this square napkin with the class abbreviations, C, A, F and P.  Then, by lifting the P corner to touch the A corner, I have a triangular structure (figure 7).  You see, the percept can be thought of as the immediate interpretant and the cognitive aspect can be considered to be the interpretant in its dynamic capacity.  In some ways they are opposite things, but in others they are related very strongly — so strongly that they can seem to be fused.  But hasn't that always, at least since Descartes, been the issue?  It was Peirce's system suggested that move,

Kathy, that elimination of mind/body by fusing the whole notion in the concept of the interpretant, which itself, cannot be divorced from its dependency on sign and object. While this system is not that of Peirce, you will find many relationships with the system and his ideas."

Kathy had stopped writing. Dr. Pearce smiled.

"So much for a theoretical overview, Kathy. I'm sure your head is spinning. What I can do now is explain how we used this structure and especially how it explains visual signs. We can make the applicability of the system tangible that way."

"At this point, Dr. Pearce, that might be a good idea." Kathy sipped her beer.

"Ok. To see how the functional web works, consider the issue from the point of view of someone who is making a mark. Let us assume a definite purpose. You want to make a sign outside your barber shop that indicates that you will cut people's hair.

"Now the first thing that might occur to you would be to show a picture of someone getting a haircut. You could, for instance, take a snapshot of someone getting a haircut and use the photo as your shop sign. The photograph is a concrete representation of a haircut.

"Further reflection dissuades you from using the photograph. There are two reasons why a photograph might not be the best sign. One is that you'd like to use your sign as a logo: that is, as a visual device that can stand always for your shop even though it be seen in different situations. Sometimes those situations will call for it to be reproduced in black and white on a small card or advertisement, so it cannot contain so much detail that it can't be reproducible. These concerns who an awareness of practice. The second reason why a photographic depiction may not be suitable is that while it is a depiction of the shop's activity, but it is somehow too specific. it shows one patron, a middle aged man, getting a haircut at a particular time. You want to your shop sign to stand for haircuts in a more general way. So somehow you must focus more on what happens and less on who it happens to. For instance, you maynot want your sign to be depicting a man or a woman, but be inclusive of both sexes. These concerns reveal awareness of other pragmatic effects such as potential implications and associations of the image.

"So you think, 'I'll try to reduce the matter to its essentials and in a way that is very versatile in how it is reproduced'. Perhaps a simple line drawing depicting the hair itself being cut will be successful. How about this? (figure 8) Immediately you see that in doing this drawing, you are going to be depicting not only an activity but also the tools that make the activity possible. How should they be portrayed? For instance, you might draw a very accurate representation of scissors. How exact should the drawing be?

A simplified drawing has the advantage of less detail which translates into easier reproduction, but a more precise rendering can better depict the kind that barbers use. However, the scissors by themselves do not necessarily imply the cutting of hair. This may be a shop that manufactures scissors. To really show the action of barbering, one must be more direct. Adding a comb and strands of hair being snipped is a way to achieve a more exact representation of barbering (figure 9). Unfortunately, the region where the snipping is happening is a very small subset of this picture. One must look rather carefully to see the hair actually being cut. If this mark where used at a small size, foreseeing a problem with practice, it might prove difficult to see the important information."

Kathy looked skeptical. "Yeah, but maybe there is a way to isolate the hair clipping action itself and make that the mark. Just zoom in."

"Gotcha covered, Kathy, and again a good observation (figure 10). When that is done, you gain the advantage of being able to use the mark in a greater variety of sizes but you lose a clear depiction of what is happening. For the scissors and comb to read as such, they must be shown almost in their entirety. They are a gestalt configuration. Only when the scissors and comb read well does the hair look like anything other than limp noodles!"

"Let's pause here to look at what is happening. In visual sign systems, there is an infinite number of increments in which things can be zoomed into or zoomed out of. This zooming can occur, ad hoc so to speak, during the viewing, when the viewer's attention is drawn from the whole composition to a detail, or from a detail to the whole. These details, while acting as subtle features to the whole configuration, can have complete and independent meaning when considered in isolation. So there is a bundling, a non-linear bundling I might add, to the visual scene. That non-linear bundling will become an issue in work with visual language, but we need to defer that problem for now.

"Ok, back to the barber sign. Amazingly, if I take the strands of hair away, leaving only the comb and scissors, I have perhaps a more successful sign (figure 11). Notice how I have adjusted the positioning of the objects in deference to formal intuition. Now we say that the scissors and comb work better for the barber sign without including hair, but in making that statement, I actually make a leap of faith that my audience will have experienced these two objects as a combination only in the context of a barber shop. So I actually tap into the associational aspects of these objects here to some extent. The sign vehicle is concrete in the depiction of the objects, but it is depending somewhat on connoatational relationships to work as a barber sign.

"The thing to notice, Kathy, as I try these different strategies, what I'm doing is moving between the four classes in subtle ways. Sometimes the moves are not so subtle. Watch this. Let's say that we go back to the concern about the photograph looking too specific. We take that as a point of departure to try to make a sign that does not portray a gender specific person. To do that, we might start with a concern with basic geometrical shapes (figure 12).

"A head is basically circle, hair stringy tendrils that emerge from the head. Perhaps it is necessary for the head to have eyes and mouth which as a configuration produce a face. Yet there is no way of knowing if it is a man or woman, young or old face. The formal relationships may well become predominant now: the proportion of masses, the compatibility of weights, the sense of balance. As the sign gets more abstract, that is, distanced from a concrete depiction, geometrical features become emphasized above all else.

"Yet, even here it is not clear that the hair is to be cut. So somehow there must be an act of cutting. We introduce elements that when combined with the others elements will be interpreted as scissors. We try to show, perhaps, the strands of hair being separated by something sharp. Still, despite the nod to concreteness that these moves represent, the formal direction remains central in the decisions to relate the geometries to each other rather than to their 'realistic' selves.

"But Doctor Pearce, this so-called 'abstract' shop sign looks silly. I mean, I wouldn't go there for the simple reason that they don't look professional. It reminds me of a smiley face or some such thing. Is this a 'kids only' shop?"

"Exactly, Kathy. What you've noticed is that the *tone* of the shop sign is all wrong. It's not so much that the forms are ugly in and of themselves (innate or free beauty!) but that when they are used in this context, for this message, they are simply sending the wrong *attitudinal* message. Your past experience has taught you to associate these kinds of simplistic minimal signs with things like children's events or, in another context, airport and international traffic symbols. So when these forms are used for something like a haircutter, they seem out of place and funny. You are classifying them, on the basis of former associations, into inappropriate categories of the culture.

"So perhaps we can achieve some sort of compromise if we try to express the appropriate attitude of the shop. This is where a great deal of research time must be spent. If the shop is striving for a stylish clientele, it had better do its homework and find out what kinds of things its stylish clientele are seeing. In other words, it is important to move into the stylistic and associational modes that will convey the appropriate tone. The connotations that will be conveyed, regardless of whether the sign is successful at depicting haircutting, are just as important to the success of the mark as any other factor.

"And underlying this whole discussion in a way that is so subtle as to seem self-evident, is that the sign has to reproduce as the sign.  Black on black might be difficult to read at night.  Even though these aspects have been only dealt with in passing, they are crucial and cannot be forgotten without the possibility of compromising the entire communicative effectiveness of the sign.  Those considerations are the domain of Practice.

"Finally, Kathy, let's take one more example of a barber's sign.  Barbers have long been represented by a red and white striped pole.  The red stripes stand for blood, but fortunately that fact is not in the consciousness of most of the people who see the barber's pole today!  The pole is a purely symbolic, ideographic, object.  It represents barbers strictly through agreement:  there certainly is nothing about the work of the modern barber that is displayed, pictured, or portrayed in the striped pole.  Instead the pole becomes, like a name, a kind of visual label that people have to learn.  But once learned, ideographs such as the barber's pole become very effective identifiers.  So if we draw a striped pole, we should be able to represent 'barber' fairly well (figure 13).

"Even here, working primarily within the symbolic arena, there are aspects of all four classes of the functional web.  Notice how difficult it is to draw a striped pole.  It is not enough to draw a pole, or a pole with 'flat' stripes: the pole simply doesn't appear to be round.  It must read as a cylinder in order for it to function.  So there is the element of concreteness in the pole looking like a pole and the stripes looking like stripes that are truly on the pole.  There is also the issue of how much detail can be included — a practice issue — and there is the issue of formal relationships of the elements as they are constructed on the pole.  When these things come together in an appropriate blend, one has a good sign for barber.  It would be a great shop sign except that it is completely generic, standing for all barbers, which makes this particular barber shop seem unremarkable and nameless.  But I will come to the concern with language soon.

"Now with that background, you can understand how we are able to produce the experiences in the semiotic theater.  Our early experiments simply tried to create the experience of seeing something.  What that entailed was making a coherent figure stand out from a background.  Then we moved to the experience of remembering something.  That allowed us to be able to have a thing be identified and also allowed us to have a subject reflect upon the object's purpose and past experiences with the object.  What we do, you see, is create for you an entire life-background, called the apperceptive mass, which you draw upon for making connections, connotations, symbolic metaphors, even having an understanding of self.  That's why you could be a middle aged man in your experience and not even find it strange.  You'd never been anything else, because the 'you' of the experience was a construction.

"What we are working on now, and it figured prominently in your experience, is a particular category of signs known as marks. We don't mean to say 'marked' as in Jakobson's theory where certain aspects of a system are distinguished by some special treatment. Instead we mean to use the word *mark* as a noun more closely to the sense Goodman gives it. Goodman, in *Languages of Art*, speaks of notational systems. Notational systems have certain requirements. One is that they invariably are composed of discrete units he calls 'characters'. A character is a position within the notational system such that any token character may be substituted for any other token character without changing the syntactic relevance of the message[7]. Goodman's mark is a particular version of the character operating in the use of the notational system. For example, the first letter of the alphabet is a character within the notational system of the English language. This mark—**a**—operates within that system. Substitute that mark for any other letter 'a' in this page and you still have a readable English sentence.

We wanted to begin with such a notion of mark, but we saw also its limitations. For example, the place where a change in the shape of the 'a' causes it not be an 'a' any longer is never clear. And how about changing its position on the line of writing? Moving it above or below the word it 'belongs' to? Is the line of writing (an invisible thing) also a mark of some kind since it is necessary for the syntax of the sentence? We felt our functional web could explain the way these things operated quite well, but we needed to investigate the slippery quality of marks in more detail.

"We decided in the end to use the term *mark* whenever two conditions were satisfied: a visual configuration that is separated as a figure against its visual background, and secondly, such a figure which proceeds to call attention to its mode of production. A mark is the trace that remains once an action has departed. In the case of a projected mark, it is a trace of a distant interaction. In either event, when you see the figure as a record, trace, or evidence, it becomes a mark. In your semiotic theater experience, we planted three particular marks. The first is the shadow of the trees projected onto the curtains of the room. When you became aware of that clear image — when you distinguished it clearly from its background, a function of aspects of the class of 'practice' — you immediately thought of the trees as existing 'out there' and of the condition of sunlight that projects their image. This referencing to the mode of production is indexical: it points to the means of production as an environmental performance. It will tend to activate the indexically controlled classes — the form, attitude, the environmental conditions of practice.

"The photograph is a second mark. It is a special case because it is also a concrete image. What happened was that you saw it as a photograph first. Seeing it 'as a photograph' is seeing it as a recorded mark, a documentation of light playing across a surface of a subject. You immediately realized that the photography was 'taken' in a certain time and place. You realized it was not your mother, but was a photograph of her. That awareness, an indexically profuse function, was the awareness of it as a mark. But you went beyond that experience and into a concrete one. In the concrete function, you see your mother. That moment involved the switching to a pragmatic function, attaining meaning for you based upon your connection with the sign, in this case, your memories of your mother. It triggered those other classes of functions that are activated by the pragmatic domain, for instance, allusions to the way your mother was in her youth. The photograph begins to be symbolic of your mother in the sense that it represents a pleasant life if she smiles or seems otherwise well-off by her mode of dress etc.

"The third mark in your experience was the handwritten letter. Here the inscriptional marks were working in a very Goodmanian sense, acting as characters in a language notational system. And yet from our perspective, what made them marks was not their articulate linguistic presence, but their articulate physical presence. They were clearly seen as figures against the background of the paper and they also carried a strong indexical reference by causing you to reflect that they were written down. The indexical power of inscriptions is especially strong in handwriting, as opposed to typography for example, because it is so rich in the information it provides about the state of mind of the writer. You noticed these things as you considered the form of the writing. And then you continued to decipher the verbal message in the writing. This is a parallel process to what happened in the photograph in that the written letter became, in a sense, concrete at that stage. It seems to drop away as record and becomes all subject. The identification and awareness of the verbal content is concrete. The attitudinal function, including all the suggestive implications that spin you outwards to other associations, memories, symbolisms and stylistic modes is brought into play as well.

"That letter from Henry's mother was the last thing you noticed in your semiotic theater experience. We wanted to make it final in the sequence because it happens to bring us back to the questions of aesthetics that grounded our semiotic theater project. Kathy, you mentioned that your hobby is calligraphy, is that right?"

"Yes, Dr. Pearce, I've always enjoyed it. I like the feeling calligraphy gives me when the rhythms of the writing are happening just right. I lose track of time sometimes and get really lost in the forms and textures."

"Well that sense of getting lost in the physical and mentally focused act of writing is what Csikszentmihalyi calls 'flow' and what others have called the zone, or chi. It is a hallmark of the aesthetic experience and it is what Csikszentmihalyi calls the experiential structure of the aesthetic experience as opposed to its cognitive content. This is a universal feeling and is also common to religious practices, trance states, and meditation practice.

"One thing that the semiotic theater has shown us is the way in which aesthetics flows seamlessly through all experience, but can become heightened in certain situations. And one of the most intriguing of those situations is to be found in the art, long underappreciated in the West, of calligraphy.

"You see, it is precisely because letterforms are 'supposed' to be characters in a verbal system that they are charged with especially strong powers to surprise when their role as mark becomes exaggerated. What happens when you have a drawing that you think might be a sentence? You struggle to read it. As you do, the word meanings begin to operate on a completely different level than the physicality of the marks. We are used to seeing our typography tamed, acting as a servant to our words. The struggle for supremacy between visual mark and word is always bitter. If the writing becomes 'uppity' in its excursions into pure formal explorations, the reader begins to get uncomfortable. This desire to read is much like the desire to see representational images in 'abstract' art, or in clouds, but is more insistent. What happens if the calligrapher decides to hide, obscure, contradict, or otherwise counter the power of the word through effervescent form? The tension is amplified, the markness — the symbolic, physical, indexical form — is emphasized, and the relation between word and mark becomes heightened.

"Jakobson and Eco talked about the poetic or aesthetic function of signs as consisting in just this sort of referencing back to the 'matter' of the sign vehicle[8]. The point is not that the artwork fails to tap the other functional classes, but by the unusually strong emphasis placed on the form, the entire experience becomes heightened, attention returns repeatedly to the materiality of the sign and it becomes what is known as an object of contemplation.

"I've brought some examples to illustrate this power. Let me show you how our model explains what is happening in the following sequence of calligraphic marks. The first is a completely illegible mark (figure 14). Letters have been written, each one legibly on its own terms, but they occupy the same space on the page. The second remains illegible, too (figure 15). Pairs of words occupy the same space in four different groupings. The third has emerging legibility (figure 16), but it is a struggle. The fourth is legible (figure 17) as is the fifth (figure 18), rendered typographically. As you might have guessed, they all use as a text the same excerpt from the Huang Hse poem, *Cold Mountain*. In this series you can see the movement from pure form, what one might call expressive or abstract art, toward verbal text. You experience the difference between looking and reading, which, for most of us happens somewhere around version number three or four and is complete by version five.

"For visual marks such as these, the power of semiotics to explain the manner in which they are interpreted is immense. We think the semiotic theater is an ample demonstration of those powers. What we have achieved in this latest semiotic theater event is to assemble important thoughts from semioticians, and, based on questions arising from aesthetics, woven them into a network of relations. That has allowed us to construct these experiences into a gestaltish whole — with the help of recent advances in nano-biotechnology of course. We have tried to understand how semiotic ideas might be applied to visual signs, and in particular to those kinds of signs that we have called marks: visual signs that clearly project from the background and come to us as records or give explicit evidence of their production.

"From here our work on the Semiotic Theater will necessarily divide. Some of us will devote time to the study of the representational concrete image. But I intend to look more closely at the scriptographic mark: typography and calligraphy. Much remains to be discovered in that area."

Dr. Pearce picked up the papers, now a small stack, from the table. She clicked them twice on the table top to align them neatly, and returned them to her briefcase. Kathy picked up her coat, thanking Dr. Pearce as she picked up the tab. As they stepped to the door of the Acorn, saying their goodbyes in the early gathering dusk, a beam of sunlight projected a pattern of shorn trees on the Acorn's white shop sign.

*Editor's note: "Figures" referred to in text follow, on pages 147-157.*

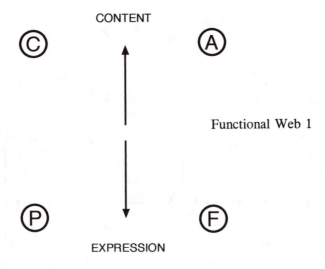

Functional Web 1

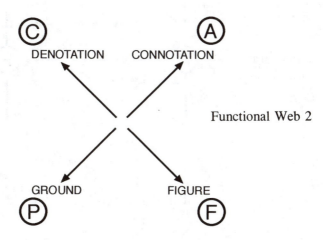

Functional Web 2

*Figures 1 & 2*

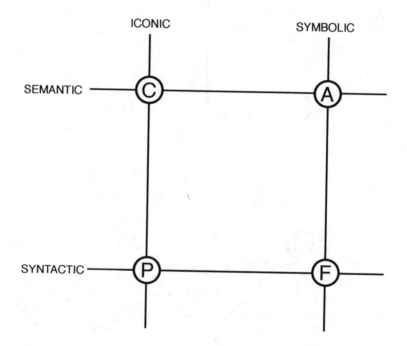

Functional Web 3

*Figure 3*

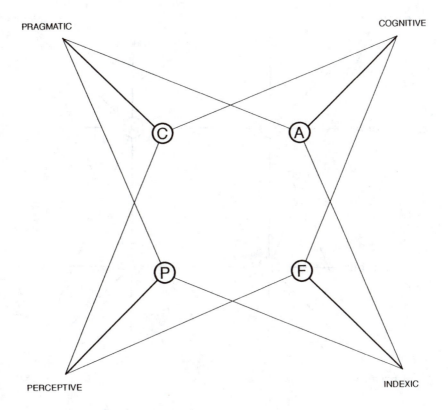

Functional Web 4

*Figure 4*

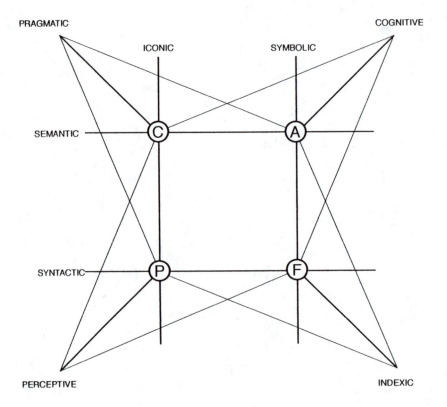

Functional Web 5

*Figure 5*

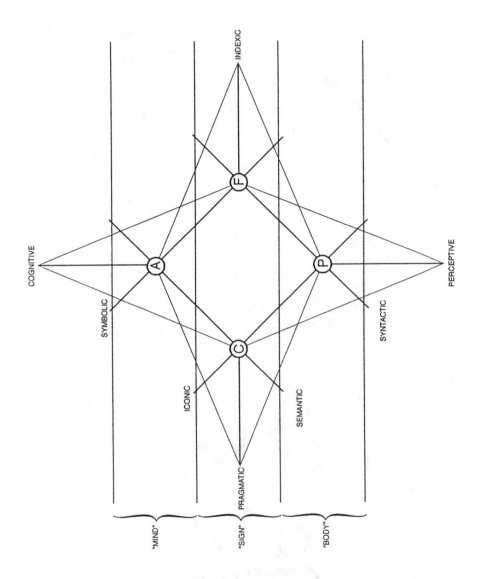

Functional Web 6

*Figure 6*

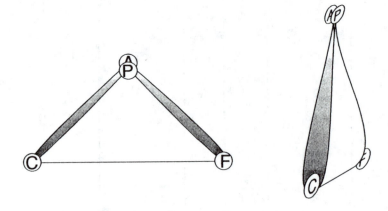

Functional Web 7

*Figure 7*

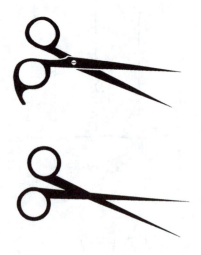

*Figure 8*

*Figure 9*

*Figure 10*

*Figure 11*

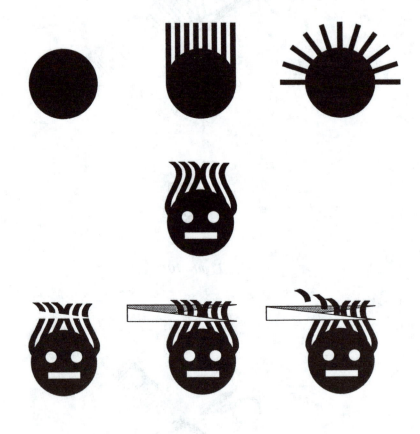

*Figure 12*

*Figure 13*

*Figure 14*                                        *Figure 15*

My heart
is not
the same
as yours.

*Figures 16, 17, 18*

* *Steven Skaggs is Professor of Design at the University of Louisville.*

## NOTES

1. See Sheppard for a concise overview of the major lines of aesthetic inquiry. Sparschott offers a more detailed discussion.
2. For a full discussion of Witelo and Aquinas, see Eco, 1986.
3. Witelo. *De Perspectiva*, quoted in Eco: *Art and Beauty in the Middle Ages*, page 69.
4. *Comm. de Anima I I*, 9, 144. Quoted in Eco: *Art and Beauty in the middle Ages*, page 77.
5. *Summa Theologiae* I, 91, 3. Quoted in Eco: Art and Beauty, page 78.
6. See the discussion of *priem ostrennenja* "the device of making strange" in Eco's *Theory of Semiotics*, page 264.
7. Goodman, *Languages of Art*, page 131.
8. See the discussion in Eco's Theory of Semiotics regarding the production of the sign vehicle. Especially noteworthy is the discussion on pages 262 to 276. The "matter of the sign-vehicle" is discussed on page 266.

## REFERENCES

Arnheim, Rudolf, 1954, *Art and Visual Perception: A Psychology of the Creative Eye*. Berkeley: University of California Press.

-----, 1969. *Visual Thinking*. Berkeley: University of California Press.

Barthes, Roland, 1977, *Image, Music, Text*. Translated by Stephen Heath. New York: Hill and Wang.

Clynes, Manfred, 1977, *Sentics: The Touch of Emotions*. New York: Doubleday.

Collingwood, R.G., 1938, *The Principles of Art*. London: Oxford University Press.

Croce, Benedetto, 1921/1983, *Guide to Aesthetics*. Lantham, Maryland.

Csikszentmihalyi, Mihaly and Rick E. Robinson, 1990, *The Art of Seeing: an Interpretation of the Aesthetic Encounter*. Malibu: Getty Center/Getty Museum.

Csikszentmihalyi, Mihaly, 1990, *Flow: The Psychology of Optimal Experience*. New York: Harper and Row.

Eco, Umberto, 1976, *A Theory of Semiotics*. Bloomington: Indiana University Press.

-----, 1984, *Semiotics and the Philosophy of Language*. Bloomington: Indiana University Press.

Eco, Umberto, 1986, *Art and Beauty in the Middle Ages*. New Haven. Yale University Press.

Goodman, Nelson, 1976, *Languages of Art: An Approach to a Theory of Symbols*. Indianapolis: Hackett.

Hjelmslev, Louis, 1943/1961, *Prolegomena to a Theory of Language*. Madison: University of Wisconson.

Kant, Immanuel, 1790/1952, *Critique of Aesthetic Judgement*. Translated by J.C. Meredith, Oxford University Press.

Kress, Gunther and Theo Van Leeuwen, 1995, *Reading Images: The Grammar of Vusual Design*. New York: Routledge.

Kuhn, Thomas, 1970, *The Structure of Scientific Revolutions*. Chicago: University of Chicago Press.

Langer, Suzanne, 1953, *Feeling and Form*. 1957. *Philosophy in a New Key*. Cambridge, Harvard University Press.

Mandoki, Katya, 1994, *Prosaica: Introduction de la Estetica de lo Cotidiano*. Mexico: Grijalbo.

Moles, Abraham, 1966, *Information Theory and Aesthetic Perception*, translated by Joel E. Cohen. Urbana: University of Illinois Press.

Morris, Charles William, 1955, *Signs, Language and Behavior*. New York: Braziller.

Peirce, Charles Sanders, 1931-1958, *Collected Papers of Charles Sanders Peirce*. Edited by Charles Hartshorne, Paul Weiss, and Arthur Burks. Cambridge: Harvard University Press.

Saint-Martin, Fernande, 1990, *Semiotics of Visual Language*. Bloomington: Indiana University Press.

Salen, Katie and Steven Skaggs, editors, 1998, *Zed.4 - Semiotics: Pedagogy and Practice*. Richmond. Center for Design Studies.

de Saussure, Ferdinand, 1959, *Course in General Linguistics*. Edited by Charles Bally and Albert Sechehaye, translated by Wade Baskin. New York: Philosophical Library.

Searle, John, 1969, *Speech Acts*. London: Cambridge University Press.

Sparschott, Francis, 1982, *The Theory of the Arts*. Princeton: Princeton University Press.

Sonesson, Goran, 1989, *Pictorial Concepts*. Lund: Lund University Press.

Sheppard, Anne, 1987, *Aesthetics*. Oxford: Oxford University Press.

Tolstoy, Leo, 1898/1960, *What Is Art?* Translated by A. Maude. Indianapolis: Bobbs-Merrill.

Williamson, Judith, 1994, *Decoding Advertising: Ideology and Meaning in Advertising*. Marion Boyars.

*Editor's note: All graphics originate with the author.*

# Chapter 10

# The Narrative of Architectural Semiotics

Shelagh Lindsey*
and Jerzy Wojtowicz*

## I

In the early seventies *Meaning in Architecture*, (Jencks, Baird, 1969), began to circulate in Schools of Architecture and ideas from the several papers were entering courses in architectural theory. Soon concepts were evident which defined *architectural* semiotics within semiotics generally. Through conferences, personal contact, correspondence, research, articles, and texts, a group of individuals, many of whom are now members of the International Association for the Semiotics of Space (IASS), have been pursuing a direction which has consistently focused on a particular set of issues. Including architectural codes, order and composition, identification of the *parti*, building analysis, and computational architectural syntax, architectural theory and practice. The work on architectural syntax of archeological sites and ruins for example had its beginning with the work of Donald Preziosi. The current direction has its ancestry in the initial work first assembled in the book edited by Jencks and Baird. My intention is to trace the formation of the current direction. There is no text which presents the early history of semiotic thinking in architecture. John Deely in *Introducing Semiotic, Its History and Doctrine,* (1982) traces the epistemological and metaphysical roots of semiotics. There is the possibility that the indirect influence of semiotic ideas would be evident in some architectural writing and design. Semiotics as a method and theory which enhances our understanding of architectural meaning, representation, and cultural expression had its *contemporary* beginning in the pioneering *Meaning in Architecture*. Among the contributors who continued to work in the area are Geoffrey Broadbent, Christian Norberg-Schulz and Alan Colquhoun. Broadbent not only had a paper in the book, but in the first section, he comments on the text. Broadbent was instrumental is bringing together at Portsmouth Polytechnic in the seventies a group of semioticians from abroad who were able to continue their work while in England. Among them are Juan Pablo Bonta, Tomas Llorens, and those who initiated school at Ulm.

From the identification of issues in architectural semiotics, some of which were identified in the Jencks and Baird volume, those that have continued to direct the discipline are composition and order, syntax, and reconstruction of built form from archeological remains in situ.   To follow narrative of architectural semiotics requires that the literature be approached as a fabric of efforts to formulate a sound methodological base and identify with some rigor the terms to be used and their meaning.

## II

Several questions emerged that would help to focus the subject to the present.
1. The possibility of the semiotic analysis of particular buildings to reveal meaning.
2. How this might be done and at what level — semantic, pragmatic, syntactic, (cf. Morris Charles, 1955).
3. What aspects of meaning are receptive to *objective* analysis?
   Legibility and imageability,
   instrumentality and functionality,
   tropes,
   historical and cultural representation
4. Should the main focus be upon architectural composition and order?
5. Could the discipline contribute to the relationship between the behavioral sciences and architectural space and functionality?
6. The possible overlap between architectural semiotics and other subject areas like geography and psychology.
7. Does semiotics have a continuing relevance to architectural theory?

Not until well-grounded research was conducted were the issues sufficiently clear except to indicate that order and composition would be fundamental to the contribution semiotics was to make to architectural understanding.

During congresses:  International Association of Semiotic and Structural Studies (IASSS), meetings: Semiotic Society of America (SSA), International Association for the Semiotics of Space (IASS), those who were developing architectural semiotics perceived themselves to be in the main stream of semiotic thinking but gradually found mutual interests.  At these functions, special efforts were made to identify research questions and possible methods to address them.  The proceedings of both IASSS, SSA, and IASS include either the full papers of abstracts of the presentations in the field.

Martin Krampen was one of the first to conduct methodologically and theoretically well-grounded research which is both relevant and replicatable using semiotics.  Krampen continues to do imaginative research.  He also has a fine sensibility about responsibility for the natural environment.  With his work, the legitimacy of semiotics for both architecture and urbanism particularly revealed that the discipline could provide insights previously inaccessible. His research includes the interpretation of children's drawings, recognition of building types, architectural connotation, and stylistic issues in semiotics. Krampen is trained in social psychology and his research reflects the value of empirical methods in research on subjects which relate social and behavioral matters to architecture.

Krampen's research interests, while somewhat different from the more formal *architectural* stream, has been seminal because of his refined sense of research and the projects themselves which often have pragmatic implications.

Alexandros Lagopoulos also began work in the field quite early. He continues his research on the *social* and architectural semiotics of settlement patterns. His papers are published primarily in journals so they are not readily available. However, the text he edited with Mark Gottdiener is a collection of seminal papers some of which had not been published in English. Prof. Lagopoulos has been particularly instrumental in bringing those who have an interest in architectural semiotics together. One of the first occasions was a conference, sponsored by the Greek Semiotic Society, on the island of Andros. From these initial contacts the International Association for the Semiotics of Space was formed. Lagopulous and his wife Karin Boklund—Lagopoulos have edited more than one set of conference papers. They have recently completed editing the papers prepared in English for the conference of the Russian Semiotic Society held in St. Petersburg during the summer of 1995. The volume is to be published along with a companion of papers in Russian.

About the same time as Krampen and Lagopoulos were establishing methodological strategies, Preziosi was applying semiological concepts to archeological sites. Starting with *Architecture, Language, and Meaning: the Origins of the "Built World" and its Semiotic Organization*, (Preziosi 1979) his work validated that composition, order, planning, and layout obscured on site by time could be made known. Using an almost poetic and mathematical strategy, Preziosi devised a method for identifying the order and structure of buildings at archeological sites. The strategies were quite productive of insight into architectural meaning. Recent work in computational semiotic analysis by Jerzy Wojtowicz and his students at the School of Architecture, University of British Columbia, Vancouver, Canada, is grounded to a certain extent, in Preziosi's work.

By the late seventies the focus was on not only order and composition, but also on geometry, and the *parti*. During classes in *Meaning in Architecture*, (1979-1995, conducted by the author at the School of Architecture, (University of British Columbia), the students developed strategies for critically analyzing buildings by identifying building elements. With *Analysis of Precedents* (1979) and the subsequent *Precedents in Architecture* (Pause and Clark, 1982) conventions became available for the semiotic analysis of buildings to identify the *parti*: i.e., the basic architectural idea of a building out of which the building is formed.

Irina Sakellaridou, while an undergraduate at the University of Thessalonika, had been trained in building analysis. With her background and the work of Clark and Pause at North Carolina, the importance of the *parti* to architectural meaning was clear.

While a graduate student at the University of British Columbia, Sakellaridou did extensive work on architectural codes. Both as the governing, conventional rules and the themes within a text of different modes governed by the rules, codes have since become a motivating idea for the relevance of semiotics to signification. The process of codification is not unlike Foucault's concept of *episteme* in the history of ideas: a rich and persuasive concept around which other ideas cluster and are structured. Codes, composition, and *parti*, as the key characteristics of an architectural semiotic, fostered also theoretical connections with literary theory. In fact, semiotics and architectural semiotics have been enriched by substantive overlaps with other subjects too.

Geographers Trevor Barnes, at the University of British Columbia, and James Duncan, Emmanuel College, Cambridge, have both interpreted particular geographic spaces from a textual perspective. Duncan in his work on the ancient and sacred city of Kandy in Sri Lanka adopted a textual method to understand the mapping of cosmological ideas onto the landscape. The adoption of intertextuality in landscape interpretation for example, continues to enrich our understanding of the hegemony of ideology as represented both in urban plans and on the landscape (cf. Lindsey, 1994, 555-566). Literary theory, especially textuality and narrativity are likely to be an ongoing direction in architectural semiotics.

Two main directions are motivating current work: the signification of buildings through the revelatory power of composition and the *parti* (Sakellaridou 1994) and computational analysis (Wojtowicz) and a group of students at the University of British Columbia.

Precursor to Sakellaridou's work is that of George Stiny. As early as 1980, Stiny was developing the ideas which would make possible the adoption of the terms to test architectural syntax. In his paper, "Introduction to Shape and Shape Grammars" (1980) and one of his subsequent papers, "Computing with Form and Meaning in Architecture" (1985) he laid the ground work for architectural syntactics which accepted architecture as an analyzable sign set.

In her doctoral dissertation "*A Top-Down Analytic Approach to Architectural Composition*" (1994) Sakellaridou *formally* and *empirically* analyzed 19 houses by Mario Botta, to establish that the identification of the process and product of architectural composition and *parti* communicates meaning and signification. Her work is characterized by a rigor which helps to legitimate architectural semiotics to understand the production and meaning of built form.  Sakellaridou was doing her doctoral work with Professor Bill Hillier at the Bartlett School of Design, University of London about the same time as Wojtowicz and his students were refining computational methods for the formation of an architectural syntax.

They were working toward showing the relationship between syntactics and signification to *reconstruct* archeological sites and remains by applying the grammars to existing material in situ.  Their work is likely to have a lasting effect on the field because of the rigor introduced by the computer into the formation of the terms and rules for an architectural grammar.

Elzbieta Zielinska (see for example www.architecture,ubc.ca), for example, not only produced a grammar based on Stiny's work, but also tested it on the remains of several medieval Silesian castles in Poland.  She was able to present visual representations of the buildings which were authenticated from other sources primarily archival.  The strength of her work is the reliability of the computational strategies to reconstruct the form of the castles.  For her, the most important reasons for introducing the computer was to demonstrate its applicability to adopt replicatable shape grammars.  Computational tools "allow for an easy and flexible manipulation of objects and parts in digital space."  Through various configurations and the constraints of the grammatical rules tests could be made from which a selection could be made from which to choose the appropriate one for castle reconstruction.

Another student, Antoineta G. Rivera, using a diverse number of sources has issued a CD on which she has reconstructed the ancient Aztec city now located in the centre of Mexico City: *The TeoCalli of Tenochtitlan: a Digital interpretation of the Aztec Ceremonial Precinct.*  Tenochtitlan was the religious and political centre of the Aztec Empire.  Rivera's digital reconstruction is based on historical, iconographical, and archeological materials.  Digital models were constructed by taking into consideration aechaeoastronomical principles bad and measuring systems. (cf Notes for CD — ROM0, 1996).  Through her understanding of these principles, Rivera was able to show convincingly what remains could be expected to be found on the ceremonial route from the main temple.

My narrative for architectural semiotics is somewhat personal.  However, a careful reading of the sources and through research of your own, the scope of architectural semiotics, past, present, and future is available.  The directions that can be anticipated are likely to include not only architectural syntax and its contribution to meaning and cultural representation but also further interdisciplinary work which pursues the mapping of geographical space, intertextuality, and ideology.

*\*Shelagh Lindsey is now a retired member of the faculty of the School of Architecture at the University of British Columbia.  Jerzy Wojtowicz is at present teaching at the School of Architecture at the University of British Columbia.*

*Editors note:  The "annotated bibliography" is provided by Shelagh Lindsey as alternative to the selected references used elsewhere in this volume.*

## ANNOTATED BIBLIOGRAPHY

A collection of papers edited by geographers which illustrates interdisciplinary work which overlaps with semiotics:

Bonta, Juan Pablo, 1979, *Architecture and its interpretation, a study of expressive systems in Architecture*, New York: Rizzoli.

A definitive study of meaning and architectural history.

Broadbent, Geoffrey, Richard Bunt, Tomas Llorens, 1980, *Meaning and Behavior in the Built Environment*, Chichester, England: J. Wiley.

Broadbent, Geoffrey, Charles Jencks, and Richard Bunt, 1980, eds., *Signs, Symbols, and Architecture,* Great Britain: John Wiley and Sons.

These two collections remain among the main sources for work on the architectural semiotics and related subjects from an historical and practical.

Barnes, Trevor J., and James S. Duncan, 1992, eds., *Writing Worlds: Discourse, Text and Metaphor in the representation of Landscape,* London, New York: Routledge.

Approach.

Clark, Roger H., and Michael Pause, and twenty students of the School of Design, 1979, Kevin Utsey, ed., *Analysis of Precedent: an investigation of elements, relationships, and ordering ideas in the work of eight architects,* Raleigh, N.C., 1982 Printing: North Carolina State University.

An excellent source book to use for the replicatable analysis of buildings.

Deely, John, 1962, *Introducing Semiotic: its History and Doctrine,* with an introduction by Thomas A. Sebeok, Bloomington: Indiana University Press.

Professor Deely interprets semiotic thinking in the history of ideas.

Duncan, James S., 1990, *The City as Text: the Politics of Landscape Interpretation in the Kandyan Kingdom,* Cambridge University Press, Cambridge, New York.

Professor Duncan maps myth, belief, and cosmology onto the landscape in the ancient and holy city of Kandy in Sri Lanka.

Göttdiener, Mark, 1995, *Postmodern Semiotics: material culture and the forms of postmodern life,* Oxford University Press, England.

Göttdiener, Mark and Alexandros Lagopoulos, 1986, *The City and the Sign, and Introduction to Urban Semiotics,* Columbia University Press, New York.

Professor Göttdiener is primarily a sociologist who places semiotics in the broader context of ideas. The text edited with Professor Lagopoulos includes papers not previously accessible in English.

Hillier, Bill, and J. Hanson, 1984, *The Social Logic of Space,* Cambridge, England: University Press.

Dr. Hillier and his colleagues at the Bartlett School of Design, University of London, contribute to the direction of the discipline through their rigorous methodology and standards of research.

Jencks, Charles, and George Baird, 1969, *Meaning In Architecture,* New York: George Braziller.

The first collection of essays which set out the major issues in the field.

Krampen, Martin, 1979, *Meaning in the Urban Environment,* London: Pion Ltd.

Dr. Krampen has made a canonic contribution to research in semiotics. This book not only presents research results but also has an excellent historical summary and bibliography.

Lagopoulos, Alexandros, and Mark Gottdiener, 1986, eds., *The City and the Sign: an Introduction to Urban Semiotics,* New York: Columbia University Press.

Lindsey, Shelagh and Irina Sakellaridou, 1981, "Architectural Semiotic Analysis, A Demonstration," in John Deely, and M. Lenhart (eds.) *Semiotics,* New York: Plenum, 383-387.

> Grounded in the studies Dr. Sakellaridou did as an undergraduate at the University of Thessalonika, this paper begins to establish the critical merit of semiotic analysis for built form.  At the time Lindsey was a faculty member in the School of Architecture, Vancouver, Canada: University of British Columbia.

Lindsey, Shelagh, 1994, "*Conflit ideologique dans la representation cartographique*", 555-566, *Figures Architecturales Formes Urbaines, Actes du congres de Geneve de l"Association Internationale de semiotique de l"espace, Antropos.*

> In this paper, Lindsey attempts to demonstrate how semiotic analysis can reveal the representation of ideology in urban plans.

Preziosi, Donald, 1983, *Minoan Architectural Design:  Formation and Signification,* New York and Berlin: Mouton.

> In this volume, Dr. Preziosi, Professor of Fine Arts at the University of Southern California, Los Angeles, elaborates the merit of semiotics for the reconstruction of ruins.

Preziosi, Donald, 1979, *The Semiotics of the Built Environment, An Introduction to Architectonic Analysis,* Bloomington, Indiana: Indiana University Press.

> A canonic book especially for undergraduates identifying many of the issues pertinent in the future.

Sakellaridou, Irina, 1982, *Architectural Codes,* (unpublished), M. Arch thesis, University of British Columbia, Vancouver.

> A definitive study of the meaning and function of architectural codes. Her work remains the best study to date of the subject.

Sakellaridou, Irina, 1994, "*A Top—Down, Analytic Approach to Architectural Composition,*" (unpublished) Ph.D., Barlett School of Design, London University.

A critical analysis of 19 houses by Mario Botta which is well illustrated and includes a thorough bibliography. Plans are proceeding to publish the work in French. Dr. Sakellaridou practices architecture in Thessalonika.

Stiny, J, 1980, "Introduction to Shape and Shape Grammars", *Environment and Planning*, B, no 7, 11—34.

-----, 1985, "Computing with Form and Meaning in Architecture", *Journal of Architectural Education*, vol. 39, No 1.

Two of the definitive papers toward computational architectural syntax.

Wojtowicz, Jerzy and W. Fawcett, *Architecture: Formal Approach,* Hong Kong, 1985.

Dr. Wojtowicz and his students at the School of Architecture, University of British Columbia are pioneering the application of semiotic computational methods to built form especially in the reconstruction of archeological sites and the remains of buildings. Two of his students have been forming and testing syntactics on archeological sites.

# Part Four

## *The Spirit of Semiotics*

# Chapter 11

# Cathartic Thinking:
# Tragic Theory from a Semiotic Point of View

Thomas O. Beebee*

## I

Semiotic studies of theater, such as that by Jiri Veltrusky (1977), tend to focus upon the interplay of sign systems in the "*Gesamtkunstwerk*" (total work of art) which the theater can provide. Gesture, dialog, lights, plastic representation, and so on each has a separate semiotic contribution to make to the play, and these systems must be combined with and juxtaposed against each other to provide a theatrical effect. This approach, however, cannot account for our very different responses to tragedy vs. comedy, which make use of the same basic sign systems. "Tragedy" in this paper refers to a form of dramatic representation where events go from bad to worse, resulting usually in the death of the main protagonist and often of other characters as well. It refers only to consciously constructed aesthetic phenomena, and not to real events which sometimes receive the designation of "tragic." If I were to have the space to discuss such real events, my point would be that they are called tragic because they fit the pattern of cathartic thinking established by a theatrical aesthetic system, rather than vice versa.

To discuss tragedy as a semiotic phenomenon, I begin with the most basic semiotic fact on which the major theorists of tragedy, from Aristotle to Artaud, agree: tragedy is a sign vehicle for a unique referent which cannot be communicated through other means. The easiest designation for what this ineffable sign might be is "the tragic," while I will be calling it, for reasons soon to be made clear, "catharsis." But naming such names is not the same as delivering their referent, which possesses a high degree of emotive content. After discussing the status of semiotic investigations into emotions, I will relate those findings to various tragic theories. For some critics, the idea of the "catharsis" has been merely a summary of certain qualities, which may or may not find their way into a particular tragedy and which can also show up in other genres. I will deal with those theorists who associate the particular sign vehicle of theatrical representation with a unique referent not found in other forms of discourse.

My hypothesis is that the referent of "catharsis" is essentially an emotional state, although one to which certain cognitive properties are also referred.

Semiotics, like Western philosophy in general, has paid far more attention to the objective world, and to human cognitive abilities and reason, than to the emotions. Investigations into "catharsis" thus constitute one of the few areas — along with eros and love — where a great deal of attention is devoted to defining an emotional state. As a propaedeutic to this investigation of catharsis, then, we must begin with a general view of the semiotics of emotion.

# II
## The Semiotics of Emotion

In his landmark essay on "Linguistics and Poetics," Roman Jakobson noted the need for semiotics to take account of the coding of emotions: "If we analyze language from the standpoint of the information it carries, we cannot restrict the notion of information to the cognitive aspect of language. A man, using expressive features to indicate his angry or ironic attitude, conveys ostensible information, and evidently this verbal behavior cannot be likened to such nonsemiotic, nutritive activities as 'eating grapefruit,'" (1960:354). Jakobson adds the simple example of the difference between [big] and [bi:g]. The elongation of the vowel conveys an affective relationship between the speaker and the object denoted as "big." The difference in Portuguese between "*mulher*," "*mulherão*," and "*mulherzinha*" is similar. The various endings (literally indicating a woman, big woman, and little woman) often do not denote physical characteristics existing in the world, but the neutrality or various kinds of emotional reaction towards the woman on the part of the speaker. "*Mulherão*" denotes an attractive woman; it is a sign of admiration and desire. "*Mulherzinha*" is often used for one's wife; it is a sign of affection. Jakobson assumes, correctly, that emotional signifieds are just as objective and systematic as any other category. Indeed, he is undoubtedly following the dictum of Louis Hjelmslev, who noted that it was dangerous to establish a theoretical distinction between grammatical and extra-grammatical elements, or between intellectual and emotional uses of language.

In applying these ideas to aesthetic objects, Umberto Eco generalizes Jakobson's idea thus: "even the material consistency of the sign vehicle becomes a field for *further segmentation*" (1979:266). In languages with free word order such as Russian, for example, the choice between several different orderings is not grammatically codified, but may produce different aesthetic effects. Variant spellings or misspellings of the same word in English, normally part of a continuum and not significant ("receive" and "recieve" refer to one concept only), become separate sign vehicles when used in "eye dialect," as by William Faulkner. Eco concludes that in aesthetic discourse "even those features that usually pertain to the continuum and that [therefore] a semiotic approach does not need to consider ... here become semiotically relevant" (1979:266).

The best example of semiotic coding of aesthetic discourse is the Indian theory of *rasa*, developed by Bharata in the sixth century C. E., the classical era of Sanskrit drama. *Rasa* literally means "juice" or "essence," but the translation of its meaning in the realm of aesthetics varies greatly, from "relish" to "emotive aesthetics." The theory of *rasa* is based upon a gamut of nine different emotions which a spectator can experience: eros; the comic; grief; rage; heroism; fear; disgust; wonder; and quietude. The last-named "emotion" is in fact an absence of what we commonly refer to as emotion, and it can only be represented in art negatively, i.e. as the absence of gesture and movement. There are, in addition, thirty-three "transient" emotions, including pity, discouragement, intoxication, pride, indignation, and deliberation. These emotions can be described as less segmented than the stable ones. They can appear together, and generally are provoked only in conjunction with a stable emotion. We note the greater state of flux for these emotions, and hence their lower degree of adabtability to semiotic analysis.

Indian theorists conceived of meaning as a referential relation between the audible word form, or the signifier, and the inaudible, mentally perceived sense or object content — the signified. Unity of meaning is also an important axiom in all Indian theories. Meanings are not confined to the linguistic form alone; they are determined by what are known as the "contextual factors." The limits of the meaning of a sentence are set by the twin criteria of completeness and logical consistency. Literature is defined by its aim rather than by its linguistic form. Literature is a kind of verbal prompting or evocation of moods (Chari 1990:5). Poetic language has the capacity of evocation, a power assumed by words, distinct from their denotative capacity by which the emotions presented in the poem are realized by the reader in a generalized form. Poetic apprehension is a form of feeling response because it induces a repeated contemplation of the object. When an emotion is rendered delectable through a representation of its appropriate conditions in poetry, it attains *rasa*hood. *Rasa* theory would be opposed to a purely cognitive view that argues that poetry is a mode of knowledge and contemplated as a pattern of knowledge and that valid cognitive knowledge rather than emotional experience is the proper aim and mode of existence of poetry. In the West, poetry has been set up as a rival to science. For *rasa*, poetry mirrors the psychic states that are already known to us and dramatizes them or presents them as something experienced — a type of recognitive knowledge, because it most generally presents what we have already known before but would like to experience again.

In addition, *Rasa* theory posits that the emotional "reading" of an aesthetic object is segmented and not continuous: one does not feel more or less eros, but simply its presence or non-presence. Two concordant emotions may be present at the same time: the comic may combine with eros and rage; quietude with wonder; and grief with fear — the latter combination reminding us of the fear and pity of Aristotle's poetics. If discordant emotions are present and not dealt with by directing them onto different objects or having them presented by different characters, then one will dominate: disgust and wonder produce only disgust; and love and fear produce only fear. This segmentation of the emotional field allows the linking of particular sign-vehicles to particular emotions.

Finally, it is worth emphasizing that the *rasa* felt by the audience of an artwork is aesthetic in nature. There is such a thing, in other words, as fictional fear, fictional eros, and so on, which are not to be confused with their real counterparts. *Rasa* theorists see no harm in admitting that poetic presentations, being emotive statements, can and do also arouse feeling responses in the readers and that these responses are felt as a vibration in the consciousness. The poet, text, and reader are all bound together in a common matrix. This assumption is vital to any conception of emotive aesthetics — affective reference.

That *rasa* is produced as a sign function is evident from the commentators' agreement that it resides in the spectator rather than in either the artwork or its producer (*Rasa* 1986:25). Considering the three possibilities, we perceive a classic case of the semiotic triangle, in which interpreter, interpretans, and interpretandum are equally responsible for the functioning of the sign. Without the correct interpretation on the part of the spectator, *rasa* cannot be achieved, just as a sign is always something representing something else *for* someone (or something) else.

When one compares *rasa* with Western theories of responses to drama, the simplicity and conceptual poverty of the latter immediately become apparent. The gamut of emotions catalogued by the Indians begin as just one: the tragic. The notions of the comic and of the sublime are added later. On the other hand, while "the comic" appears in both systems, "catharsis" is nowhere to be found in the Indian system. This stems in part from the theory's rootedness in the practice of Indian drama, which did not produce tragedies (as opposed to certain types of Japanese *noh*, which seem quite similar to Greek tragedies). In attempting to reconcile the two approaches, Chari reads the tragic as the *rasa* fear subordinated to pity (1990:70). In any case, the absence of a tragic emotion suggests that "catharsis" is a referent emotion produced by the genre of tragedy and not found in any other context.

# III
## Aristotle and Catharsis

The last section ended with the suggestion that "catharsis" is a referent produced by the genre of tragedy and not found in any other context. An examination of the earliest treatise on tragedy, Aristotle's "Poetics," confirms this linkage in an interesting way: Aristotle makes catharsis the central effect of tragedy, yet does not give the word a definition or explain it further, as though it were a sign produced by tragedy and only comprehensible in that context.

We do not know the precise date of the composition of the "Poetics" (ca. 330 B. C. E.), nor whether Aristotle intended it for publication, or merely as lecture notes. The text which has come down to us is undoubtedly corrupt, and more importantly, much of it is missing. The text was apparently intended to treat, at the very least, all forms of *mimesis* or imitation, including, besides theater, music, dance, epic, painting, and history. Aristotle promises to give a treatment of comedy as extensive as his treatment of tragedy, but this is nowhere to be found. The core of Aristotle's thinking about tragedy (as opposed to other dramatic forms) is contained in the definition he gives the genre in book six:

> A tragedy, then, is the imitation of an action that is serious and also, as having magnitude, complete in itself... [I]n a dramatic, not in a narrative form; with incidents arousing pity and fear, wherewith to accomplish its catharsis of such emotions. (1947:631)

We can imagine that if Aristotle had gone on to write of comedy, it would have shared with tragedy the first part of this definition, except that the action of comedy is not serious. Comedy may have also effected a catharsis, but through ridicule and amusement rather than pity and fear. It is clear that for Aristotle, tragedy's linking of pity and fear to catharsis forms the crux of what the genre is supposed to accomplish. However, he never again mentions catharsis in what has come down to us of the "Poetics"!

Brunius, who supplies a useful brief history of the term "catharsis," states the problem of interpretation succinctly when he points out that "the translation of these last words [pity, fear, catharsis] is difficult not because we do not know the meaning of pity and fear and catharsis but because we do not know how they are related to each other" (1977:265). In true semiotic fashion, the meaning of any term in the triad is dependent upon the meanings of the other two. In addition, before Aristotle "catharsis" did not have, so far as we know, a technical, "lit-crit" meaning such as he apparently wishes to give it here. The word had both a medical meaning (of purging the system) and a religious one (of cleansing or washing away sins), and scholars surmise that Aristotle is using one or the other of them metaphorically. However, our interpretation of catharsis is helped greatly by another passage where Aristotle discusses the term, in book eight of the *Politics*. There catharsis is the product of another mimetic form, namely music. Greek musical theory strongly associated different modes (roughly, musical keys) with different emotions. Socrates had banned certain of these modes from his Republic on the basis of their producing unwanted emotions or being effeminate. "These two modes [Dorian and Phrygian] — a violent one and a voluntary one, which will produce the finest imitation of the sounds of unfortunate and fortunate, moderate and courageous men — leave these" (Plato III.399b, 78) Plato assumes that the music produces in the listener the emotions which it semiotically represents. The result is to further strengthen that emotion, so that a positive feedback loop is created; courage is the referent whose sign is the Phrygian mode, which produces more courage in the listeners. Aristotle accepts the reference theory of the musical modes, while with his notion of catharsis, he seems to be subtly countering his teacher's views on music:

> music should be studied ... with a view to ... purgation [catharsis]....
> In education the most ethical modes are to be preferred, but in listening
> to the performances of others we may admit the modes of action and
> passion also. For feelings such as pity and fear, or, again, enthusiasm,
> exist very strongly in some souls, and have more or less influence over
> all. Some persons fall into a religious frenzy, whom we see as a result
> of the sacred melodies — when they have used the melodies that excite
> the soul to mystic frenzy — restored as though they had found healing
> and purgation. Those who are influenced by pity or fear, and every
> emotional nature, must have a like experience, and others in so far as
> each is susceptible to such emotions, and all are in a manner purged and
> their souls lightened and delighted. (*Politics* 1943, VIII. 7, 335)

The music does not produce, but purges (catharts) the emotions which it represents. Imitative forms arouse emotions in the spectator which, if they were to occur in their raw form, would be dangerous, but which, once experienced in their artistic form, will not recur in their "real" form. Unlike Indian theories of *rasa*, Aristotle does not discuss the possible difference between "fictional" and "real" emotions. (Plato specifically denies a distinction.) He seems to extend the medical notion of catharsis to the realm of the psyche.

Aristotle's discussion of music's ability to achieve catharsis suggests that he meant that the emotions of pity and fear should be experienced by the spectators, who will then experience relief from those emotions. Pity and fear are complementary terms. Presumably incidents of fear alone, such as in slasher movies, will not produce catharsis; nor will an actor emoting on stage and making us pity him, without our being able to see the fearful incidents which have brought him to this. Terrible events linked through a strong plot produce a mixture of fear and pity in the audience. This mix of emotions (which we have seen in Indian *rasa* theory), if we follow Aristotle's reasoning in the *Politics*, acts like a vaccination against the bad effects of these emotions in real life.

To summarize, catharsis appears to be a specific kind of mental process produced only in aesthetic contexts. In one sense, this mental process can be defined as that by which the sign of tragedy is interpreted by the spectator. Its semiotic nature can be summarized in a few points.

Aristotle's concept fulfills Charles Peirce's definition of the sign as having three references. Every sign refers "*to* some thought ... *for* some object ... *in* some respect or quality (Peirce, CP 5.283). Here, pity and fear in their respect of representational events stand for catharsis to the spectator (and not necessarily for the actors or for the characters they portray). Catharsis itself, as an emotion, is "the *material quality* of a mental sign" (Peirce, CP 5.292), but Aristotle does not specify further the *to* and *for* of that sign, though we will see that Nietzsche, Benjamin, and Artaud do. Peirce's notion of the sign as mediation is important here. Unlike Plato, Aristotle does not admit of "emotional infection" in aesthetic contexts. It is the artistic structure of tragedy which produces catharsis. Thus, catharsis is understandable only within an aesthetic sign system.

Neither Aristotle's nor my own explanation of the term can actually produce the sign of catharsis. The system of the modes, or the complex structure of a tragedy are necessary contexts for producing the sign of catharsis. Only tragedy can work catharsis in the spectator. Furthermore, in book six of the *Poetics*, Aristotle notes that tragedy consists of six elements: plot; character; thought; diction; song; and spectacle. These elements must all work together to produce the complex sign-vehicle of catharsis. A rousing march played when Oedipus emerges wtih his eyes gouged out may prevent the communication of catharsis. This sign system of tragedy must be learned; it is not intuitive or natural. Finally, the sign of catharsis seems to be fully segmented. It is all or nothing, present or not present. Aristotle does not seem to feel that one can experience just a little catharsis.

# IV
# Nietzsche and Benjamin:  What the Words Don't Say

Friedrich Nietzsche's (1844-1900) *Geburt der Tragödie aus dem Geiste der Musik* (Birth of Tragedy from the Spirit of Music) shocked his fellow classicists when it appeared in 1872.  Among other of its perceived deviations from scholarly truth, the book did not once mention Aristotle's theory of tragedy.  In its lack of footnotes and Greek quotations, the text differed greatly from standard publications in the field.  Its subsequent rejection by the scholarly community caused Nietzsche to abandon classical studies and become a hermit "philosopher."

Nietzsche deliberately wrote the book in a "popular" manner, because he intended it not as an antiquarian exercise in recovering Greek views of tragedy, but as a quasi-political appeal to the Germans to construct a tragic mythology around which they could orient their lives.  The latter parts of *The Birth of Tragedy* refer to the operas of Richard Wagner as the conceivable basis of such a mythology.  Nietzsche's fundamental intuition was of the phenomenon which Adorno and Horkheimer were to call the "Dialectic of Enlightenment":  ever-increasing rationalizations of life imposed by culture, while they help free humans from necessity, also alienate them from their essential, emotional being.

Nietzsche's proposed solution for what he saw as a consequent alienation and lack of purpose in the bourgeois classes was the use of art — and particularly of the Wagnerian operas — to instill a national myth and tragic sense of life in people.  Only myth and tragedy could enlighten people to the illusory nature of societal values and to their need to look within and create their own values out of a life force which Nietzsche would eventually formulate as the "will-to-power."  Nietzsche's overall goal explains why he felt compelled not only to reject Aristotle, but to avoid mentioning him altogether.  Aristotle himself was a post-Socratic propagator of reason and the dialectic of enlightenment.  In addition, eighteenth-century readings of "catharsis" had "reduced" Aristotle's concept to one of moral refinement and the tragic hero's conversion to societal norms — the exact opposite of what Nietzsche felt tragedy should achieve.

According to his purpose, Nietzsche does not investigate catharsis as an emotional or moral effect on the audience of tragedy, but rather locates the essence of tragedy in a drive, which he terms the Dionysian.  His definition of this drive is carried out through through binary opposition with another which he calls the Apollonian.  Nietzsche associates the Dionysian with certain phenomena such as nature, drunkenness, the disappearance of the ego-principle, and music, while the Apollonian invokes culture, dream, individuation, and poetry.  Nietzsche locates the tragic in the Dionysian, musical portion of tragedy, carried out by the chorus. The Apollonian drive, which emerges as a reaction to the horrors of Dionysian "truth," brings forth the individual actors of tragedy, who are like a dream or illusion of the chorus. Life is only possible in the Apollonian world of illusion: "only as an *aesthetic phenomenon* is existence and the world eternally *justified*" (1974:50).

Music is, in Nietzsche's view, the sign of something primordial whose ceaseless turnings are otherwise unrepresentable:

> By no means is it possible for language adequately to render the cosmic symbolism of music, for the very reason that music stands in symbolic relation to the primordial contradiction [*Urwiderspruch*] and primordial pain [*Urschmerz*] in the heart of the Primordial Unity [*Ur-Einen*], and therefore symbolises a sphere which is before all appearance and phenomena. Rather should we say that all phenomena, compared with [music], are but symbols, (1974:55).

Nietzsche's point here is fundamentally semiotic: humans are never in direct contact with the world's phenomena, which are referred to them through mediatory sign systems such as language. Nietzsche almost seems to except music from this mediatory function. Music, he claims, is not a symbol, but an index of the dark forces of nature within us. An index can be described as a sign that stands for what has produced it. Smoke for fire and animal tracks are commonly used examples. The difference lies in the principle of arbitrariness: unlike language, where any set of sounds could conceivably represent a given concept, the choice of musical sounds to represent emotional states is not arbitrary. His constant evocation of primordial functions denies the possibility of segmentation of the emotions; music symbolises something prior to the emotions: life itself, the bodily pulsions or turning on and off of hormones, as we might explain it today. As opposed to Aristotle and Plato, Nietzsche does not accept the segmentation of musical meaning — Phrygian for heroism, Dorian for misfortune.

Like Aristotle, however, Nietzsche gives the play's actions a far more significant role in catharsis than the diction and thought. The action of tragedy points to a meaning beyond words:

> The heroes of tragedy speak, as it were, more superficially than they act; the myth does not at all find its adequate objectification in the spoken word. The structure of the scenes and the conspicuous images reveal a deeper wisdom than the poet himself can put into words and concepts: the same being also observed in Shakespeare, whose Hamlet, for instance, in an analogous manner talks more superficially than he

acts, so that the previously mentioned lesson of Hamlet is to be gathered not from his words, but from a more profound contemplation and survey of the whole.  (1974:129)

The teaching of Hamlet is given in the gap between his actions and the words which are continually searching for meaning, but there is a further twist: Nietzsche had noted earlier that the chief action of Hamlet was his inaction, which in Nietzsche's interpretation derives from his Dionysian insight into the world as a place of horror and cruelty.  Indeed, Hamlet is the perfect example of Dionysian man:  both figures "have for once seen into the true nature of things — they have perceived, but they are loath to act;  for their action cannot change the eternal nature of things;  they regard it as shameful or ridiculous that one should require of them to set aright the time which is out of joint.   Knowledge kills action, action requires the veil of illusion" (1974:62).  In this sense, the sign of the tragic is doubly displaced: we must take it as whatever in the action serves to complement what the superficial words of the drama convey;  and, at least in the case of Hamlet, we must be prepared to interpret inaction as a highly significant action.

This idea of tragic inaction was taken up by Walter Benjamin (1892-1940) in *Der Ursprung des deutschen Trauerspiels* (The Origin of German Tragic Drama) and turned into a notion of tragic silence.  Agreeing with Nietzsche that tragic thinking has become impossible in a modern world governed by rational and scientific thinking, Benjamin differentiates tragedy proper from tragic drama (*Trauerspiel*) on the basis of the silence vs. the garrulousness of the hero.  Both are dramatic forms with terrible incidents ending in the death of the protagonist.   The casual observer may not be able to distinguish between the two forms, but for Benjamin, only tragedy produces cathartic thinking due to the poetic relationship of its protagonist to his or her fate. Tragic heroes may possess the poetic *logos*, but this *logos* belongs to and confirms their destiny.   They do not attempt to place language between themselves and their fate.  Rather, language is prophecy, the *logos* of their destiny.      Drawing on Nietzsche's blaming of Socrates for the death of tragedy through the introduction of analytic, prose-like discourse as opposed to poetry, Benjamin makes Socratic dialog the culprit for the division between the forms of tragedy and *Trauerspiel*: Socrates is the first martyr (the martyr being, along with the tyrant, the typical heroic type of *Trauerspiel*, but alien to the concept of tragedy), a tragic hero with a voice.  Socrates and his later reincarnations replace the wordless suffering of the tragic hero with the endless ponderings of destiny found in the *Trauerspiel*.   The silent relationship of the tragic hero to his or her fate depends upon the very different notions of the world which motivate martyr and hero:

In the terms of the martyr-drama it is not moral transgression but the very estate of man as creature which provides the reason for the catastrophe. This typical catastrophe, which is so different from the extraordinary catastrophe of the tragic hero, is what the dramatists had in mind when — with a word which is employed more consciously in dramaturgy than in criticism — they described a work as a *Trauerspiel* (1977:89).

Unlike tragedy, which creates its own semiotic system which produces catharsis as a sign, *Trauerspiel* is comprehensible within the "ordinary" realms of politics and religion, from which it draws its heroes. A fallen, "creaturely" world, a ruined landscape whose redemption is only hinted at through the process of allegory, such are the "features" which make of *Trauerspiel* a "mourning-play" rather than a tragedy. The loquaciousness of the *Trauerspiel*'s protagonists points dialectically towards language's inability to imbue their fates with a meaning:

What is tragic is the word and the silence of the past, in which the prophetic voice is being tempted, or suffering and death, when they redeem this voice; but a fate in the pragmatic substance of its entanglements is never tragic. The *Trauerspiel* is conceivable as pantomime; the tragedy is not (1977:118).

Redemption is possible only through the *logos*, which cannot be represented visually. Since the world depicted in *Trauerspiel* is abandoned by the gods to the vagaries of history, its events can be reconstructed as mere phenomena, and hence represented in pantomime.

In semiotic terms, tragic silence and non-action are what Roman Jakobson, following the lead of Charles Bally, calls the "zero sign" or "*degré zéro.*" The linguistic basis of this concept is the fact that most languages have situations where the absence of any marker is itself significant. In English, for example, the first person of any verb is marked by the absence of any ending: "I go_," whereas "he go_es_." In Russian and Latin, the copulative (X is Y) can be given by the absence of any verb in the sentence: "*deus _ bonus*" (God is good). As Jakobson points out (1971:216), the absence of "*est*" in Latin, as a stylistic choice, is understood as a "zero coupling" according to its form, but as a signal of expressive language according to its function. The absence of the verb acquires stylistic value. A lack of action by the hero, for Nietzsche, is a sign of Dionysian insight and hence a stylistic marker of catharsis. Similarly, for Benjamin, the absence of a pragmatic entanglement of the hero is necessary for catharsis to occur.

Benjamin's version of catharsis goes beyond the emotional realm of Aristotle, and seems closer to the Dionysian insight of Nietzsche:

> As is suggested by the open theatre and the fact that the performance is never repeated identically, what takes place [in tragedy] is a decisive cosmic achievement. The community is assembled to witness and to judge this achievement. The spectator of tragedy is summoned, and is justified, by the tragedy itself (1977:119).

Benjamin describes tragedy's essence as the hero's and audience's relationship to *logos*. In contrast, Benjamin discusses *Trauerspiel* as the hieroglyphic of a nature-history which reveals only decay and death. Not the cosmos, but history is the setting for the events of *Trauerspiel*. Allegory as a form of writing is contrasted with tragedy's living speech:

> When, as is the case in the *Trauerspiel*, history becomes part of the setting, it does so as script [Schrift]. The word "history" stands written on the countenance of nature in the characters of transience. The allegorical physiognomy of the nature-history, which is put on stage in the *Trauerspiel*, is present in reality in the form of the ruin. In the ruin history has physically merged into the setting. And in this guise history does not assume the form of the process of an eternal life so much as that of irresistable decay. Allegory thereby declares itself to be beyond beauty. Allegories are, in the realm of thoughts, what ruins are in the realm of things (1977:177-8).

Benjamin here posits a different semiotic process — which he designates as Allegory — for interpreting the signs of *Trauerspiel*. This process is not equivalent to cathartic thinking. Again, the movement seems to be from poetry as indexical to prose as symbolic or, in Benjamin's word, allegory. Allegories are signs of signs (letters as the signs of words), not thought itself, but the ruins of thought. The mention of ruins corresponds to the overwhelming emphasis of the *Trauerspiel* on mortal suffering and material decline which, in Benjamin's novel view, hides within it the hope of redemption.

In summary, both Nietzsche and Benjamin are more specific about the referent of catharsis than is Aristotle, and both describe the cathartic process as in some sense cognitive, though bound up with an emotional content. For Nietzsche, music reveals the Dionysian aspect of reality and exposes the illusionism of Apollonian cultural existence. Benjamin seems to be arguing that tragedy reveals human beings' essential place in the cosmos, as opposed to the *Trauerspiel* which reports on their historical and material conditions of their existence. Neither writer can be clearer than this because the sign of catharsis belongs to a different semiotic system than the logical-discursive one they are using. In addition, both thinkers posit the signs of tragedy as being more motivated and less arbitrary than the conventional signs of language. I have used the term "index" for this kind of sign meaning that the sign necessarily reminds us of what has produced it as its referent, as music reminds us of emotion.

# V
## Antonin Artaud:  What the Body Says

Antonin Artaud's (1896-1940) theory of drama deals primarily with the rearrangement of the sign relations mentioned in the last section.  Artaud called for a "theater of cruelty" in the early twentieth century in much the way Nietzsche had called for a tragic vision of life in nineteenth-centry Germany.  Artaud saw his problem in formulating a new theater in a way similar to Martin Heidegger's view of his problem in trying to write philosophy.  The weight of the Western tradition had left both theater and philosophy with vocabularies which amounted to petrified forms of thought. Only the invention of a new vocabulary could allow either thinker the possibility of developing a discourse at all adequate to the specific problems of modernity.  Hence, Artaud, like Nietzsche and Benjamin, avoided using the term "catharsis" as part and parcel of theater's metaphysical baggage which he was trying to destroy.  Our semiotic point of view, however, allows us to argue that really Artaud is asking for catharsis to happen again in a theater which has become petrified.  Artaud rebelled against the conventions of bourgeois drama, in which all stage representation based on following a prewritten script, and which can thus only fulfill what an author has already said;  theatrical signs are grounded in authorial discourse, which is in turn grounded in Western metaphysics and transcendental signifieds, such as God.

Hence, Artaud posits the possibility and the necessity of subverting the theater's sign function and achieving an originary catharsis through a theater of cruelty.  We have seen Nietzsche and Benjamin starting in this direction by making the cathartic sign fundamentally different from those of language. For Artaud, the theater first must divest itself of the sign function: "The very objects, props, and scenery on stage must be understood in an immediate sense, without being transposed.  They must not be taken for what they represent, but for what they really are."  However, Artaud reinstates the sign function in the next sentence: "Production as such, the actors' movements, must be considered only as the visible signs of an invisible or secret language. Not one theatrical gesture should be devoid of the fatality of life and the mysterious happenings that occur in dreams" (1971, 2:23). While in the latter sentence the sign function seems to be restored, it becomes the vehicle for a "secret language." This process is without segmentation; referents cannot be delineated one from another. Artaud calls this "illegibility." The result is a theater between the thing-in-itself (someone eating a grapefruit) and a semiotic act. To put it in semiotic terms, in theatrical illegibility "the sign has not yet been separated from force. It is not quite yet a sign, in the sense in which we understand sign, but is no longer a thing, which we conceive only as opposed to the sign" (Derrida, 1978a: 189). Derrida implies here that there is only one kind of sign, but his discussion of the force-sign can probably be accomodated under the notion of indexical signs. Again, this sounds remarkably like Nietzsche's account of the role of music in tragedy.

Like Nietzsche, Artaud attempts to arrive through theater at a notion of Life (*Sein*) which is not merely the summation or reduction of a series of Lives (*Dasein*). Illegibility and force stem from the fact that in Artaud's theater, something on stage engages in the process of becoming. Artaud uses the world "cruelty" as a catachresis for what he seeks: "I have therefore said 'cruelty' as I might have said 'life' or 'necessity,' because I want to indicate especially that for me the theater is act and perpetual emanation, that there is nothing congealed about it, that I turn it into a true act, hence living, hence magical." (1971, 4:87). As Jacques Derrida interprets this, "the theater of cruelty is not a representation. It is life itself, in the extent to which life is unrepresentable. Life is the nonrepresentable origin of representation" (1978b:234). The zero sign of catharsis has life as its referent.

The clearest metaphor for the zero sign of catharsis is the notion of plague as an unseen, unpredictable alteration in the body and the body politic. One of the primary meanings of the word "semiology" is the method of relating medical symptoms to their causes. Artaud uses this method, describing both the epidemiology and the pathology of plague. That plague can erupt anywhere without discernible vectors, coupled with the observation that it leaves the organs intact while killing its victims, demonstrates for Artaud that this disease is metaphysical, that its sufferings originate, like those of the actor, in a metaphysical rather than physical condition: "The condition of the plague victim who dies without any material destruction, yet with all the stigmata of an absolute, almost abstract disease upon him, is in the same condition as an actor totally penetrated by feelings without any benefit or relation to reality" (1971, 4:14-15). Without tangible origins, the actor's fury has no chance of being cured or dispersed: "Compared with a murderer's fury that exhausts itself, an actor of tragedy remains enclosed within a circle. The murderer's anger has accomplished an act and is released, losing contact with the power that inspired but will no longer sustain it. It has assumed a form, while the actor's fury, which denies itself by being detached, is rooted in the universal" (1971: 4:15). This universality, which Artaud posits here as the cause of tragedy's sound and fury — Aristotle's pity and fear — is in fact tragedy's signified, as we have learned from Benjamin.

Artaud's referent for theater also sounds like Nietzsche's Dionysian impulse, with its mixture of horror and extasy:

> If the essential theater is like the plague, it is not because it is contagious, but because like the plague, it is the revelation, the bringing forth, the exteriorization of a depth of latent cruelty by means of which all the perverse possibilities of the mind, whether of an individual or a people, are localized (1971, 4:19).

As Noriko Miura reads it, "The aim of [Artaud's] theater is not to present and resolve moral or psychological conflicts, but to awaken in the mind of the audience an emergent power of darkness, and to transform and renew its audience through the battle with their demonic forces" (1996:18).

Artaud's theories, which he himself was mostly unable to realize through actual practice, had an important effect upon drama, leading to unconventional forms such as the theater of the absurd, guerilla theater, and psychodrama. In these forms of theater, to a greater extent that in any discussed so far, emphasis is shifted away from the words of a preexisting script and onto the body and voice of the actor. Performance is not repetition, but the production of a unique, unrepeatable sign of catharsis which passes into the audience, is consumed, and lost forever.

# VI
## Summary

All the tragic theories we have examined make the point that catharsis is a sign produced only through the semiotic processes of theatrical representation. All agree that it is the sign of an emotion which brings with it significant cognition. We might call it an "emotion-thought." All the theories examined imply that the cathartic sign is indexical, standing for what has produced it. For Aristotle these are fearful and pitiful events, for Nietzsche the Dionysian "*Urschmerz*," for Benjamin a cosmic event, and for Artaud the emerging event on the stage itself.

Catharsis appears to many people as a vague concept for two main reasons. The first is that its aesthetic sign is not translatable into other discursive systems. To understand this point, consider the word "four." It is not really comprehensible except as a translation of the number 4. In turn, the number 4 is really only comprehensible within the highly segmented arithmetic series 1, 2, 3, 4, 5 .... Though it may seem to be possible to intuitively grasp that there are "four" of something, in fact such a comprehension depends upon the entire array of the counting numbers, that is, upon the possibility that there be more or less than four of something. Though "four" certainly is able to function as a sign in both language and mathematics, certain higher mathematical concepts, such as the different types of infinity, can truly only be understood within their mathematical sign system. Similarly, the chief weakness of theories of catharsis, from a semiotic point of view, is that they do not segment aesthetic signs, and hence do not mention what the neighboring signs of catharsis might be. In other words, what are other emotion-thoughts which dramas might produce in the audience in place of catharsis — simple sadness, for example, or pity and fear which do not quite come together? Aristotle may possibly have meant to discuss two kinds of catharsis — tragic and comic — while Nietzsche notes the difference between Dionysian (cathartic) and Apollonion emotion-thoughts. Benjamin and Artaud are least helpful in this regard. In this sense, Indian *rasa* theory provides an excellent contrast to theories of catharsis, explicitly segmenting the emotions and noting which emotions are more likely to appear in the context of others. Unfortunately, this highly sophisticated theory of the aesthetic emotion-thoughts has no room for cathartic thinking.

*Thomas O. Beebee is Professor of Comparative Literature at The Pennsylvania State University.*

## NOTES

1. I have emended Osborne's translation in two places: to "put to the test" instead of "tried out"; to "when they redeem this voice" instead of "when they *are redeemed by* this voice."

## REFERENCES

Aristotle, 1947, "Poetics," in *Introduction to Aristotle*, ed. Richard McKeon. New York: Random House, 624-67.
-----, 1943, *Politics,* trans. Benjamin Jowett. New York: Modern Library.
Artaud, Antonin, 1971, *Collected Works*, 4 vols., trans. Victor Corti. London: Calder & Boyars.
-----, 1958, *The Theater and Its Double*, trans. Mary Caroline Richards. New York: Grove.

Benjamin, Walter, 1977, *The Origin of German Tragic Drama*, trans. John Osborne. London: New Left Books.

Brunius, Teddy, 1977, "Catharsis," in *The Dictionary of the History of Ideas*. Ed. Philip P. Wiener, 5 vols. New York: Scribner, I:264-70.

Chari, V. K., 1990, *Sanskrit Criticism*. Honolulu: University of Hawaii Press .

Derrida, Jacques, 1978a, "La parole soufflé," trans. Alan Bass, in *Writing and Difference*, ed. Alan Bass. Chicago: University of Chicago Press. 169-95.

-----, 1978b, "The Theater of Cruelty and the Closure of Representation," trans. Alan Bass, in *Writing and Difference*, ed. Alan Bass. Chicago: University of Chicago Press, 232-250.

Eco, Umberto, 1979, *A Theory of Semiotics*. Bloomington: Indiana University Press.

Hjelmslev, Louis, 1928, *Principes de grammaire générale*. Copenhagen: A. F. Host.

Horkheimer, Max, and Theodor Adorno, 1987, *The Dialectic of Enlightenment*, trans. John Cumming. New York: Continuum.

Jakobson, Roman, 1960, "Linguistics and Poetics," in *Style in Language,* ed. Thomas A. Sebeok. Cambridge Massachusetts: MIT Press, 350-77.

-----, 1971, "Signe Zéro." *Selected Writings II: Word and Language*. The Hague: Mouton.

Miura, Noriko, 1996, "Marginal Voice, Marginal Body: The Treatment of the Human Body in the Works of Nakagami Kenji, Leslie Marmon Silko, and Salman Rushdie," Ph.D. diss. The Pennsylvania State University.

Nietzsche, Friedrich, 1974, *The Birth of Tragedy from the Spirit of Music*, trans. William A. Haussmann, in *The Complete Works of Friedrich Nietzsche*, Vol. 1., ed. Oscar Levy, 11 vols. New York: Gordon Press, 17-187.

Peirce, Charles S., 1931-35/1965, *Pragmatism and Pragmaticism*, in the *Collected Papers*, Vol. 5., eds. Charles Hartshorne and Paul Weiss, 8 vols. Cambridge: Harvard University Press, at pp. 213-357.

Plato, 1968 edition, *The Republic of Plato*, trans. Allan Bloom. New York: Basic Books.

*Rasa: Les neufs visages de l'art indien*, 1986, Paris: Ministère de Relations Exterieures, Association français d'action artistique.

Veltrusky, Jiri, 1977, *Drama as Literature*, Semiotics of Literature 2. Lisse: Peter de Ridder.

# Chapter 12

# Cryptology

Laurence A. Rickels*

## I
## Introducing Loss

Psychoanalysis was the first "science" to take the detour through literature for its premier inspiration and findings. It therefore contains, at or as its origin, a poetics within the zone of destabilized boundaries linking and separating literature, science, and our mass culture, our media sensurround. The nature of this psychoanalytic poetics is conveyed best, up front, by the name "cryptology." Cryptology designates, officially, since the seventeenth century, and thus ever since the onset of our modern technological era, secret communication or, more recently, in our century of total media wars, the encoding and decoding of messages practiced against and with opposing institutions of espionage or diplomacy. Without foregoing these outer senses of the term, a psychoanalytic poetics which bears the name cryptology focuses first of all on the genealogy of the crypt, a unit of signification, a "family" unit — it comes in individual, couple, or group sizes —, one that contains and transmits relations of long distance, relations with the long distant, the dead or undead. In the beginning of "making" — whether in the sense of poetry or of fetish —, a beginning that opened up our first prospects for civilization and science, there was loss (Freud 1959 [1915] 309-308). But not just any loss. This is where the paradoxical — because ruinous — materialism of psychoanalytic poetics begins.

The association of death with signification is as old as it gets. But psychoanalysis skips the beat of death, a metaphysical beat that philosophical systems and institutions of higher yearning are given to police, and instead consigns death, one's own death, whatever that is, to its unconscious reception as precisely unimaginable for oneself. Psychoanalysis thus puts through the direct connection with the dead, the dead other, whose passing both confirms the profound conviction we hold, bottomline, of our own immortality and installs in us a need to mourn, and unmourn, against the odds of our mounting suicidal impulses.

As is confirmed by the inclusion of "tomb" in the group of its original or primal meanings, every "sign" is constituted by the possibility that it marks or will mark the spot of an absence, the spot we as survivors among signs are in, an at once undeniable and unacknowledgable absence, one that either refers to a missing body or presses to be given a body. Psychoanalysis sets up the "work of mourning" (*Trauerarbeit*) as model for analysis, both in session and in theory, and, by extension, for all forms of work or making. These extensions and applications of Freud's model of mourning network an uncanny interchangeability between psychoanalysis and our mass media culture. Was Freud right all along or have advertising technicians, for example, or the imagineers simply been reading their Freud? It is not a question of influence or causation, at least not one that can ever be properly answered. But just the same psychoanalysis has become the owner's manual to our ongoing technologization and group-psychologization.

The sign that mourns a designated object, also kills it (again). Only that which we have killed, killed a second time, can we successfully mourn. But there are also signs (often the same signs) which, by dint of their function (the proper name for instance) or via literalization and fantasmatization, withdraw from circulation, translation, substitution in order to hide away and thus preserve an undead relation (Derrida, 1986: xxi-xxiii). Such a literalized or demetaphorized sign, word, or phrase assumes the status of unmetabolized object, vestige, part object, ruin. A crypt of concealment and preservation is built up out of these mutated signifying units. Through psychoanalytic decoding, excavation, or ghostbusting, these same building blocks or blockages comprising the crypt can also be seized upon or confiscated as the passwords leading into the secret space of unaknowledgable loss. These crypts are therefore completely vulnerable to the forces against which they have been set up to defend their secret ingredients (Abraham and Torok 1980). Like the vampire lying in his crypt during the daytime programming of his undead existence, who for the duration must rest in place, absolutely vulnerable to the first hunter who stumbles across the entry way to the tomb, so the language crypt can only keep up disappearances, its utter concealment from view or knowledge of those living, circulating, and substituting among signs, through generation of diversionary signs or whole discourses in the secret service of detour. In the context of psychoanalytic discourse, the diversion function cannot but pass through a relay of Oedipal interpretations and constructions.

Loss takes us down to and hits us hardest in pre-Oedipal zones where the original dual bond with the mother's body, which we also take to be our own body, remains the best union we never had. The only frame of reference available at this stage of unmetabolizable separation is that of double or nothing. This is the zone of a literalized and destablized "between:" "being two." The space-between is always also a place of doubling, a placeholder of total loss or of loss retention. To be two or not to be two, that is our first question.

Inside the Oedipus complex, loss gets redefined via the third person, the "he," "she," "it," as just the kind of conflict around absolute but unattainable desire that leads to sublimation and identification. That the mother's body is declared off limits by law skews our phantasmatic relationship to this body and to our own body, and opens up prospects, terrifying or gratifying, for the near-missing fits of substitution. The mother's body was the one we wanted to eat and have too. But the third person transforms the edible object into the Oedipal object. The author of separations, the third person, the father, the law, or the Name-of-the-Father, figures as the anti-body of the same conflict it invites, a conflict that cannot be won by little one. We cannot fight the law and win, so we take "it" in via identification (Lacan, 1977: 217).

We join what we cannot lick. The father (or third person) is thus set up as the first object of successful mourning. To take the bite out of the third person, one has already swallowed the metabolic enzyme of substitution and circulation, just as one has already assimilated the intake in part and digested or eliminated the rest in equal parts. The father, again as anti-body, embodies a death or loss that does not annihilate but can be survived down the line of transmission of the name, in the name of which the third person functions. But there's a catch, like the catch in our throats: the father function can break down. Indeed, when Freud suggests that the Oedipal interpretation does not lose in importance even if it is but the "construction of psychoanalysis," we are given to understand that this paternal function is more a saving fiction, an anti-body in the inoculative sense, one that requires careful, therapeutic adminstration or injection (Freud 1959 [1919], II, 179-180). But there are unmournable losses that do not meet match and maker in the antibody's disposable containment.

Inside the Oedipus complex mourning is already the happening and ongoing event. Loss comes in always only second to guilt, the abstract currency of p-unitive relations with father, our internal and eternal standard of mournable death. In juxtaposition with a plot of secret burial or unburial, the Oedipal plot is never simply simulated. But it can function at the same time as diversion away from the crypt with which it shares one system, psyche, or body. When this is the case, the crypt of unmournable loss remains in displaced control of all signification.

The extremes of mourning (inside the Oedipus complex of relations with father) and melancholia (inside a pre-Oedipal zone of unmetabolizable loss) do not cancel each other out, nor do they admit each other's synthesis or assimilation. The complex of their relations corresponds to the ultimate frame of Freud's thought experiments, that of a greater mourning, in which inevitable moments of successful integration and substitution must in turn be mourned. Along the lines of Freud's understanding of the "uncanny" (Freud 1959 [1919], IV, 377), we might refer thus to "unmourning" as our basic concept, which describes the interminable process whereby mourning gets accomplished but is also undone, is mourned and unmourned.

# II
## Loss Transmission

What's past or gone gets transmitted two ways, either as transference or as telepathy. For Freud the difference comes via analogies which are noteworthy in their own writing and work. In the metalanguage of psychoanalysis, at the origin of the transmission of Freud's science, we find a work of analogy that is also always the work of mourning. Freud's first analogies for the transference — the fundamental in-session experience of the way the past gets relived in or as the present — came from the printing press medium and from the lexicon of haunting. Freud compared transference to a photographic cliche that could be reprinted always the same but for so many different occasions and contexts (Freud 1959 [1912] 313). The transference that keeps bringing back an earlier relationship, intact and undisclosed, also announced the arrival of a specter. Freud in turn rewired telepathy through analogy with the telephone and concluded that both occult and technological transmissions could be received only now, thanks to Freud's understanding of the unconscious (Freud 1964 [1932] 36). Occult telepathic transmissions (like the live transmission of the phone) forward foreign bodies outside all recognizable contexts of communication. But Freud also recognized that, unconsciously, what can be picked up as thought transference, and then fulfilled in the form of a fortune-telling medium's prophecy (whether or not ever realized as true in the future), is a wish, an Oedipally informed wish for union or a death wish, to give two recurrent examples. But between the lines of these main examples Freud recounts a foreign-body transmission between mother and child which cannot be explained but only wished away by recourse to the Oedipal wish or command.

Transference as the main medium of analysis, analogized with and coconstituted as technical medium of legibility, presses in the course of analysis toward the successful outcome of a work of mourning. Telepathy resides within a live — or a life's — transmission of secret layovers and stopovers, a whole network of unacknowledged losses which begin again, however, according to Freud's interpretations or constructions, as unacknowledged wishes. Freud turns to telepathy as to the phone to functionalize or already mediate our first contact with the long distant, the dead or undead.

The ghosts in transference and in the foregrounded examples of telepathy are ghosts of mourning who represent (and repress) our mixed emotions regarding the living persons we have known and from whom we must now part, in time, with sweet sorrow over our stray bad thoughts and wishes. But telepathy also admits the secret transfer of foreign bodies belonging to some other's context of mourning or unmourning. In the example that slips out of the Oedipal fold, Freud presents the thought transference of a gold coin, a "foreign body," from the mother to her son for safekeeping (Freud 1964 [1932] 56). But what if the foreign body were a body? Thus a mother who cannot mourn her dead child can, unconsciously, slide that little corpse (and the mourning assignment attached to it) inside the body or psyche of another, living child, who must follow out the signals of this fantasmatic life or unlife entrusted to or rather installed within the survivor. The age of the survivor and the age difference from the deceased sibling preclude a context of mourning between these two figures alone: it's bigger than the two of them, bigger than life.

## III
## The Example of Mary Shelley's Frankenstein

Mary Shelley settled a transferential score by writing her monster novel. To be an author was her legacy assignment: both parents were renowned authors. Her partnership with Percy Bysshe Shelley redoubled this pressure of inheritance. Like her father he acted as her ghost writer, as when he intervened in her name with the 1818 preface to *Frankenstein. Or, The Modern Prometheus*, a piece of PR packaging about how amiable and domestic the novel really was. The father claimed the right of final cut for any one of his daughter's manuscripts, which she would dutifully forward to him for approval. In one instance he exercised this right to the full extent of prohibiting publication of one of her works (Knoepflmacher 115).

Mary Shelley's birth had been the sad occasion of her mother's death by blood poisoning from the unreleased placenta. By the time she wrote the work that made or remade her — for every subsequent novel she identified herself as "the author of *Frankenstein*" — she had spent her young life attempting restitution and replacement duty for the circumstances of her birth. The father had remarried in the meantime. Up to this point we can recognize only Oedipal props and conditions for Mary Shelley's invention of her monster novel. The pre-Oedipal or encrypted scene of its conception came about, as recognition value, only after the fact, after the first version or artifact. But then, again, forever after, there came the final confirmation of Mary Shelley's own crypt bond with the novel (which was not just the same as the protagonist's undead bond with his monster).

Already the author's identification with the novel and, in her 1831 preface, of the novel with the monster occupies a borderline zone between the Oedipal conditionings and the encrypted text. Just follow the bouncing name

"Frankenstein." Is it the mad scientist, is it the monster, the novel, or Mary Shelley's chosen name? In the 1831 preface the author describes, this time in her own writing, her "conception" of the novel within the same lexicon of light, lightning and electricity in which Dr. Frankenstein's creation of his monster gets spelled out. She further specifies that invention never proceeds out of nothing: it is always the practice that makes imperfect combinations of pre-existing elements (Shelley x). This of course at the same time describes Dr. Frankenstein's method of body building.

*Frankenstein* is bound to what it hides: a melancholic fit between Victor Frankenstein and his dead mother, whose unacknowledged loss goes down, encrypted, inside her son and between the lines of the novel. The outlines of the crypt are discernible by default, via Victor's inability to fulfill two Oedipal contracts (or transferences). The first one was negotiated with his father and binds him to marriage with Elizabeth, who has been positioned by family history, destiny, or conditioning as the cure-all substitute for all losses in the Frankenstein household. Following the death of Victor's mother, Victor's father repeatedly enjoins him to enter or reenter the "house of mourning" (Shelley 88). The entry ticket is marriage to Elizabeth, the consummation of substitution for an Oedipal mother who was off limits before she was lost. The second contract, another self-unfulfilling prophecy, is proposed by the monster, who asks his maker to produce the mate or match he has been looking for in all the wrong places, namely, in the scenes of loss he keeps on visiting upon the Frankenstein family. In exchange the monster will swear off his vengeful interventions in Victor's circle of family and friends.

The undead loss inside Victor — figured, for example, by the fiend inside the creature which his first act of premeditated murder releases — is not at rest but haunts the crypt and crypt-bearer. Victor follows out the beam of haunting through a series of externalizations. When his mother dies, we catch Victor giving lip service — it is his one-time offer — to the economy of mourning, the household he will in fact never enter, no matter how often his father entreats him to do so. The subterfuge is brief. Victor lets on that the dead should bury the dead (Shelley 43). But then the next sentence starts up: "My departure for Ingolstadt." Thus, without matching the act to any running commentary, he in fact doubles and internalizes his mother's departure by departing for the university or alma mater where he will build the creature in place of the work of mourning he could not even begin to contemplate. The monster ultimately duplicates the uncontrollable loss of the mother as the long distance, the gap, and the murderously, vengefully remote-controlled relationship between Victor and his monster, the agency henceforth of all subsequent losses, losses which are no longer uncontrolled or random, but which, however, must, all right already, be gotten on or over with.

The monster is also built up out of Oedipal lines the reader is given, in large part, though never consciously, as diversion. The outer narrative frames all certain acts of transgression against a father's injunctions, which thus produce certain consequences which appear transferentially legible in the reversed or cautionary mode. However at the same time there would appear to be, between frames, no father function or fiction around with the authority (or anti-body) required for maintaining substitution of a safer course for all-out, double-or-nothing abandonment to risk. The first version of the novel began with the creature's Oedipal scene of abandonment. The creature appears as child forsaken by a self-absorbed father who, like Mary Shelley's father, William Godwin, obsessively contemplates prospects for the creation of "new men." An Oedipal line can also be seen as the opener which the monster grabs hold of when he claims his first victim. Victor's younger brother William crosses the path of the artificial being, who has followed his creator home for a surprise visitation. When the little boy boasts to the stranger about his powerful father, the raging monster gives him the rest. But between those lines of rivalry there is also the medallion William wears which contains an image of his dead mother. Within the unburial plot, in contrast to the Oedipal plot, this locket (which includes the injunction: Lock it!) also keeps the monster locked onto its beam. The monster takes the image from the neck of the dead boy and, when he later chances upon the sleeping form of Justine, whom he recognizes as the dead mother's lookalike, he slides the same image deep inside her pocket. The creature at once frames Justine for the murder of William (within a series of framed images of the mother) and is born or reborn at this penetrating or encrypting point of transmission of the mother's legacy as the fiend within, as the monster. At the end of his university training, along a finish line where the thesis is customarily signed, but which in Victor's case throws out a life line to the body he built, it is time to return home, enter the house of mourning, and marry Elizabeth. Now it's time. Following the creature's animation and abandonment or repression Victor has the following dream, which also looks forward to the homecoming:

> I thought I saw Elizabeth, in the bloom of health, walking in the streets of Ingolstadt. Delighted and surprised, I embraced her, but as I imprinted the first kiss on her lips, they became livid with the hue of death; her features appeared to change, and I thought that I held the corpse of my dead mother in my arms; a shroud enveloped her form, and I saw the grave worms crawling in the folds of the flannel. (Shelley 57)

The dead mother blocks the son's embrace of his future wife. That fits the Oedipal frame. But this frame is exceeded by the literalness of the image and of its meaning: Victor can embrace the substitute only if — only when — she in turn is superimposable onto the dead mother. He will indeed embrace Elizabeth, which is as far as the consummation of their wedding night goes, only after she is the dead victim of his monster.

To love the dead is to love to death. But this remains within the zone of the first death. Drawing on the rites and beliefs of so-called primitive cultures, Freud argued that every deceased loved one becomes at first a vampire, a ghost, a monster whose considerable undead powers of haunting hold sway for the duration of the mourning period (two years in length on average is Freud's estimate). At the end of this period the deceased, first exhumed and then reburied, is believed to die a second and conclusive death (Freud 1955 [1912-1913] 51-63). You only die twice. But in order to mourn the dead you must insure a second death, you must kill the dead. From within Victor's melancholic perspective, substitution for loss represents a murderous imposition of the second, decisive death. And Elizabeth can indeed be seen, along the lines of Victor's perspective, as murderous: her mother died giving birth to her; she survived the same illness she gave in fatal form to Victor's mother; she placed around William's neck the medallion, the draw for the monster's stranglehold along its dotted line; her self-less speech in Justine's defense psychologically fine-tunes a contrast that seals the condemned woman's fate. It is far easier to let the murderous substitute go than to attend to the second death of the dead.

Victor's second contractual or transferential relationship binds him to create a bride for his monster. He sets out to build the second body under the cover of yet another departure, this time for England. His father and Elizabeth are convinced that Victor is on his way to being restored to himself. There were already qualms, on Victor's part, before the storm of protest he acts out by destroying the creature-in-progress. At first Victor's resistance checks in with the Oedipal register. The construction of the bride, the wife, the figure from the outside, would introduce an element of uncontrollability. He has his contractual relationship and his duo dynamic with the original monster. Mate makes three. The mate would be on her own, pulling the first monster into her alien orbit of reproduction and murder. The monster couple might reproduce to the point of creating a fiendish race that would beat the human race at its own finish line. Victor may think globally, but he reacts locally, in some other place. The unspoken but motivating condition of relations between Victor and his monster is the control release of all Victor's subsequent losses, and the relegation of the first uncontrolled loss to a prehistory of monster relations where there was nothing to lose. By promising, in exchange for a mate, that he will withdraw from the orbit of Frankenstein's suffering, the monster leaves his maker only one move to avoid check mate, the Oedipal ending that would be the beginning of the end in sight, the beginning of mourning. The original male monster was made at a safe remove from the lost body Victor had retained on the inside. With the continuation of the labors of body building, in place of the mourning work that was never to go down, and this time with a female focus, Victor would be getting too close to matching the external body with the internal one, a match that would identify the body as the mother's corpse, whose loss could no longer go unacknowledged. Before completion of a task that would mark the beginning of mourning Victor destroys the second creature. As he prepares to leave the lab he is arrested for a moment by the scene of murderous, material ruin from which he then extricates his instruments, his belongings, and himself. At this point, the metaphorical (and metaphysical) collapses onto the literal: "I paused to collect myself" (Shelley 163).

As the novel comes to a close around the complete reduction of Victor's frame of reference or relationship to all-out pursuit of his monster, the crypt begins to emerge both in names given in passing and in palpably missing names. For example, when Victor gives us his succinct recollection of his entire existence just as it flashes before his eyes, the reduced frame fits the life that was always there between the lines:

> I repassed, in my memory, my whole life — my quiet happiness while residing with my family in Geneva, the death of my mother; and my departure for Ingolstadt. I remembered, shuddering, the mad enthusiasm that hurried me on to the creation of my hideous enemy, and I called to mind the night in which he first lived. (Shelley 175)

So these are the events of his life: happiness, the death of the mother, the departure for Ingolstadt. When he adds the monster's creation to the list, the flashback has already ended, subsumed by the present tense and tension of the relationship to the monster, the diversion that is back on course. But just as he resolves to leave the past behind, to leave Geneva forever, in order to chase down the monster to the end of one or the other's existence — an I for an I — he takes along with him a deposit, a respository, not only cash but something else that he can carry: "I provided myself with a sum of money, together with a few jewels which had belonged to my mother, and departed" (Shelley 192). But on his way out of town, he doubles back once more, before completely taking off, and visits the cemetery. He goes to the family plot marking the spot where his loved ones are properly buried: "As night approached I found myself at the entrance of the cemetery where William, Elizabeth, and my father reposed. I entered it and approached the tomb which marked their graves" (Shelley 192). At this point the unacknowledged loss is in our typeface: even the mother's grave is missing. The novel thus names, silently and literally, what has gone unburied within a psyche, corpus, or text, gone without saying or naming and without commemoration.

But at the end the work of mourning does begin, both by displacement, since Victor never mourns, and by an after-the-fact identification which completes the novel as a whole as work of mourning. And this completion as work of mourning takes place twice, once for Victor, once again for Mary Shelley. When Victor Frankenstein dies, the monster returns to the scene and grieves over the maker. But it is as the mother that the monster mourns her dead son. And then the monster, no longer bound to Victor as his retainer and fiend, can put herself to rest. Mourning will take place, even if the creation mobilized by the refusal to mourn must deliver the mourning rites of passage.

There is a second after-the-fact identification that fulfills itself as acknowledged throughout the novel, one that hurtles through the space-between of telepathy rather than proceeding down the lines of transference. After the monster or mother of a secret identification has turned around into the maternal corpus of mourning there was still, for Mary Shelley, a secret deposit accidentally tagged "William." William, Victor's younger brother, is the monster's first victim. Inside the novel that binds him, beyond the diversions represented by narrative frames held together by transgressions against a father's injunction, to his dead mother, Victor too registers alongside William's passing a fundamental change in his reception of his monster which he now recognizes to be a relationship, one that is projectively binding, making the monster the innocent bystander's responsibility. On his way back home for William's funeral, Victor identifies the monster in the light show of an electrical storm that has them surrounded:

> I remained motionless. The thunder ceased, but the rain still continued, and the scene was enveloped in an impenetrable darkness. I revolved in my mind the events which I had until now sought to forget: the whole train of my progress towards the creation, the appearance of the work of my own hands alive at my bedside, its departure. Two years had now nearly elapsed since the night on which he first received life, and was this his first crime? Alas, I had turned loose into the world a depraved wretch whose delight was in carnage and misery; had he not murdered my brother? ...

> I considered the being whom I had cast among mankind and endowed with the will and power to effect purposes of horror, such as the deed which he had now done, nearly in the light of my own vampire, my own spirit let loose from the grave and forced to destroy all that was dear to me. (Shelley 74)

What connected Mary Shelley to the name William was some bad ambivalence. In Oedipal zones William was her father's name. And it was a name he had already bestowed on her half brother before she could give it to her own son, her first child to survive infancy. But then, with the completion of the novel, her son died. Her grief on this occasion alarmed her ghost writers, husband Shelley and father Godwin. One asked the other to intervene. Godwin dropped his daughter a note of warning about her selfish and ugly grieving and how it would put off all those who still cared for her. This was Mary Shelley's invitation to enter the house of mourning. And it was as it was already written. After the completion and between the lines of *Frankenstein* and subsequent works Mary Shelly just had to recognize the telepathic forecast, what she would address as the prophecy, of the death of someone close to her. With the uncanny confirmation of a reservation made in her first novel for William's death, another primal scene had caught up with her. Once upon the time before she wrote *Frankenstein*, she had a dream: her infant girl, who had just died, was not dead, but only cold; she warmed her back up to life by the light of an open fire.

William had also served as her secret name or double within her own prehistory. When her mother and father were contemplating the child that would be Mary Shelley they were already so sure they would be having a son that they referred to the upcoming child in their correspondence as William. William is a name tagging or lagging behind multiple disappointments. The mother, looking forward to the birth of William, produced Mary Shelley. And then she died.

Writing to Jung on October 13, 1911, Freud refers to a belief still current in so-called primitive societies that the placenta is always the twin of the baby. The placenta is therefore cared for after birth until its manifest decay requires disposal or burial. This, then, is the repetition or rehearsal of what Freud would call the uncanny: every baby is shadowed at birth by a dead double (Freud/Jung 1974 449). The name of Mary Shelley's double loss was William. She tried to make a big reproduction out of cutting her losses when she recycled the name for her first survivor. But sometimes losses just double on contact. In the meantime, however, she had conceived and carried to term the novel or work of mourning which would henceforward mediate and control-release the blows. And it was time.

# IV
# Afterimages

By chance or dictation the most lasting extra-literary representation of the monster (in the two films directed by Whales) reduced the range of the monster to infancy, from the stammering of first words to the baby steps of learning to walk. But the baby that bounces back to mark the spot of unmourning Mary Shelley was in, had been part of a representation and repression of the underworld of identification. The Oedipal diversions dominate the outer-corpus trajectory of the Hollywood reception of Mary Shelley's novel. In *Frankenstein* and *Bride of Frankenstein*, the monster serves to interrupt the consummation of marriage, the continuation of the father's line. The monster's destruction in turn gives safe passage, for the surviving characters and for the members of the audience, out of the underworld of haunting into the happy ending of symptoms of sexual repression inside a comfort zone of accomplished coupling. In the movies, the mad scientist is linked and limited to his obsessive creation with his own hands of a monstrous body of part objects all alone in his phallic tower. It is the hand job of solo sexuality that gets associated with the piecing together of a fantastic body out of parts, which, just as in the imagination or technology of pornography, each exceeds the whole. In *Frankenstein* one reference is made, in passing, to the missing mother. Father has kept her bridal garland intact under the glass of its small Snow White's coffin. The son's bride will wear it down the aisle of the family line's perpetuation. But then the monster interrupts — a little girl has been murdered and, it appears, molested by the creature — and the film rushes to its end in the monster's destruction. In what must have been the premier Hollywood horror sequel, *Bride of Frankenstein*, the whole movie must begin again, overlapping with the replayed footage of the first movie, which has in a sense been incorporated at the opening of the new film. Between the lines of this recycled material, the monster is reanimated as survivor of the attempt to torch it. The second film must make it to the reunion of the couple at the end. The monster releases the couple from imprisonment by mad science and then puts himself and his bride to rest. But before this restoration comedy or happy ending could take place, the bride had to be transformed. In the course of creating the monster's mate, a confusion between brides has sparked Elizabeth too with the status of techno-liveness. When Dr. Frankenstein listens to the beat of the new creation's heart he exclaims: "It's alive! It's alive!" Just his words exactly when he is connected via another new electrical device — the phone, by any other name — with Elizabeth, who is being kept hostage in exchange for the maker's second creation: "She's alive! She's alive!" She's live. She survives, between the lines, as the double "bride of Frankenstein," a techno body, an undead or live outlet for Dr. Frankenstein's perpetually arrested state.

# V
# Leaving an Opening

In time Mary Shelly had allowed herself to benefit from her work of mourning, her novel *Frankenstein*, and it was in this sense, and not from inside the dolorous space of the crypt, that she identified herself as "the author of *Frankenstein*." To benefit from one's losses is the most difficult and the most determining assignment of successful mourning. But mourning did not rest upon its successes. The first double-feature reception of Frankenstein illustrates this unrest, even or especially between the projected lines of what is so manifestly aimed away from the story of melancholia inside the novel towards a more upbeat case study of sexual repression in the couple and the inevitable busting of its monstrous symptoms for the big screen. A greater mourning takes over where the success of mere integration took place, and mourns on, over each substitution or disposal. This does not have to be an infinite process. But it always exceeds the lifetime of one corpus, or, in other words, that of the two bodies of life's work in the couplified context of loss and mourning. Mary Shelley's corpus turns the ghost writing once administered to it around and against her father's corpus: she deferred completion of her biographical essay on her father for his posthumous collected works edition, thereby postponing the publication of that collection for her life time (Knoepflmacher 119). She never did complete it: the incompletion of that assignment continues to inhabit her collected works.

*\* Laurence Rickels is Professor of German Literature and Adjunct Professor of Film Studies and Art Studies at UC Santa Barbara.*

## REFERENCES

Abraham, Nicolas and Maria Torok, 1980 [1972], "Introjection — Incorporation: Mourning or Melancholia." *Psychoanalysis in France,* ed. Serge Lebovici and Daniel Widlöcher. New York: International Universities Press, Inc., 3-16.

Freud, Sigmund, 1959 [1919], "'A Child is being Beaten.' A Contribution to the Study of the Origin of Sexual Perversions." *Collected Papers,* ed. Joan Riviere. New York: Basic Books, Inc. Volume II, 172-201.

-----, 1964 [1932], "Dreams and Occultism." New Introductory Lecutres, XXX. *The Standard Edition of the Complete Psychological Works,* ed. James Strachey. London: The Hogarth Press, 31-56.

Freud, Sigmund, 1912, "The Dynamics of the Transference." *Collected Papers*. Volume II, 312-322.

-----, 1915, "Thoughts for the Times on War and Death." *Collected Papers*. Volume IV, 288-317.

-----, 1912-1913, *Totem and Taboo*. The Standard Edition 1955. Volume XIII, 1-161.

-----, 1919, "The 'Uncanny.'" *Collected Papers*. Volume IV, 368-407.

Freud, Sigmund and C. G. Jung, 1974, *The Freud/Jung Letters,* ed. William McGuire, trans. Ralph Manheim. Princeton: Princeton University Press.

Derrida, Jacques, 1976/1986, "Fors: The Anglish Words of Nicolas Abraham and Maria Torok," trans. Barbara Johnson. Foreword to Nicolas Abraham and Maria Torok, *The Wolf Man's Magic Word: A Cryptonymy*. Minneapolis: University of Minnesota Press, xi-xlviii.

Knoepflmacher, U. C., 1979, "Thoughts on the Aggression of Daughters." *The Endurance of Frankenstein*. Essays on Mary Shelley's Novel, ed. George Levine and U. C. Knoepflmacher. Berkeley/London: University of California Press, 88-119.

Lacan, Jacques, 1966/1977, "On a question preliminary to any possible treatment of psychosis." *Ecrits. A Selection,* trans. Alan Sheridan. New York and London: W. W. Norton & Co., 179-225.

Shelley, Mary, 1831/1965, *Frankenstein. Or, The Modern Prometheus*. New York: Signet Books.

# Chapter 13

# The "Science" of Law as Justiciable Speech: Notes from the Psychoanalytic Underground

Bruce A. Arrigo*

## I
## Introduction

The "scientific" practice of law rests largely on the conviction that facts are observable, that truth is knowable, that culpability is discernible, and that crime control is therefore possible.[1] In this essay, the problem of the "scientific" practice of law as privileged justiciable speech is revisited. To facilitate this exploration, several semiotic contributions from the French psychoanalyst and social commentator Jacques Lacan are enumerated.

The work of Lacan is useful to this project in that many of his theoretical formulations represented a deliberate attempt to tease out the subtle interdependence found among the variables of subjectivity, discourse, and knowledge. For Lacan, this triadic relationship was best captured in his notion of desire or *desir* (i.e., one's unconscious longings) (Lacan, 1977). For purposes of this inquiry, Lacan's broad thematic observations on (1) semiotic production and (2) the structuring of discourse will serve as conceptual anchors for the analysis of the science of law as justiciable speech.[2]

## II
## Lacan and Semiotic Production

Much of our understanding regarding Lacanian psychoanalytic semiotics stems from the seminars which he delivered in Paris, France, re-worked, refined and re-wrote during the 1950s to 1980 (e.g., Lacan, 1977; 1985; 1988; 1991). A prominent feature of his inquiry considers the origin of intrapsychic and intersubjective thought processes, resulting in the encoded articulation of one's desire.

A focal point for Lacan's investigation includes the mellifluous and polyphonic voices of the unconscious or "Other," understood to be layered much like a language, embodying multi-accentuated desire, and seeking expression and legitimation in the act of naming (*le donner-nom*) (Tiefenbrun, 1986: 152; for applications in law and psychiatry see Arrigo, 1996a; 1997a; 1997b). The discourse of the primary process region (the unconscious or "*Autre*") becomes articulated speech (e.g., utterances, words, phrases,) by way of a binding of excitatory (psychical) energy, in which primordial sense data (unidentified objects in the world) undergo linguistic structuration (identity formation) (Milovanovic, 1992b: 35). Put another way, intra- and interpsychic semiosis begins with the naming of mnemic traces (phenomenal or sensory data) through that language representing the knotting of the three semiotic axes (i.e, paradigm-syntagm; condensation-displacement; metaphor-metonymy axes). This knotting or binding assumes a uniquely encoded  form of  desire  and signifies meaning for the speaking being (Lacan's *l'etre parlant*). This meaning is expressed, is thematized, through a series of signifier-signified formations. These signs are the product of that intrapsychic and intersubjective semiosis issuing forth from the interdependent and overlapping effects of the axial interaction at work in the repository of one's unconscious. In order to appreciate the operation of these axial mechanisms in relation to the science of law as justiciable speech, a more detailed description is presented below.

**Paradigm-Syntagm Semiotic Axis**. In his posthumously published treatise *Course de Linguistique Generale*, (1966) Ferdinand de Saussure originally developed the paradigmatic-syntagmatic axis understood, however, in terms of "selection" and "combination." In order for speech to occur, certain linguistic forms must be selected from an available range, subsequently coordinated in some coherent pattern. Thus, words cannot be randomly placed in a linear-oriented sentence structure if meaning is to be communicated. Following his schematization, discourse (*parole*) is selected from the horizon, the community, of language (*le langue*). The paradigmatic level corresponds with the vertical axis in which words are grouped together by their "*comparability*" (Metz, 1982:188-189). Comparability refers to the associative relationship words share. Saussure indicated how the clustering of different words (or phrases) along the paradigmatic axis typifies degrees of similarity or dissimilarity (i.e., inter-relatedness) (e.g., cool, cold, frigid, freezing; scintilla of proof; preponderance of evidence; clear and convincing evidence; beyond a reasonable doubt). Thus, the paradigmatic axis provides a range of possible word choices from which the speaking subject may select.

The syntagmatic plane is the horizontal axis in this paired trope. It is the sequence of speech, or the chain of discourse, reflecting the process of word placement in a sentence, yielding a stream of signifying practices. In the courtroom setting, attorneys persuade (introduce) juries and judges to the justiciable speech which will be consistent with that discourse through which storytelling in law is construed (Granfield and Koenig, 1990). The precise words chosen (paradigms) and their careful placement in a particular phrase or string of sentences (syntagms), are uniquely constructed (encoded) in order to convey to the trier of fact that flow of speech consistent with how to engage in appropriate or acceptable (scientific) legal reasoning. The discourse constituting appropriate legal reasoning, then, serves as the basis for practicing "good" law.

Relying upon a more psychoanalytic semiotic perspective, conspicuously absent from this Saussurean reading are those contextualizing factors — including verbal, extra-verbal, and non-verbal cues — which significantly contribute to the structuration of the paradigmatic-syntagmatic axis (Milovanovic, 1992b:36; see also, Vygotsky, 1972:199; Bakhtin, cited in Todorov, 1984:42). In other words, shifting a descriptor from one part of the sentence to another profoundly alters the courtroom message. The use of such words or phrases as "Ahh!", "So!", "I see" or modal techniques such as gestures, glances, facial expressions can accomplish the same dramatic variance. Following Metz (1982:180-187, 263), there are "degrees of linguistification" or *secondarisation* which point out how shades of logic (rather than one logic) are more accurately represented in the juridical process. As I have argued elsewhere (Arrigo, 1996b), this feature of secondarisation serves as a basis for constructing alternative, more inclusive, images of (juridical) meaning.

**Condensation-Displacement Semiotic Axis**. The operation and complexity of this second paired trope was originally developed in the Freudian (1914, 1916, 1965) schema and although accepted in the Lacanian model is much less integral to his enterprise. The phenomena of condensation and displacement are situated in the realm of the unconscious, activated as primary logic. For Lacan, the seminal issue remains the same; namely, an exploration of the psycholinguistic journey by and through which the desiring subject communicates meaning but at the expense of being. Condensation signifies desires (wishes) prohibited from one's conscious thoughts which find embodied expression as manifest signifiers. These encoded verbalizations are indicators of one's deeply felt wishes and when deciphered identify latent signifieds. In the Freudian topography we speak of "parapraxes" or *slips of the tongue*. Displacement refers to the transfer of internalized energy (unconscious longings) from unacceptable/inappropriate objects or persons to acceptable/appropriate objects or persons. In the Freudian model we speak of neuroses or hysterical symptoms. The following, seemingly innocuous, statement is illustrative of the joint effects of the condensation-displacement axis: "I would characterize the witness's direct testimony before the court as *critible*." Here we have the presence of condensation because the words "critical" and "credible" have been joined. The speaker's seemingly benign comment regarding the witness's testimony can more accurately be linked to an unconscious signified in which some (subjective) evaluation relevant to the dispositive worth of the evidence is made manifest. This is the activity of displacement. Similar questions could be asked if the subject had declared the testimony to be *relaughable, sexifactory, insevere* (i.e., reliable + laughable; satisfactory + sexy; insincere + severe). Again, the point is not only what meaning is intended but, moreover, how does one's being (or some unconscious clue about it) reveal itself in each instance of semiosis.

**Metaphor-Metonymy Semiotic Axis**. This paired trope negotiates the condensation-displacement and the paradigm-syntagm semiotic axes (Silverman, 1983:110; Lemaire, 1977:199-205). The subtleties of the metaphoric-metonymic axis and its relationship to semiotic theory were originally developed by Jacobson (1971; see also, Tiefenbrun, 1986:130-2) and subsequently re-examined by others (e.g., Lacan, 1977; Metz, 1982; Silverman, 1983; Milovanovic, 1992a; Arrigo, 1993b). Metaphor is a literary device which creates "meaning by understanding one phenomenon through another in a way that encourages us to understand what is common to both" (Morgan, 1983:602; see also, 1986:321-344). Put another way, metaphor establishes a linguistic equivalence (the same signifier) by invoking two entirely different signifieds.

Examples of metaphorical speech in the law are particularly prevalent in the free speech area (Arrigo, 1993b:47-8). In *Whitney v. California* (1927:376), Justice Brandeis invoked the image of slavery to explain the affective or sensory state of fright: "[I]t is a function of speech to *free* men from the *bondage* of irrational fears" (emphasis added). In *Cohen v. California* (1971:25), Justice Harlan selected the poignant metaphor of song writing to account for the differing views on the use of profanity: "[o]ne man's vulgarity is another man's lyric." In the first instance, we have reference to slavery and fear (two signifieds) used to explain one signifier (free speech). In the second instance, we have reference to song writing and vulgarity (two signifieds) used to explain one signifier (free speech). In each case, although the signifieds are different, they are brought under one signifier. Thus, metaphor as a "constructive falsehood" (Morgan, 1980:612), provides us with a creative vehicle for "seeing things *as if* they were something else" (Manning, 1979:661; emphasis in original). As Milovanovic (1992b:37-8) reminds us: "metaphor is a structuring mechanism....[It} structures our thoughts, perceptions and actions."

Metonymy is also a literary device. It creates meaning by referring to a (whole) object by the naming of its (isolated) parts or attributes. Put another way, metonymy is the substitution or reduction of an object by relying upon the constituents of that object to convey meaning (Morgan, 1983:602; see also Manning, 1979:661). Examples of metonymical discourse are endless. In the quasi-legal sphere conversational expressions such as: *lock 'em up behind the wall and throw away the key*, refers to a lifetime sentence in a penitentiary; *giv'em the ax*, substitutes for sentencing the person to death.

In the science of law as justiciable speech there are also entire principles which assume a metonymical function. Consider, for example, the explanation of police search and seizure practices and their prosecutorial implications, predicated upon procedural mishaps. American courts refer to this situation as the *fruit from the poisonous tree doctrine*. Here the word "fruit" refers to a particular ("juicy" or criminally culpable) piece of evidence and the expression "poisonous tree" alludes to the thoroughly contaminated nature of that evidence's source (i.e., the process for obtaining the information/material was tainted). In the courtroom milieu, the trier of fact more than likely associates the 4th Amendment violation (the signified) with the phrase, rather than with the location or identification of such a tree (for example, as in the Garden of Eden and the Biblical Fall from Grace).

Finally, consider the manner in which a litigator builds a criminal/civil case. Bits and pieces of evidence are strung together, establishing a series of events in a trial supportive of a particular theory of culpability or wrongdoing. The advocate hopes that his/her presentation of evidence will create that imaginary space, filled in by jurors, in which they will conclude that the chain of events (the sequencing of the pieces of evidence) as construed, signify a fuller picture — one that categorically proves the litigator's theory of the case.

In the Lacanian topography, the metaphor-metonymy semiotic axes are located in the repository of one's unconscious, understood as the Symbolic Order. The Symbolic Order is that saturated realm, embodying phallocratically-conceived language and culture. As the central mechanisms of the Other's discourse, metaphorical and metonymical speech assume that ideologically-derived and materialistically-based content consistent with the prevailing political economic order. In other words, this axis reflects the mode, means, and relations of production consistent with the *zeitgeist*. Accordingly, for example, when we invoke the metaphorical phrase "She's a real dynamo!," the technology of advanced state regulated capitalism supplies the raw data sufficient to construct this machine image. The figurative phrase is selected from among the floating sea of signifiers inhabiting the primary process region. As such, metaphorical and metonymical images anchor discourse. They represent the discursive linguistic parameters of a society's current history, culture and science.

## III
## Lacan and Discourse in Law:
## The Science of Justiciable Speech

In addition to Lacan's schematizations on the intrapsychic and intersubjective dimensions of semiotic production, are his formulations on how discourse is varyingly structured to reproduce certain conceptions of subjectivity, knowledge, and truth. Lacan (1991) was to elaborate upon this discursive activity in his notion of the *four discourses*. In this section, I wish to analyze this process by paying specific attention to how the science of legal practice as justiciable speech gets re-legitimized through everyday constructions in law. In order to effect this outcome, a review of the constitutive elements pertaining to the four discourses is warranted. Subsequent to this, application to the *discourse of the master*, the Lacanian structuring mechanism most consistent with the operation of law (Milovanovic, 1992a; Arrigo, 1996a), will be summarily presented.

Lacan's discursive structures include four critical terms or factors assuming position in any one of four locations.

**The Four Terms/Factors**. The four terms can be identified as follows:

$S1$: the master signifier
$S2$: knowledge
$\$$: the divided or slashed subject
$a$: *le plus-de-jouir*

Master signifiers embody strongly held and central ideals with which the subject identifies. Once these principles assume linguistic form, they possess the illusory potential for one to experience fulfillment (Lacan's *jouissance*) through the speech act. In law, for example, such phenomena as "the reasonable wo/man standard," "due process," "equal protection," etc., satisfy this function. What makes these master signifiers illusory is that they symbolize only a circumscribed (partial) knowledge — one which is both materialistically-based and phallocratically-contrived. For Lacan, the development of one's master signifiers can be traced to two unconscious yet interrelated processes. First, during the girl/boy's early childhood, key figures such as the mother and father symbolize the child's signifying sphere and represent a focal point for identification. Thus, the child's repository of streaming signifiers (situated in the unconscious) and her/his signifying practices (paradigmatic-syntagmatic speech chains and semiotic anchorings) are steeped in parental associations. Second, following entrance into the Symbolic Order subsequent identifications take on prominence (including dominant linguistic codes and socio-cultural ideals) coordinating the girl/boy's identity formation but which, nevertheless, remain rooted in and conditioned by the fundamental identifications of the parents.

S2 symbolizes the knowledge factor. For Lacan, knowledge is delimited within the coordinates of a given communicative market and is therefore embedded within a battery of signifiers. In this context, knowledge is always and already *mediated* by language which is itself self-referential. Hence, in the legal sphere that which we claim as knowledge finds expression and support through the pre-configured limits of a specialized code (e.g., the juridico-linguistic communicative market or the law).

To illustrate, following a harrowing automobile accident in which multiple parties are injured and/or killed, a criminal suit filed by a surviving spouse will be semiotically cleansed and reconstituted as *vehicular homicide*. If the same party petitions in civil court, all of the trauma, horror, and devastation of the event is once again neutralized and will be re-codified as a *wrongful death* cause of action. The point here is that there is a certain left-out knowledge or *pas-tout* (not all) seeking embodiment in a host of master signifiers not yet valorized, declared non-justiciable, in the law. This *pas-tout* has been the source for much discussion among French postmodern feminists, both as a rejection of phallic *jouissance* as well as the potential basis upon which to construct a woman's sign system or *ecriture feminine* (e.g., Sellers, 1991. Grosz, 1990; Ragland-Sullivan, 1986). In the sociology of law, some efforts have been undertaken which incorporate the insights of Lacan, moving in the direction of constructing a postmodern feminist jurisprudence (Cornell, 1991; 1993; Arrigo, 1992:18-21).

$ signifies the de-centered or split subject. Following Benveniste's (1971) elaboration of Lacan, we note that there are two levels or spheres upon which the $ can be identified. One level represents the more hidden subject of enunciation (*le sujet de l'enonciation*). This is the plane of "the speaking subject, the speaker, writer — the producer of the discursive chain (Milovanovic, 1992b:47). The other level symbolizes the subject of an utterance (*le sujet de l'ennonce*). This is the plane of the subject in speech, the grammatical subject or "*I*" in discourse. Thus we have the speaking-being (*l'etre parlant*) engaged in discourse and the subject of the utterance's production (*le parletre*), the *cogito,* who speaks.[3]

Desire in language announces itself in each moment of speech when an absence is made manifest. Here we refer specifically to the absence or lack (*pas tout*) of the subject of the utterance (*le sujet de l'ennonce*) which disappears in the act of naming. The subject or "*cogito*" is not so much stable, unified, organized; rather, it embodies overlapping and contradictory expressions of desire awaiting articulation and fulfillment (Lacan, 1977:166). The divided subject, submitting to and being inserted (situated) within a stream of signifying practices finds that its cacophony of voices are momentarily consolidated, temporarily unified, by way of a dominant and ossified linguistic code. As we have already indicated this language system is itself subject to systemic semiotic production and intra- and interpsychic semiosis both of which are phallocratically-based and governed by the logic of capital.

Applying Lacan's notion of the $ term to the experience of the science of law as justiciable speech, both attorneys and fact finders situate themselves and are inserted within the juridico-linguistic communicative market. There is an ongoing interplay between the Imaginary and Symbolic Orders in which a manifest, though illusory, unity is articulated, ostensibly representing the subject's *plenitude*. However, what is articulated is the desiring voice of *lawspeak*; that is, a coherent stream of meaning is uttered by the subject but one which, in the act of naming, negates or represses *le sujet de l'ennonce*.

In order to engage in "good" legal reasoning, in the science of law as justiciable speech, enactors of legal discourse find that they must suspend their own longings, aspirations, fears, suspicions and the like while in the courtroom. Further, the legal arena is conceived of as a place in which such emotionality (i.e., subjectivity) arguably detracts from the fairness and impartiality esteemed in legal practice. Indeed, as Bourdieu (1987:85) explains, "legal qualifications comprise a specific power [which] allows control of entry into the juridical field by deciding which conflicts deserve entry, and *determining the specific form in which they must be clothed to be constituted as proper legal arguments*" (emphasis added).

In the unfolding process of discovering legal facts and truths, agents of the system are temporarily shut off from their unconscious; that is, they are closed off from their discordant voices embodying mellifluous desire. Consequently, judges, jurors, and litigators remain faithful to the coordinates of lawspeak by participating, unwittingly, in the production of (juridical) meaning (i.e., appropriately clothed speech). I contend that the cost for this conveyance of meaning is the suspension (or loss) of one's (essential) being.

The fourth and final term is the *a* with its *le plus-de-jouir* character. Although Lacan tells us that this term is subject to interpretations dependent on context, the *a* mostly symbolizes the excess in enjoyment (*jouissance*), defying symbolization in the signifier. In intersubjective communication, words (*objets petit a*) signal meaning but always with something left out; that is, a not-all or *pas tout* (Lacan, 1985:150-56,, 167-68). The presence of the *a* in any of Lacan's four discursive structures identifies the emergence of the subject as $ (divided). The *a* is the manifestation of what is left out in the interaction of one's master signifiers (S1) with the coordinates of one's knowledge (S2).

**The Four Positions**. The four terms/factors can assume position in any one of four locations. These positions can be identified as follows:

agent     other

_____     _____

truth     production

The left-hand structure, agent/truth, is occupied by the transmitter or sender of a message. It signifies those factors (**S1**, **S2**, **$**, **a**) at work or dominant in the person conveying the message. The right hand structure, other/production, represents the recipient or receiver of the message. Here, we see what factors are at work, activated, or aroused in the listener. The bar located in both structures helps differentiate the more conscious, manifest, and conspicuous factors (i.e., the positions above the bar), and the more unconscious, latent and repressed factors (i.e., the positions below the bar).

Starting with the mechanisms of the left-hand structure and moving to their counterparts, we can see the fluid manner in which each position operates in discourse. The *agent* is that position most active in intersubjective communication. Put another way, the agent assumes that station responsible for generating the message. The lower left-hand position, *truth*, signifies the hidden or concealed factor endorsing the induction of the message sent by the agent. In the right-hand structure, the *other* represents what message is received by the listener. More subtly, it signifies what is aroused/activated in the recipient of the message conveyed by the agent. In order for the coded message to be understood, or for the transmittee to mobilize a response, the listener must be responsive to that which is communicated. This very attentiveness makes possible a profound sociolinguistic transformation. In short, the autonomous receiver of the message becomes an *interpellated* subject (Althusser, 1971). Alternatively expressed, the other, situated within and entering the coordinates of a particular communicative market (such as legal discourse), must become receptive to the transmitted message. The effect of this process fosters a certain *production*, located in the bottom right-hand position.

Following my provisional assessment of the four factors and positions, application to the *discourse of the master* is now possible. The structuring of this discourse is depicted as follows:

$$\underline{S1} \text{ ------} > \underline{S2}$$
$$\$ < \text{------} \; a$$

The science of law as justiciable speech includes several master signifiers (e.g., "due process", "interest balancing", "intent", "duty of care"), assuming the position of agent and arousing certain effects in the receiver of the coded message (e.g., the fact-finder). These master signifiers while embodying the logic of legal discourse symbolize an imaginary and fragmented construction of desire. The stated signifiers are imbued with ideological content and are filled in with specialized meanings, representing a circumscribed knowledge consistent with the system-maintaining iterations of the juridical apparatus.

In the courtroom setting a story (criminal/civil case) unfolds constructed as a coherent narrative based upon a believable (plausible) sequence of events (Jackson, 1991). The juror, situating him/herself and being inserted within the pre-configured coordinates of the legal sphere, relies upon the elements of the narrative (i.e., its actors, settings, motivations, injuries) and weaves together a logical chain of circumstances so that a "series of ideas is built up in the perception and consciousness...of the spectator (juror), [resulting in] a whole image" (Eisenstein, 1975:18). This composite image, however, is typically culled from contradictory, inconsistent and incomplete information. After all, there are at least two parties in the dispute presenting with incompatible interests. The ambiguity is intensified particularly where the claims of both disputants seem plausible. In such instances,  the litigator, communicating meaning from within the coordinates of law-talk, creates an imaginary space, to be filled in by others,  where legitimation of the master signifiers are embodied with juridical desire. The selection of particular pieces of information constituting *the facts*, the sequencing of these elements, and the semantic domain used to communicate both will foster a metonymical system of expression constitutive of lawspeak. This (juridical) knowledge, passed on from lawyer to fact-finder, represents a certain product. What is absent in the product (i.e., other or more bits of information, alternative readings of *the facts,* different sequences for both), although seeking affirmation in the law, is declared non-justiciable. This data represents that left-out knowledge or *a,* denied symbolization in the master signifiers — signifier/signified anchorings affirming a truth which is itself provisional, positional, fragmented but which is, nonetheless, the law.

# IV
# Conclusions

What this essay endeavored to show was how the "science" of law as justiciable speech represents a partial explanation for engaging in sound legal decision making and good juridical practice. To advance this claim, selected contributions from Jacques Lacan's expansive psychoanalytic-semiotic topography were utilized. Both his notion of intra- and intersubjective semiosis (semiotic speech production) and the process by which discourse is structured and reproduced (the *discourse of the master*) represented key theoretical insights into the nature of legal reasoning and juridical desire. The work that remains is to assess how speech in courtroom contexts can be justiciable outside the pre-configured parameters of the juridical code. To affect this outcome may produce greater possibilities for advancing our knowledge of the law. This, in turn, may lead to fuller, more complete expressions of individual realities embodying, once articulated, new and different socio-legal truths. This is the challenge that awaits semiotics, science, and the law.

*Bruce A. Arrigo is Professor of Criminology and Forensic Psychology; he is Director, Institute of Psychology, Law, and Public Policy at the California School of Professional Psychology-Fresno.*

## NOTES

1. The reference to science and law is also a comment about the precision, accuracy, and certainty with which many modernist jurisprudes engage in claims-making resulting in the construction and articulation of legal truths that are partial and incomplete constructions of reality. For a postmodern critique of this phenomenon see Milovanovic, 1994; 1992a. For a postmodern feminist assessment of law as science advancing a Foucauldian analysis (1972) see, Smart, 1989.

2. The early Lacan (pre-1969) believed that the *language* of psychoanalysis was crucial for developing a science of helping, yielding certainty or *mathematical knowledge* Lee, 1990:191-95, Bracher, 1988:47; 1993). The later Lacan (post-1969) was to pursue not a reductionistic, deterministic science of psycholinguistics but, rather, a remarkable open-ended and dynamic form of *mythic knowledge* (Lacan, 1985:143-147; see also, Arrigo, 1992:24-27; 1993a:33-37; 1994:28-32 on *imaginative discourse*). In this latter period, Lacan emphasized the interplay between the *imaginary* (illusory identifications of self and others) and the symbolic (language). This new vision of the psyche and what might be was more intuitively grasped and subject less to prescriptive mathematical interpretation. Thus, for purposes of this chapter, Lacan's mathematical organizing principles must not be interpreted as his (or my) rigid identification with hard linguistic determinism; rather, they must be construed as conceptual tools (descriptive generators of ideas) where the lexicon of the unconscious (i.e., the intrapsychic and intersubjective processes which constitute the "science" of law) can find fuller, more unencumbered, expression and voice.

3. A much more elaborate and fluid analysis of Lacan's notion f subjectivity is found in his *Graphs of Desire* (Lacan, 1977:310-6).   However, additional commentary can be traced to his acclaimed *Schema L*.  In this conceptualization, a quadripartite depiction of human agency (the desiring subject) is outlined (Lacan, 1977:193-4; 1988:243; see also Milovanovic, 1992b:46; 1993:318; Lemaire, 1977:237-8; Ragland-Sullivan, 1986:2).

## REFERENCES

Althusser, L., 1971, *Lenin and Philosophy and Other Essays*. New York: New Left Books.

Arrigo, B., 1977a, Transcarceration: Notes on a Psychoanalytically-informed Theory of Social Practice in the Criminal Justice and Mental Health Systems." *Crime, Law, and Social Change: An International Journal*, 27(1): 31-48.

-----, 1977b, "Insanity Defense Reform and the Sign of Abolition: Re-visiting Montana's Experience." *International Journal for the Semiotics of Law*, 10(29): 191-211.

-----, 1994, "Feminist Jurisprudence and Imaginative Discourse: Toward Praxis and Critique," in R. Janikowski and D. Milovanovic eds., *Legality and Illegality*, pp. 23-46. New York: P. Lang.

-----, 1993a, "An Experientially-informed Feminist Jurisprudence: Rape and the Move Toward Praxis." *Humanity and Society*, 17(1)): 28-47.

-----, 1993b, *Madness, Language and the Law*. Albany, New York: Harrow and Heston.

-----, 1992, "Deconstructing Jurisprudence: An Experiential Feminist Critique." *Journal of Human Justice*, 4(1): 13-30.

-----, 1996a, "The Behavior of Law and Psychiatry: Rethinking Knowledge Construction and the GBMI Verdict." *Criminal Justice and Behavior*, 23(4): 572-592.

-----, 1996b, *The Contours of Psychiatric Justice: A Postmodern Critique of Mental Illness, Criminal Insanity, and the Law*. New York/London: Garland.

Benveniste, E., 1971, *Problems in General Linguistics*. Coral Gables, University of Miami Press.

Bourdieu, P., 1987, "The Force of Law: Toward a Sociology of the Juridical Field." *The Hastings Law Journal*, 38: 814-853.

Bracher, M., 1993, *Lacan, Discourse, and Social Change: A Psychoanalytic Cultural Criticism*. Ithaca, New York: Cornell University Press.

Bracher, M., 1988, "Lacan's Theory in the Four Discourses." *Prose Studies*, 11: 32-49.

Cornell, D., 1993, *Transformations: Recollective Imagination and Sexual Difference*. New York: Routledge.

-----, 1991, *Beyond Accommodation: Ethical Feminism, Deconstruction and the Law*. New York: Routledge.

Eisenstein, S., 1975, *The Film Sense*. New York: Harcourt Brace Jovanovich.

Foucault, M., 1972, *The Archeology of Knolwedge*. New York: Pantheon.

Freud, S., 1965, *The Interpretation of Dreams*. New York: Avon Books.

-----, 1916, *Wit and Its Relation to the Unconscious*. New York: Brentano's.

-----, 1914, *The Psychopathology of Everyday Life*. New York: MacMillan.

Granfield, R. and Koenig, T. "From Activism to Pro Bono: The Redirection of Working Class Altruism at Harvard Law School." *Critical Sociology*, 17: 57-80.

Grosz, E.A., 1990, *Jacques Lacan: A Feminist Introduction*. London: New York: Routledge.

Jackson, B., 1991, *Law, Fact and Narrative Coherence*. Liverpool: Deborah Charles Publications.

Jakobson, R., 1971, "Two Aspects of Language and Two Types of Aphasic Disorders," in R. Jakobson and M. Halle eds., *Fundamentals of Language*. Paris: Mouton.

Lacan, J., 1991, *L'envers de la Psychanalyse*. Paris, France: Editions du Seuil.

-----, 1988, *The Seminars of Jacques Lacan, Book II, The Ego in Freud's Theory and the Technique of Psychoanalysis 1954-1955*. Cambridge: Cambridge University Press.

-----, 1985, *Feminine Sexuality*. New York: Norton.

-----, 1981, *The Four Fundamental Concepts of Psychoanalysis*. New York: Norton.

-----, 1977, *Ecrits: A Selection*. A Sheridan trans., New York: Norton.

Lee, J.S., 1990, *Jacques Lacan*. Amherst: University of Massachusetts Press.

Lemaire, A., 1977, *Jacques Lacan*. D Macey trans., New York: Routledge and Kegan Paul.

Manning, P., 1979, "Metaphors of the Field: Varieties of Organizational Discourse." *Administrative Science Quarterly*, 24: 660-671.

Milovanovic, D., 1994, *The Sociology of Law* (2nd.). Albany, New York: Harrow and Heston.

-----, 1993, "Lacan, Chaos, and Practical Discourse in Law," in R. Kevelson (Ed.), *Flux, Complexity, Illusion*, pp. 311-337, New York: Peter Lang.

Milovanovic, D., 1992a, *Postmodern Law and Disorder: Psychoanalytic Semiotics, Chaos and Juridic Exegeses*. Liverpool: Deborah Charles.

Milovanovic, D., 1992b, "Rethinking Subjectivity in Law and Ideology: A Semiotic Perspective." *Journal of Human Justice*, 4(1): 31-53.

Metz, C., 1982, *The Imaginary Signifier*. Bloomington: Indiana University Press.

Morgan, G., 1986, *Images of Organizations*. Beverley Hills: Sage.

-----, 1983, "More on Metaphor: Why We Cannot Control Tropes in Administrative Science." *Administrative Science Quarterly*, 28: 601-607.

-----, 1980, "Paradigms, Metaphors, and Puzzles Solving in Organizational Settings." *Administrative Science Quarterly*, 25: 605-622.

Ragland-Sullivan, E., 1986, *Jacques Lacan and the Philosophy of Psychoanalysis*. Chicago: University of Illinois Press.

Saussure, F. de., 1966, *Course in General Linguistics*. New York: McGraw-Hill.

Sellers, S., 1991, ed., *Feminist Criticism, Theory and Practice*. London and New York: Routledge.

Silverman, K., 1983. *The Subject of Semiotics*. New York: Oxford University Press.

Smart, C., 1989, *Feminism and the Power of the Law*. London: Routledge.

Tiefenbrun, S.W., 1986, "Legal Semiotics." *Cardozo Arts and Entertainment Law Review*, 5: 89-156.

Todorov, T., 1984, *Mikhail Bakhtin: The Dialogical Principle*. Minneapolis: University of Minnesota Press.

Vygotsky, L., 1972, "Thought and Word," in P. Adams ed., *Language in Thinking*, pp. 180-213. Middlesex: Penguin Books.

## LEGAL CASES

*Cohen vs. California*, 403 U.S. 15 (1971).

*Whitney vs. California*, 274 U.S. 367 (1927).

# Chapter 14

# Semiotics and Law

Vivian Grosswald Curran*

*One can always put new questions to old material.*
                                    Robert Darnton
                        *The Great Cat Massacre and*
                *Other Episodes in French Cultural History*

## I

Semiotics developed independently in Europe and in the United States at around the same time. In the early years of the twentieth century, Ferdinand de Saussure, a Swiss professor of linguistics, was developing the science of "semiology," while the American philosopher and logician Charles Sanders Peirce was constructing a theory of signs to study both language and non-language systems.

According to Saussure, the fundamental characteristic of language is difference. A sign is that which is different from other signs, and difference is the enabling force behind communication. Differentiation is also comparison. Comparison increasingly has been recognized by cognitive scientists as a necessary building block of understanding (Lakoff 1987). Legal analysis, like other forms of analysis, is permeated by comparison or differentiation. In common law countries, law is formed by judges engaging in a process of comparing a pending case to similar and different aspects of prior cases. The law of a prior case will apply to a pending one if the judge considers the prior case to be sufficiently similar to the pending one merit the application of the former's rule to the latter.

Comparison and differentiation also operate at deeper and invisible levels in legal analysis. Law can be likened to a language system in that it has deep, although invisible, sets of rules. These are not rules of law, such as statutory directives against murder or for paying one's taxes. These rules, rather, form a complex web or network underlying the functioning of the legal system. They are the "grammar" of law, and indeed law has many "grammars" because law is a heterogeneous system, just as most actual languages have many grammars, although often only one is recognized officially. In semiotic terms, law's "grammars" consist of interacting signs.

Saussure's idea of the sign was a binary construction, consisting of a signified object, the *signified*, and a *signifier* to represent the signified. Peirce, on the other hand, conceived of a three-part structure, including the sign itself, or the *representamen*, relating to an *object*, with this relationship necessitating an *interpretant*, the mental conception of the sign, to be distinguished from the person who interprets, as would be understood according to the common, lay definition of the word.

Semiotics can help us to see, among others, how law is dependent on language, and, therefore, subject to the complex consequences of not existing independently in essence from the words with which it is enmeshed. The nature of language involves fluctuations in meaning over time, and at any given time among various users who do not use words identically. Consequently, law fluctuates in meaning according to the inevitable disparities in meaning of the language in which law is framed and with which it is connected inextricably, conveying something different to different groups of people, to different individuals, and undergoing shifts in significance and connotation with the passage of time and events. These fundamental characteristics of law undermine and refute traditional claims for the legal field of unicity of meaning and limited connotations.

The following comments of Peirce are relevant in terms of the interactive, dialogic relationship of influence between the legal field and the language of law: "Men and words reciprocally educate each other; each increase of a man's information involves and is involved by, a corresponding increase of a word's information... Does not electricity mean more than it did in the days of Franklin?" (Peirce 1992:54). Thus, language is integral to law, but that relation is also dialogic or mutually influential, as words take on acquired meanings due to the development of the legal concepts they both represent and help to shape.

The sign is a generative phenomenon. The sign in the mind (the interpretant) has its own object, thus triggering a new interpretant. Traditionally, law has been conceived of as a set of static, given rules, frozen, existing autonomously, and waiting to be applied. In one way or another, and despite numerous different legal philosophies that have dominated legal thinking and scholarship at different times in history, this conception of law has been an enduring myth. The field of semiotics can help us to understand the generative nature of law.

In addition to law's being subject to characteristics of human language, law is also subject to special relations that have developed in the legal field in particular, and that can be described metaphorically as a language of its own. Law is a field in which it is vital to understand the inner workings, for otherwise one cannot assess or hope to justify the power of life and death, freedom and confinement, it carries in its wake. Semiotics offers a method, a process, for examining how law functions in ways that are not apparent, and that must be teased out of the apparent. As the semiotics scholar, Roberta Kevelson, has put it, semiotics is "a method of inquiry into the process of inquiry" (Kevelson 1988:30).

If we can understand the way in which legal signs are produced, how one sign generates another, then we will gain new insights into legal culture, for we will begin to see the process of legal thought-formation. Just as frameworks of meaning vary from one officially distinct language to another, so they vary from field to field, both despite and because of mutually influencing systems of signs among various fields.

Semioticians have likened meaning-producing sign systems to networks or webs (Sebeok 1975:1-63). Seen semiotically, law is better understood as an ever-changing process, continually being created. This does not mean only or primarily that legal rules are changing, but also that, on a more subtle level, the meanings of legal concepts are also not static, but continually fluctuating.

The fluctuation of legal significances is a function of who interprets them, of the law's audience. Some scholars believe that legal concepts can find stability in particular interpretive communities at particular moments in history. This raises the problem of how to define an interpretive community. Traditionally, the citizens of nation states have been treated as though composing a single interpretive community. In recent years, diverse sub-communities within what used to pass for single communities have been increasingly vocal in articulating their differences. One of the greatest challenges to constitutional states today is the extent to which the law is capable of protecting the rights of constituencies whose self-understanding involves difference from the majority.

The semiotic focus on audience can increase sensitivity to the varying legal discourses competing in what otherwise might seem to be a single community. It may also help us to challenge traditional categorizations and even to explore the implications of each individual's having individual interpretants, and consequently, distinct sign generations. Different values and ways of conceiving suggest that differing interpretive modes separate many groups in every society, just as differing physical make-ups and environments separate groups, and even all individuals. These differences further implicate traditional ideas of communication and meaning, as the meaning of signs is never identical between any two human beings, just as meaning gaps widen from community to community. The multiplicity of meanings which semiotics implies may cast doubt upon the possibility of judgment or of ethics. Some scholars of jurisprudence, such as the legal philosopher Ronald Dworkin, nevertheless believe that there are correct answers in law; Dworkin maintains that they depend on a harmonious interpretive community.

The very words which might seem to pin down meaning to regulate conduct, and to ordain specific results, are catalysts for different significances because different groups and individuals have their own way of framing reality. The legal semiotician Bernard Jackson has suggested that "law may be regarded as a dual semiotic system, the language in which is expressed, and the discursive system expressed by that language" (Jackson 1997 [1995]:3).

Semiotics implies the contextuality of meaning. Contrary to popular misconceptions, it cannot by this nature be aligned with political views. It does not logically imply any particular political stance. Rather, meaning is situated in particular and ever-changing contexts. One legal scholar who has drawn attention to this phenomenon calls it "ideological drift" (Balkin 1993; 1989). A current example is the concept of law as color-blind, as this was the position liberals espoused in the United States to end discrimination against blacks. They hoped that mandating that the law be color-blind would result in equal treatment under the law for all citizens, without reference to race. Today, changing circumstances and contexts have yielded a right-wing political valence to the position that law should be color-blind. The idea that was promoted as fundamental for integration now is advocated by those who argue for the end of affirmative action programs.[1]

Further undermining the traditional concept of the autonomous existence of meaning is the analysis of one thing in terms of another, as existing *in relation* to others. Peirce and Saussure both stress the omnipresence of relations. This is part of the related concepts of differentiation and comparison as being intrinsic to understanding. It is a crucial concept for law at many levels. The semiotic search for the rules of underlying meaning-generation might be analogized to the Freudian search for latent causes of manifest symptoms, (Freud 1950).

Legal semiotics focuses on the processes of legal analysis. In this way, it is inherently self-conscious. It is the study of the kinds of arguments that surface and succeed in law, the elements that compose viable, cognizable legal discourse; *i.e.*, the law's syntax and grammar. On one level, we tend to think that judges make rules of law. In the United States, they make rules of law in the context of actual cases, which in turn arise from actual controversies that have caused the parties to litigate their disagreements. The very concept of a rule of law is thus profoundly relational, since the rule which is born of a case emerges from within, never departs from, and belongs to, a particular, unique confluence of facts and events: the facts and events of what happened to the parties. Further complicating this scenario is that the set of facts and events which define a particular controversy are that subset which has qualified for entry into the record. The overweening judicial context selects and triages facts for survival: those facts that are both reported, and not disqualified from becoming a part of the events inscribed in the record; *i.e.*, in the recorded version of a reality of events. The law thus frames the realities perceived by the parties and witnesses in a distinctive manner.

No matter how abstractly a judge may phrase a rule of law in a given case; no matter how broad the rule may sound; and no matter how clear the words of a case's rule may seem to be, the rule necessarily is a function of the case, of the controversy, as produced by the record which generated the rule, and by the judge's interpretation thereof. Thus, rules of law cannot be severed from the facts; they cannot exist autonomously of the individuals' controversies that spawn the articulation of rules. The concept that a rule of law cannot be severed from the facts of record is itself enshrined in the legal principle that a court decision only binds with respect to the particular issues the judge adjudicated, such that a judge who purports to set forth the law with respect to other issues is not creating law.

We might take as an example a case in which a plaintiff successfully sues a defendant for the tort of false imprisonment. Let us suppose that evidence of record indicates the male defendant had told the female plaintiff he had a gun, and that he would shoot her if she refused to go to his apartment with him. She went, and he confined her there. Let us suppose that the court found the defendant liable under these facts, and proceeded to say in its opinion that the law of the relevant jurisdiction would have mandated a finding of liability even if the defendant had not threatened the plaintiff's physical well-being, even if, for instance, the defendant had been an IRS agent, and had succeeded in getting the plaintiff to follow him to his apartment under the mere threat of a tax audit.

Under the principle noted above, however, the court can not make law with respect to the latter situation. It is only empowered to make law with respect to the situation which did, in fact, occur in the particular case the court decided. Thus, the rule it has created is limited to and defined by the facts of the case in controversy. A future case involving an IRS agent's threat of an audit and involuntary confinement of a plaintiff on the basis of such a threat, might *not* yield a finding of false imprisonment, because a future court would reason under the totality of admissible facts of the future case, including other variables which may alter the significance of the facts the first court emphasized in its reasoning. The future judge will have to interpret all of the circumstances of the second case to evaluate how closely the new situation resembles the old one. Consequently, if in the future case an IRS agent makes the threat of an audit to someone who knows she has nothing to fear because she has never been employed, then the future judge might not follow the guidance set forth in the initial case. Thus, what we call a rule of law, theoretically applicable outside of the factual context of the case which yielded the rule, nevertheless is bound by those facts, and does not attain an existence autonomous of them. It is thus questionable if we have "rules of law" at all, or if we have, rather, "rules of fact."

In another example, we might have an ordinance passed in a high-crime area providing that it is a violation to possess life-threatening weapons. An energetic new prosecutor may want to charge a museum curator who has displayed an exhibit of ancient gold scimitars. Under some interpretations of the law, and perhaps particularly to a young prosecutor eager for cases, the law might seem to warrant convicting the curator. A judge who does not convict the curator will have to find an interpretation of the law which allows for a verdict of innocence. In all cases, however, the judicial decision stands in inextricable relation to the phenomena which are known as the facts of cases. Once again, we can interpret the rule of law as a rule of facts, just as, conversely, the judicially found facts are reflections of preexisting law, of the law's cognizance of selected phenomena and rejection of others. We can, thus, further question if facts exist in our legal system, or if each alleged fact is itself a legal phenomenon to which law is internal, transformed and defined by preexisting legal principles in the trajectory facts undergo from occurrences to transcriptions in legal records.

As suggested above, a semiotic analysis of the process of adjudication will yield the conclusion that, for good or for bad (and semiotics itself will not reach the question of whether it is good or bad) judicial interpretation is an inevitable aspect of judicial decision-making. Whether judicial freedom to interpret is considered good or bad depends on the particular legal culture. Some legal cultures associate judicial interpretation with liberalism. The role of judges in the United States in promoting integration and civil rights has tended to make judicial interpretation and activism be associated with liberalism and countermajoritarian protection of civil rights.

The opposite; namely, judicial preclusion from interpretation, has been widely associated with liberalism in other legal cultures. The German political scientist Franz Neumann describes as a fundamental characteristic of a liberal society a judiciary with a purely mechanical role, composed of judges forbidden to do more than automatically apply the laws a legislature has passed, and who are strictly subordinate in power to the legislative branch (Neumann 1996 [1937]: 101-141). Neumann's frame of reference was nineteenth and twentieth-century German legal culture, in which the judiciary had supported ultra-nationalism and Nazism by engaging in a decision-making methodology that depended on amorphous "general principles" of law (*"Generalklauseln"*), and that granted scant attention to the particulars of laws which might have militated for different results.

Neumann's view of the positive correlation between judicial interpretation and the failure of liberal democracy is akin to the French one, but for different historical reasons. In pre-Revolutionary France, judges could and often did rule arbitrarily. They could issue enforceable orders without offering any explanation of reasons to support their decisions. Moreover, judgeships could be sold during a judge's lifetime, or bequeathed to another by will. Public disenchantment with judges had reached a high pitch by the time of the French Revolution, and the revolutionaries, realizing that they could not dispense with judges entirely, determined to place the judiciary in an inferior status. Under French law, the judiciary to this day is an unequal branch of the government, a mere "authority" (*"autorité"*), while the executive and legislative branches are "powers" (*"pouvoirs"*).

We see that deeply entrenched categorizations which originated in each legal culture's history created different unchallenged, automatic associations with the concept of judicial interpretation in the United States, Germany and France. A related issue is whether any legal culture has the option of preventing judicial interpretation. A close look at legal systems in which judicial interpretation is prohibited suggests that it is inevitable, whether legal or illegal.

The formalities of law, such as the rhetorical framework of court opinions, differs sharply in a state like France from one like the United States. French court opinions are formally constructed to reflect the purported absence of judicial interpretation. They set forth decisions allegedly consisting of purely mechanical applications of preexisting law. In contrast, American court opinions are lengthier and convey in detail the path the court's reasoning took from the issues and facts of the case, as understood and assessed by the jury or court *qua* trier of fact, to the court's ultimate decision.

The rhetorical composition of the two judiciaries' court opinions is so different that one might be led to conclude that French judges function in a very different fashion from their American counterparts. A closer look at the way French judges decide cases, a study which is beyond the scope of this chapter, suggests that the form of French judicial opinions reflects France's prohibition against judicial interpretation, but couches an active interpretive process.

We find that not only do laws contain structures, but also that structures contain laws of their own. Legal semiotics means the study of the laws of laws. Structure itself, however, is not static, but, like language, also evolves. Semiotics for Peirce was not so much just the mother of all methods, as we might put it today, but, as Kevelson points out, the *method* of methods (Kevelson 1988:15). As semiotics teaches us, the law exists in a complex universe. The fluidity implicit in semiotic theory permeates law. Law, like language, inevitably escapes the human efforts of centuries to pin it down, reify and concretize it. Laws are erected as structures, but everywhere their deep structures subvert their apparent ones; everywhere they surprise and evolve.

We have seen how laws exist within a framework of society and history. Societal systems of signs are based on categorizations that often may be unquestioned tenets, and whose contingent nature may well go unrecognized, as where, for example, a fundamental and unchallenged credo may be that liberalism depends on judges' not being allowed to exercise interpretive powers, even though this assumption may have originated in historical coincidences rather than in connections compelled by logic. One of the great historical influences on the understanding of laws is prior laws. Traces of old laws infiltrate and affect a legal culture's conceptions of new ones.

Many scientists and philosophers have noted that discoveries are a function of the questions we ask, and of how we ask questions, of our method of inquiry. By focusing on relations, semiotics opens new possibilities of inquiry and of discovery in law. Often we discover that relations exist in different senses from what they are said to do. In this context, one tenet of the United States' legal system is that legislation trumps court decisions. Thus, if courts have created a body of law that is controversial or unpopular, the legislature may pass a statute that contradicts and supersedes the case law, rendering the case law null and without legal force or effect. Even in such a situation, however, the new statute has no effect in practice until a court explains its meaning by ruling on how it affects the issues raised in a case involving the statute. Consequently, it is highly questionable if the law of statutes, allegedly superior to judicially created case law, exists at all before judicial decisions are rendered. We may wonder, then, if judicial decisions apply statutes or create them. If cases precede statutes, for the reasons just stated, then statutes can not precede cases, despite the official rule that statutes do precede cases.

Semiotic analysis can thus help us to realize that law has categories of which most practitioners are unaware. The process can lead to new discoveries, but even new discoveries will be colored by the questions we ask, and the questions we ask remain a function of our sign systems. Communication, the making contact with others' signs, will enlarge our capacity, but the process will be an inching forward, and always dependent on interaction with our own network of signs, and the categorizations we have constructed for the reception of data.

The generative aspect of two signs meeting and creating something new is akin to the function of metaphor. It is precisely where two domains of meaning meet and generate new significance, and where they are underlying and not manifest, that they also can be most powerful. The two domains which meet through metaphor are mutually influential. Fundamental to semiotics is its dialogic nature. Peirce spoke of the semiotics web as "a cable whose fibers may be ever so slender, provided they are sufficiently numerous and ultimately connected" (Peirce 1992:52).

Semiotics is a process of logic through which the internal relations of parts can reveal signification that is not apparent. While semiotics does not permit us to emerge outside of ourselves for purposes of framing questions, it allows us to progress in assessing whether connections we see are logically required or merely historically contingent: *i.e.*, associated because of the happenstances of the past. For example, in the field of comparative law in the United States, scholars have tended to search for and discover human commonalities. A closer look at comparative legal analysis suggests that it has operated on an unchallenged belief that findings of difference, of otherness, must lead to pernicious discrimination and exclusion of the different.

This association that recognizing differences will lead to unfair, exclusionary treatment, may be due to the fact that comparative law in the United States largely was created and led by refugees from Hitler's Europe, and that Hitler's legal system singled out Jews and other minorities as different, and purported to justify discrimination under law on the basis of difference or otherness. Thus, similarly to Franz Neumann in the example discussed above concerning the import of judicial interpretation, comparatists assumed that the association they had observed in Nazi law between difference and exclusion was a necessary, immutable connection, rather than merely a possible or historically contingent one.

The goal of United States comparatists to prevent exclusion based on otherness caused them to exclude otherness itself, by erasing it from the realm of human possibility, by defining humanity as universal and fundamentally similar. As a result, the discourse of comparative law has been ever more distinctive from that of other fields of legal analysis where in recent years a dissociation between otherness and pernicious discrimination has been an increasing trend.

The parameters of inquiry into the nature of law were suggested by Peirce in his articulation of the following principles:

1. We have no power of Introspection, but all knowledge of the internal world is derived by hypothetical reasoning from our knowledge of external facts.

2. We have no power of intuition, but every cognition is determined... by previous cognitions.

3. We have no power of thinking without signs.

4. We have no conception of the absolutely incognizable.

(Peirce 1992:30)

These principles imply that, no matter how familiar we deem the object of our study, we would do best to treat it as an anthropologist would treat a foreign civilization, for fear otherwise of missing connections our legal culture has put in place unobtrusively, connections and categorizations we so take for granted that we do not notice them, but which may contain the key to the law's grammars. Peirce's principles also suggest that newness, difference, otherness, are hard to assimilate, but that learning is about developing the capacity to assimilate the previously incognizable. Indeed, elsewhere he also articulates the possibility of an "indefinite increase of knowledge" (Peirce 1992:52).

The contextuality and relationality of meaning, the derivation of identity and definition from dissimilarity and contrast, do not imply that there is no reality. They do imply that, although we may know things as they are in reality, we never can be sure that we do. The manner in which humans can acquire understanding, because it is a relational process, also implies a multiplicity of realities among humans. As Peirce put it, "there is no thing which is in-itself in the sense of not being relative to the mind, though things which are relative to the mind doubtless are, apart from that relation" (Peirce 1992:52).[2] As the anthropologist Clifford Geertz affirms, "the real is as imagined as the imaginary" (Geertz 1980:136).

The relational characteristic of meaning itself implies another conclusion important for law. It suggests that values themselves, the good(s) that legal cultures set as their goals, such as justice, inclusiveness, and equality, are themselves relational and, therefore, not good in an absolute sense. Rather, a particular value will diminish the possibility of another value, and the good to be derived from its realization must be weighed against inevitable trade-offs. This semiotic implication has been developed most fully in the writings of the late Isaiah Berlin, whose profound and brilliant insights shed light on complexities at work in legal systems, and on the paradoxes both inevitable to and inherent in human societies. To Berlin's emphasis on competing substantive claims and value pluralism, we might add that semiotics also reveals the inherence of discursive conventions and of dramaturgy to law's meaning.

*Vivian Grosswald Curran is Assistant Professor of Law at the University of Pittsburgh, School of Law.*

## NOTES

1. See Balkin, 1989, 1993.
2. *Accord*, Lakoff, 1987.


## REFERENCES

(and additional selected suggestions for further reading)

Balkin, J.M., 1991, "The Promise of Legal Semiotics", 69 *Texas Law Review*.

-----, 1989, "The Footnote", 83 *N.W. U. L. Rev.* 275.

-----, 1993, "Ideological Drift and the Struggle Over Meaning", 25 *Conn. L. Rev.* 869.

Freud, Sigmund, 1950, *Interpretation of Dreams*, New York: Avon.

Geertz, Clifford, 1980, *Negara: The Theatre State in Nineteenth-Century Bali*.

Goodrich, Peter & Yifat Hachamovitch, 1991, *Time Out of Mind: An Introduction to the Semiotics of Common Law, in Dangerous Supplements: Resistance and Renewal in Jurisprudence*, ed., Peter Fitzpatrick.

Jackson, Bernard S., 1997, 1995, *Semiotics and Legal Theory*, Liverpool: Deborah Charles.

-----, 1995, "Making Sense in Law", esp., Chapter 5: *Semiotics*.

Kevelson, Roberta, 1988, *The Law As a System of Signs*, New York: Plenum.

-----, 1990, *Peirce, Paradox, Praxis: The Image, the Conflict and the Law*, Amsterdam: Mouton.

-----, ed., 1991, *Peirce and Law: Issues in Pragmatism, Legal Realism and Semiotics*, New York and Bern: Peter Lang.

-------, ed., 1992, *Flux, Complexity and Illusion*, New York and Bern: Peter Lang.

Kristeva, Julia, 1989, *Language: the Unknown*.

Lakoff, George, 1987, *Women, Fire and Dangerous Things: What Categories Reveal About the Mind*.

Neumann, Franz L., 1996, *The Change in the Function of Law in Modern Society, in The Rule of Law Under Siege: Selected Essays of Franz L. Neumann and Otto Kirchheimer*, ed., William E. Scheuerman. Originally published in *Zeitschrift für Sozialforschung* 1937.

Peirce, Charles Sanders, 1992, *The Essential Peirce: Selected Philosophical Writings,* vol. 1, ed. Nathan Houser & Christian Kloesel, Bloomington: Indiana.

Sebeok, Thomas A., 1975, "The Semiotic Web: A Chronicle of Prejudices", 2 *Bulletin of Literary Semiotics*.

Tiefenbrun, Susan W., 1986, "Legal Semiotics", 5 *Cardozo Arts & Entertainment* 89.

# Chapter 15

# Reality and the Games of Wizards: Religious Semiosis and Universal Vision

Terry J. Prewitt*

## I
## Semiotic Disclaimers

Discussions of religion in Western Civilization tend to remain "disciplinary" and belief-oriented. Classic works of theology, sociology, anthropology and psychology construct religion in terms of quite different human functions and interests — metaphysics, social needs, cultural consistency, emotion, well-being, desire, ethics, and even salvation in any of its guises. Beyond these murky fundamental differences, theories of religion become doctrinal. Denominations, sects, and paradigms vie for authority. Conflict-theorists, functionalists, culture materialists, symbolic interactionists, Jungians, Freudians, phenomenologists, and hosts upon hosts of others vie for recognition as *the* valid perspective. Religious systems have become the games of wizards, playing across the mystical landscape of the human mind. On this roiling conceptual surface, one might easily come to the opinion that semiotics has nothing clarifying to contribute. The semiotic terrain, unfortunately, remains quite overgrown with its own competing philosophical species (some would say specious philosophies), so we often find ourselves rushing through the definition of *semiotic*, skimming or skipping along the way in the interest of getting to some accessible point of opening.

Let us recall, however, that religion is the consummate praxis of "symbology" — the exploration of the potentials of arbitrary convention expressed through action. And how does one explore the conceptual space beyond the specific conventions human imagination has created? I justify *semiotic* for this task on several grounds. First, as Deely has suggested in several works (especially Deely 1990, 1994), semiotic may offer a metaphysical corrective for modern philosophy, a redirection from certain dispositions about the trajectory of Western philosophical tradition. More to the point of this essay, semiotic provides an efficient (but not hermetical) separation of substantive issues from the processual underpinnings of anthroposemiosis (or "human experience through signs"). More specifically, semiotic helps us depart from the idea that the spawn of Western monotheism — orthodox varieties of Judaism, Christianity, Islam, and their real or imagined Satanic counterparts — are synonymous with "religion" in human culture. For semioticians, the important discourses are not about the nature of received experience, certainly not about the actual symbolic conventions operative in any particular human community.

Semioticians explore human experience as sign forms and processes (Deely 1982, 1990). Sign process takes the form of a never-ending play of emerging meanings. We speak of "unlimited semiosis" as the potential of sign systems to create endless forms from manipulation of finite means, as with language where a definable set of words produces myriad meanings. At that same time, we speak of a "perfusion of signs", which means that sense and perception "cover up" the world with signs and symbols as a means of making our practical tasks more direct and efficient. The process is rather like leaves covering the forest floor; they do not so much belie its surface as they do redefine it. Just so, semiotic systems obscure at the same time they elucidate, and this has the effect of producing a bewildering and unlimited array of coverings on the world. Balancing these diverse visions are conventions of "tradition", constantly second-guessing themselves, and yet compulsively forming new connections. Such habitual reflexivity and reconnectivity are not simply the hallmark of language, but underlie all of human action and experience (see Pike 1967, Eco 1976, Deely 1994).

To introduce semiotic through exploration of religion is not such a perfectly absurd idea as it might at first seem. In this essay, my semiotic-theoretic backgrounds are merely cited, while I directly pursue a vital experiential thread linking what we know to what we believe. The trick of reading what follows is to relax a little, and to find the many signifying natures of religious experience *without* owning "Western" or "civilized" biases. At the same time, we must maintain the pregnant recognition that under the proper circumstances *anything* can call to mind *anything* to someone. My lesson, then, is rather unorthodox and metalogical — think of the essay as a gift in an indirect exchange of values paralleling the Trobriand *kula* exchange described by Bronislaw Malinowski (1922). We seek an equivalence of experience through quite different conceptual tokens, our intersubjective parts in the exchange signifying immediate and transcendental values. If this text is expansively-signed, then, it is to challenge the reader to discover the systematics of semiotic consciousness: *the human critical mode of reflecting upon universal experience as derived from signs and sign processes.* In such a pursuit we make "ancestors" or "progeny" of our fellows, and draw minds distanced from us by centuries into an immediate and proximous kinship.

# II
## Premises about "Reflection" and "Religion"

Until human consciousness began to "reflect" upon experience, animal life was bound to immediate conditions and consequences. Our human experience of existence emerged as an eruption of possibilities, a dimensional leap, a plethora of new connections, and a continual "becoming" of relations which, ironically, founded a nagging questioning and doubt (see Deely 1994, 83-119, esp. paragraphs 216-230). The evolution of human culture has expanded the contexts of our experience from proximous and inescapable events and entities to the subtle immediacies of social time, to the dominant signatures of constructed social space, to the symbolized energetics of the larger ecosystem, to "Nature" as a family of systems and processes, to the World as its local expression, and presently to larger entities which lie beyond these nested "heres" and "nows".

Given our means of communication, the contemporary World appears as an immediately significant but well-bounded whole. We are as locked to the World as-a-whole as the people of the Megalithic were locked to their continental regions. The "Mother Earth" of our time (indeed, of "our time" in the sense of Earth's life-cycle as a whole) is a relatively isolated Creatrix within which our individual existences have emerged and function (Campbell 1983:18-19).[1] From the Earth comes, and into the Earth passes our substance, as we transform our sustaining energy and ultimately spend the organization of our physical and intellectual existence. Of course, evolution and ecology recognize differences within populations and species as natural developments of the organizing forces of nature, including the adaptive system we call culture. This is as strong a basis for spiritually embracing all of humanity (and life beyond humanity) as may exist in religious practice. Let us also realize that human beings had fit themselves to the world symbolically long before they came to reflect upon the deep nature of such conceptual experiences (Eliade 1964, Abram 1997). The foundational colorings of the world remain strong preconditions of our contemporary view.

Are ongoing scientific discoveries about our origins and nature, however, not also a basis of spiritual connection? Much depends upon how we define "spirituality" and "consciousness". Common culture tends to use the word "spiritual" to refer either to immaterial qualities of existence or to "religious" action. Entailed in the representamen[2] is a paradigm of objects relating to action, souls, deity, and the connections of material and immaterial powers. "Consciousness" calls forth relationships of "awareness" and "existence" which attach inextricably to the constructions of the spiritual. The problem is that we often do not think very hard about any of these heavily interbedded concepts as foundations of contemporary experience. We rely instead upon the pro forma solutions of tradition.

We cannot say what the first systematic connections of human consciousness were like. Certainly, at first, there was an evolved experiential "all" which had come into existence through the situated Primate heritage, the *umwelt* of qualities (quali*signs*) sensed and read in an *innenwelt* of sign relations as stark presences and imminent consequences (Deely 1994, paragraphs 21 and 149). Grounding the discursive departure of humanity, there were the "names" manifest in such direct actions as seeking-out and avoidance within social groups (Sebeok 1994:37-38). There were also qualities sensed and perceived through an unreflective presence, and the action-motivating feelings, appetites and drives of the body (for full discussion of operative semiotic terms and processes, see also Sebeok 1979:42-43, and the entire argument of Deely 1994:53-82). Upon these substantial grounds, then, symbols piled upon symbols, conventions on conventions, and the directness of animal semiosis (i.e., animal *experience through signs*) was forfeit to a wider vision, an experience of universal things and processes constructed of insubstantial relations and correlations. The unreflective "reality" of animal being became perfused with a highly inter-referential and ubiquitous symbolic lense. Human signs, like stone tools, restated and redirected the energetics of raw animal existence through the Lamarckian-structured human *umwelt* that semiotic theory calls *lebenswelt* (see Deely 1994, paragraph 174).[3]

Can any experience of "universe" can take in the whole? We are not everywhere, everyone, everything, even in our most collective expressions. Extraordinary as the human use of signs may be, anthroposemiosis remains an ever partial apprehension of either the recurrent possibilities or the long play of actualities. Constructed from traces extracted from the World in species-specific ways, our *lebenswelt* only hints at solutions of what is, and rarely, upon deep reflection, lets us believe we have encountered the "all" of which we utter conscious dreams. The continuing problem of human experience is its apparent inadequacy. What we collectively sense with the keenest urgency is the limitation of our knowledge. We know that we do not know. And thus we should not be surprised, that when human consciousness began to "reflect" upon possibilities, our remotest ancestors developed, sustained, and expressed an overwhelming sense of awe of the world in which they realized they were participants.

Animate nature, in the biblical conception of *Genesis* 1, comprises the motions of the sun, moon, stars and planets, the teeming action of the birds and fishes, and the identities and life-cycles of animals, including human beings. Curiously excluded from animate status are the plants, which are "provided" within the creation of spaces for the animate animals on the third day (see Gen. 1:11-13, and Vawter 1977: 36-56; cf. also the "preoperational" consideration of the animate suggested by Piaget, as discussed in Segelman and Shaffer 1995:42-43). However, in its representation of primal conditions of creation, the Hebrew myth explores connections of anciently recognized fundamental "powers":

> In the beginning when God created the heavens and the earth, the earth was a formless void and darkness covered the face of the deep, while a wind from God swept over the face of the waters. Then God said, "Let there be light"; and there was light.

Earth, wind, and water — elements we now see as initial conditions *before* the Hebrew God's first symbolic act of creation — express animate nature in a way which resonates with imminent presences rather than with material presences. Yet in this conception of the text, God merely calls into existence the fourth and final primary element, light (inextricably linked to fire), which even in its inception remains undifferentiated from the precedent chaos. God must act to separate light from dark, water from sky, earth from sea; and in the end God must join "earth" and "spiritwind" (Heb. *ruach*) to form the living man. "Life", then, becomes metaphorically linked to other dynamic phenomena in nature — soil, wind, rain, sunlight, and their powerful manifestations like the earthquake, the dust-devil, the monsoon, or the forest fire (or, as in *Exodus*, a plague, a powerful cloud, a parting of waters, a burning bush).

The astute observer will find in all these elemental manifestations a cyclic quality. Life moves through waves of activity we call seasons, pushing forth from nothing, waxing, savoring vitality, waning, wasting to nothing. For much of human history, for most of humanity, life has been conceptually connected to more than mere individual biological process. Life has been linked to a never-ending pattern of cyclic renewal that operates on scales both petite and grand. It is natural, too, that life's indisputable presence as an earth process makes us meditate on our origins, both immediate and remote.

# III
## Religion as a Reflection of Expanding Mind

Each contemplation of life resolves the question of origins and life's continuing presence in its own way. Human consciousness, bound as it is to reinterpret itself in the context of its own creations, has evolved "religious" solutions consistent with expanding means of production and systems of social integration. In my general anthropology classes, loosely following the lead of Frazer's *The Golden Bough* and subsequent ethnographic treatments of "traditional" religious culture, I distinguish a progression of forms:    (a) totemic animism, (b) ancestor worship, (c) chthonic polytheism, (d) anthropocentric monotheism. Each of these systems forms its claims about the origin of humanity, as understood in immediate context, and some surrounding universal vision of time and space.    If we consider each construction of the world, even only briefly, we discover that the four forms offer transformations of each other (see Figure 1).

The so-called "primitive" animistic-totemic solution claims that each social "we" rose from some genus of animal or plant form.    If society emerges as a lineal progression from, and symbolic microcosm of, non-human nature, then it is possible to conceive of religious action as directly connected to the continuity of the natural world. Animistic thinking engages in a mimesis of the chthonic world (an imagined original existence from which humans emerge) in order to express kinship and equality with the surrounding world.    Though substantively incorrect in asserting specific lineal-biological relationships of nature, animism asserts a quite defensible connection among the living species of the planet.    Animism proceeds from the first holism in human conceptions, a perspective which places humans within nature and accounts for everything and everyone as playing a part in the grand design.

Human consciousness, nonetheless, has never missed the evident extraordinary character of human culture — our myth and folklore struggle to explain the uniqueness of human difference from other species.    Moreover, in connecting the present to our created mythic pasts, we have required intermediaries.    The universal tendency has been to relate the immediate and the primal through our departed ancestors — relatives known to us only through the testimony of our elders.    What more natural sign of connections between the present and the remote past might we choose?    And what a spectacular progression of consciousness, to step beyond the personal experience to a faith in analogous testimony of others, and beyond by faith to a primary other who differed not only in time, but in kind.

Note that social and material exchange systems, relying as they do upon indirect relationships among "families" of partners who do not know everyone within the system, mimic temporal connections with spatial connections.    In traditional cultures like those of the Massim district of Melanesia (see again Malinowski 1922), trade partnerships constitute a very formal version of this mimesis.    Society and action in society are linked with lineal connection and participation in the creative continuation of the family, the clan, humanity, and the systematic world.    Thus, magic and ritual are part of ongoing human relationships as much as they are an expression of relationships with the ancestors and chthonic forces of the world.

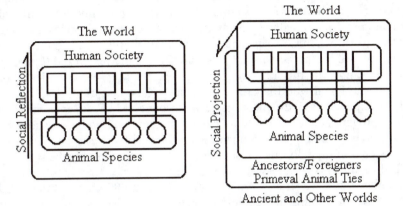

a. An Animistic Structure

b. Projection to Ancestor Worship

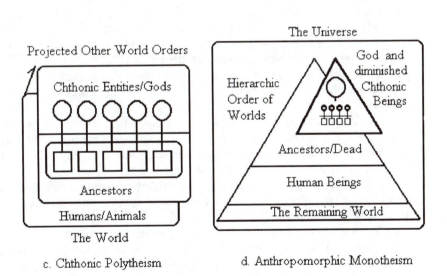

c. Chthonic Polytheism

d. Anthropomorphic Monotheism

Figure 1. Conceptual Structures of Socially Defined Religious Systems.

When ancestors became conceptual links to the gods (or with the "foreign other"), then it became easier to conceive of the chthonic as anthropomorphic.   The solution of the origins question offered by anthropomorphic analogy asserts that the ancestors or foreigners, taken as other-worldly beings, shape and influence this world.  Among the prominant examples of this process from history are Cortez in Mexico and Captain Cook in Hawaii.[4]   In this kind of religious experience, the experience of the "everyday" real world is gained through the land and its stories.  In such an intellectual climate, the ancestors become connected to "super-human" deeds. The progenitors — the chthonic beings, heroes, and gods — exceed human capacities while retaining human motivations and sometimes physical form. This kind of mythopoetic construction of space and time fits the stories to the land in universally accessible, though culturally specific, signs of being (see Propp 1968; Lévi-Strauss 1963a, 1963b; Prewitt 1990, and Abram 1997).

Now, paralleling the relationship between animism and ancestor worship, a special case arises of human "projection" from anthropomorphic bias: *monotheism claims a universal power for a single God.* God is born as much from a social expectation as from a cultural construction.  God is the ever-imminent other beyond the horizon, the ever-once-removed ancestor under the ground or beyond the sky (again see the related broad debate between and Obeyesekere 1992 and Sahlins 1995).  Construed either as an over-arching anthropomorphic creator who instigates the Earth and its surrounding physical and spiritual "realms", or as a singular progenitor whose "spirit" is uniquely shared by humanity, God is born of expectation and expressed through the known.

Within all these human constructions, religion may express the wonder of what we do not know.  But religion typically accomplishes the task by reference to the familiar.  As Joseph Campbell asserted throughout his career, language conventions yield countless religious metaphors for fundamental connection between the predictable, established experiences of the known world, and the unpredictable, intrusive encounter with difference (see especially Campbell 1972).

Contemporary evolutionary theory asserts that humans rose from hominid/hominoid ancestors over the past 15 million years.  This solution connects us in a chain of emergent organization which looks back to the remote past of life's origins on this planet, and which embraces the surrounding diversity of forms that share in the principle of life.  Evolution also suggests that life could, and probably has, emerged independently in other places throughout the universe.  Thus, beyond the actual physical connection we possess with all life here, we may share a connection in principle (in whole or in part) with other forms of life in other parts of existence.

The evolutionary perspective leads us to celebrate the extant connections of living things on our planet. Ecosystems, communities of inextricably linked lives, share destiny from the level of the "habitat" to the level of "world", and beyond. The emphasis of this celebration is mainly upon the "here and now", but it may still entail some connection with origins. The two interests, indeed, are much the same in evolutionary perspective: *at the foundation of life are the elemental principles which sustain the present*. Photosynthesis is the conceptually cooked notion of Earth, Air, and Water (the chthonic powers) bound up through the process of Fire (the God) to create living matter. Animal metabolism is a similar form of burning. We have, in the long term, risen from these grounds in very slowly reanimating processes of emergence. There is, for life in our part of the universe, still only one source, bound up in the continuing interactions of Earth, Air, Water, and Fire.

Perhaps a neo-animistic consciousness serves the ritual celebration of these connections extremely well. This may account for the scientifically-steeped but mystically connected appearance of a strong new "pagan" community amidst complex, technically-rich cultures such as ours. When we identify with an animal or plant species, we recognize and celebrate a distant kinship with that species. Remote though such genealogical relationships may be, our ecological interdependance always remains immanent at some level of community. And if recognition of the "other" is the key of all spirituality, then "religiosity" is not enhanced when the focus of spiritual connection is narrowed by the progression through animism, ancestor worship, chthonic polytheism, and monotheistic anthropocentrism. Crucially, we need to recognize that when spiritual awareness is confined to the "human community", loss of connection with the world and rampant destruction of ecological relationships may follow. Such a spiritual failing can easily become totally self-destructive, hence "unspiritual" even within the anthropocentric view of the world.

## IV
## Inauguration

A "semiotic" of religion can engage cultural forms in an especially general way, comparable to the science of the most creative contemporary natural philosophers, but taking as moot the pillared differences typically expressed by such high-cultural constraints as "primitive/civilized" or "revealed/natural". Today, I celebrate the emerging synthesis of a postmodern religious consciousness, namely, an "evolution-ary animistic spirituality". This spiritual praxis regrounds the action of religion in signifying processes linking expanding scientific knowledge to the inherent "desire for the other" religious symbolism has always entertained. In short, we possess a potential for knowledge and empathy unparalleled in human history, but this capacity derives from discoveries which lie beyond the institutional notions of monotheistic religion, Eastern religion, and the folk religions of traditional societies.

"Postmodern religion" has become fiercely syncretistic, empathically "folding-in" different beliefs and customs as they prove valuable for metaphorically expressing the known world. On these grounds, the future of religion seems less needful of institutional or doctrinal expressions, and more demanding of creative play, particularly when such play inscribes culture "within nature" rather than "above nature". This is not to say that the dominant religious forms of Western culture will disappear, or even much diminish. The old traditions served humanity reasonably well, in their time, and will probably continue to serve many people. After all, even the Christian-dominated tradition of Western Europe kept conceptually reworking the world until they finally delivered up empiricism, logical positivism, and a lasting commitment to science. And there are Christian churches that have embraced and incorporated all these philosophical perspectives into their theologies. Even with such precarious modernist failings infecting "revealed" Christianity, the core ways of Western religion will likely give only gradual ground to religious expressions more suited to our time. On the other hand, we can only imagine how broad the syncretistic capacities of Christianity might become.[5]

Our postmodern world provides access and understanding of so much, however, that the global culture challenges the self-secure, but unsubstantial, theological distinctions between such diverse (but in most ways comparable) texts as the *Iliad*, the *Odyssey*, the *Upanishads*, the Oedipus plays of Sophocles, *Genesis*, the gospels of St. Mark or St. John, or the *Koran*. Given the rich multi-cultural and scientific backgrounds of contemporary civilization — and appreciating that our hubris is also tempered with deep awareness of how much we do not know — we seem quite likely to continue making up new stories. At the least, we are likely to create new versions of the old stories as a comforting complement to our knowledge. Signs still offer us a soothing universe of wonders.

Through evolution and anthropology, many people have returned to animism in order to explore and appreciate our fuller human heritage and our animality — our ecumenical position in existence. Through medicine and psychology, we have engaged the distinctions among such ends as death, isolation, rapture, and annihilation. But we have engaged more than our *being* and our *end*. Through comparative literature and folklore studies founded in one or another form of semiotics, we have begun to *know* the minds behind our textual idols. And on this last point we should observe a critical lesson. Joseph Campbell's (1991) last essay, a sweeping account of Old World cultural connections for very familiar biblical texts, exposes two *different* and generally unrecognized pre-Judaic numero-astronomical foundations for the year counts recorded in the priestly genealogies of *Genesis* 1-11. Standing alone, Campbell's insights would have been profound, for much of what he explains has long been considered either uninterpretable or so esoteric as to warrant exclusion from modern consideration. Yet we have begun also to shape such understandings alongside, to name but one salient example, such texts as the *Popol Vuh* (Tedlock 1985) and more ancient Mayan documents also long thought to be uninterpretable (Schele and Freidel 1990).

The textual clues and astronomical knowledge necessary to deduce the deep meanings of ancient cultures have been available, for the most part, all along. As for the richer interpretation of the Christian gospels, we are only now beginning to understand connections essential to basic historicity (see Crossan 1989, for a superb example of what biblical scholarship can become). Unfortunately, few recent scholars ever possessed sufficient knowledge, much less the philosophical or practical inclinations, to publicly place non-Western texts on the table with Hebrew and Greek texts of the biblical canon. There is much information about the world that modern religions have simply assiduously avoided, when not actively keeping knowledge from public scrutiny (see Eisenman and Wise 1992, and Baigent and Leigh 1991).

The word-spells we weave freshen our humanity. They sustain us in an appreciation that the magic of the "All" is an ever-expanding show. The world-text and its potential stories lie before us as a microcosm of a universal text, much in the way primitive social organization once asserted itself as a microcosm of a universal ecology. Postmodern consciousness represents a paradigm shift subsuming the "knowledge vs. interpretation" contrast that divides epistemology from hermeneutic in modern philosophy. The emerging postmodern system (of which semiotic forms a part with contemporary hermeneutics, existentialism and phenomenology) performs all the old religious functions, yet allows expression and exploration of wholly new questions and solutions concerning humanity and life. We have finally begun to realize and chart the universals inherent to our myriad cultural constructions. We have awakened to the idea that our approaches to consciousness and empathy can yield a future in which humanity "knows" primarily as an expression of universal self-knowing. We have adjusted to the limitations of positivist science, choosing instead to set out on a family of paths toward imperfect, but quite satisfying appreciations of our world and universe. Now we may hope to create the right stories to signify such understandings in all we accomplish.

*Terry Prewitt is Professor of Religion and Human Sciences at The University of West Florida.*

## NOTES

1. Among Joseph Campbell's diverse popular treatments of religion and myth in culture history, *The Way of the Animal Powers* engages the theme of life-cycles and earth-cycles on the grand scale consistent with the direction of this essay. Because of Campbell's consistent exploration of the broadest substance of religious culture, we may revisit his arguments as a means of weighting our philosophical claims against the crushing solipsism of "Western" monotheology.
2. Here, I use the Peircean term "representamen" because Peirce's triadic sign elements (including also "object" and "interpretant") all rely on substantial individual texturing, intersubjective construction, and syntagmatic shaping. The sign is not a constant replay of a fixed Saussurean "signifier" and its supposed immutable underlying reality, the ideal, the "signified". Let the neophyte realize that these key Peircean and Saussurean terms may be encountered in other writings, quite incorrectly, as apparent glosses of each other.
3. I will employ, following Deely, "semiotic" as a loose cover for a contemporary philosophical doctrine of signs. In this instance, Deely's use of *lebenswelt* is tied to anthroposemiosis, and is thus consistent with phenomenological definitions of this term.
4. Gananath Obeyesekere (1992) and Marshall Sahlins (1995) have developed and debated this idea in book-length works. I also simply point to the parallel of ancestral kin and once-removed *kula* partners in Malinowski (1992).
5. Of course, there is always the possibility of a cultural revolution instigated by the religious-right. Though this is mainly a North American potential, such an event would create world political, economic, and social turmoil to rival an all-out Islamic war against Western Europe and the United States. Long-scale institutionalized fundamentalisms pose tremendous threats to humanity.

## REFERENCES CITED

Abram, David, 1996, *Spell of the Sensuous: Perception and Language in a More-than-Human World*, New York: Pantheon.

Baigent, Michael and Richard Leigh, 1991, *The Dead Sea Scrolls Deception*, New York: Touchstone.

Campbell, Joseph, 1972, *Myths to Live By,* New York: Viking Press.

-----, 1983, *The Way of the Animal Powers*, New York: Harper and Row.

-----, 1991, "The Mystery Number of the Goddess," in Joseph Campbell and Charles Muses, eds., *In All Her Names: Explorations of the Feminine in Divinity*, San Francisco: Harper.

Crossan, John Dominic, 1989, *Jesus: A Revolutionary Biography,* New York: Harper Collins.

Deely, John N., 1982, *Introducing Semiotic: Its History and Doctrine*, Bloomington, Indiana: Indiana University Press.

-----, 1990, *Basics of Semiotics,* Bloomington, Indiana: Indiana University Press.

-----, 1994, *The Human Use of Signs, or: Elements of Anthroposemiosis*, Savage, Maryland: Rowman and Littlefield.

Eco, Umberto, 1976, *A Theory of Semiotics*, Bloomington, Indiana: Indiana University Press.

Eisenman, Robert, and Michael Wise, 1993, *The Dead Sea Scrolls Uncovered*, New York: Barnes and Noble.

Eliade, Mircea, 1964, *Shamanism: Archaic Techniques of Ecstasy*, Princeton, New Jersey: Princeton University Press.

Frazer, James George, Sir.,1890, *The Golden Bough: The Roots of Religion as Folklore*, orig. 2 vols, London: Macmillan.

Ihde, Donald, 1993, *Postphenomenology: Essays in the Postmodern Context*, Evanston, Illinois: Northwestern University Press.

Lévi-Strauss, Claude, 1963a, *Structural Anthropology*. Translated from orig. French by Claire Jacobson and Brooke Grundfest Schoepf, New York: Basic Books.

-----, 1963b, *Totemism*. Translated from orig. French by Rodney Needham, Boston: Beacon Press.

Malinowski, Bronislaw, 1922, *Argonauts of the Western Pacific; An Account of Native Enterprise and Adventure in the Archipelagos of Melanesian New Guinea*, London: Routledge and Sons.

Obeyesekere, Gananath, 1992, *The Apotheosis of Captain Cook: European Mythmaking in the Pacific*, Princeton, New Jersey: Princeton University Press.

Pike, Kenneth L., 1967, *Language in Relation to a Unified Theory of the Structure of Human Behavior,* The Hague: Mouton.

Prewitt, Terry, 1990, *The Elusive Covenant: A Structural-Semiotic Reading of Genesis*, Bloomington, Indiana: Indiana University Press.

Propp, Vladimir, 1958, *Morphology of the Folktale*. Orig. published as part of the *International Journal of American Linguistics*, Volume 24, No. 4, Pt. 3, Indiana University Research Center in Anthropology, Folklore, and Linguistics, Bloomington, Indiana: Indiana University Press.

Sebeok, Thomas, 1979, *The Sign and Its Masters*, Austin, Texas: University of Texas Press.

-----, 1994, *Signs: An Introduction to Semiotics*, Toronto: University of Toronto Press.

Sahlins, Marshall, 1995, *How "Natives" Think: About Captain Cook, For Example*, Chicago: University of Chicago Press.

Sigelman, Carol, and David R. Shaffer, 1995, *Life-Span Human Development*, Second Edition, Pacific Grove, California: Brooks/Cole.

Tedlock, Dennis, 1985, *Popol Vuh: The Definitive Edition of the Mayan Book of the Dawn of Life and the Glories of God and Kings*, New York: Simon and Schuster.

Vawter, Bruce, 1977, *On Genesis: A New Reading*, Garden City, New York: Doubleday.

## SUBJECT INDEX